Monisha K Gumber

Teen Trilogy

Three Graphic Novels in One !

ILLUSTRATED BY Pankaj Singh Rathour

ISBN 978-93-5438-285-7
Copyright © Monisha Gumber, 2021

First published in India 2021 by Inkstate Books
An imprint of Leadstart Publishing Pvt Ltd

Sales Office:
119-123, 1st Floor, Building J2, B - Wing,
Wadala Truck Terminal, Wadala East,
Mumbai 400022, Maharashtra, INDIA
Phone: +91 96999 33000
Email: info@leadstartcorp.com
www.leadstartcorp.com

Disclaimer: All characters, events and ideas in this book are a figment of the author's imagination and bear no resemblance to anyone, dead or alive. You must not rely on the story in this book as an alternative to professional or medical advise in case of any symptom or issues regarding learning difficulties or psychological illnesses.
The author respects all religions and communities and has no intention whatsoever to cause offence to the sentiments of anyone. Unintentional mistakes, if any are regretted.

Editor: Padmini Smetacek
Cover and Illustrations: Pankaj Rathore
Layouts: Ashwini K Verma

It was the best of times, it was the worst of times- From a Charles Dickens' novel, A Tale of Two Cities

Starry Starry Night- by American singer and song writer Don McLean in a song about Vincent Van Gogh

PART-1
TEEN
RILOGY
TARA

SICK OF BEING Healthy

Monisha K Gumber

A Novel with pictures

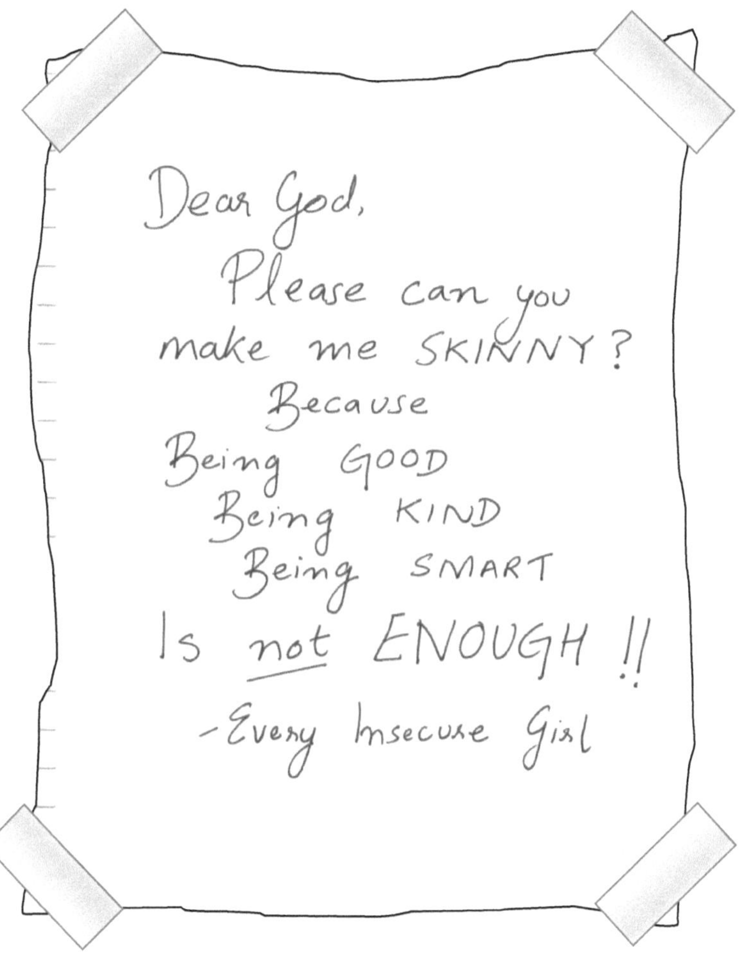

Dedicated to all the young girls in the world-

Hope you never get

Sick of being healthy

For Anusha

December, ages ago

Life begins with murder.

Chill.

You did not pick up
a horror or suspense
thriller set against the
backdrop of a haunted
bird sanctuary and I
have no skills to write
one either.

Still.

That night something happened.

Which I could have explained in detail had I been older,
more philosophical and with better language skills. But
since I am just a young schoolgirl, I will play it straight.

This wasn't a classroom or I would have called it a 'pin-
drop' silence. I was returning home with my family after
watching *3 Idiots*. For a family that gets uncomfortable just
being with each other, the silence was unbearable. But that's
what Mr Aamir Khan does to people. Even if we are quiet
about it initially, he does make us think and have our 'group
discussions' for the next few days. If a statement made by
his wife could become national news, imagine what this
controversial super-hit had done!

Anyway, back to the car. Yeah, so Papa's eyes were fixed
on the road but his mind was probably elsewhere. *Didi* was
releasing her usual tension through the touchscreen of her
new smartphone, while I, considered too young for these
fancy gadgets, was counting each lamppost passing by.
Mama, who carried the sole responsibility of making things

better for all of us in moments like these, decided to break the ice by commenting on the movie.

Mama: I loved it, what about you guys?

Papa: That's what I always say – Life is a race . . .

Dadi: Raj Kapoor *di poti* – what's her name again, Kareena – *badi soni kudi!*

Mama: How about you, Tara, what do you think?

Me: Too good, Mama. Really, it makes me want to give up everything and follow my dream.

Mama: Give up what? And what dream?

Me: You know how much I am into films; maybe I should make them my career.

Didi: Like what? You want to be a heroine?

Me: Is that all your small mind can think of? An actress!

(I could have said 'actor' but it didn't sound feminine. I didn't really have much of an idea what else I could do in films, but I sounded like I did, which was what counted.)

Didi: Since when?

Me: Since now.

Didi: Ha ha ha! Oh really? Do you even know how hard you have to work – on your looks, dialogue delivery – Ms Lazy Bum? And who will be your godfather? And who would tolerate you on a casting couch?

Me: MAAAAAMAAAAAAA!

Didi: Oh, help me, help me, Mummy. *Didi* is troubling me again . . .

Me: OK, Ms Google, give it to me, now that you can surf the Net anywhere you like.

Didi: I earned it, OK? Ask Mama! I am not like you who needs tuitions even for a subject like Hindi!

Me: Yeah, so? At least I am not a desi like you! Yuck!

Didi: And this from someone who watches Hindi movies all the time! Bloody hypocrite!

OK, so *Didi* was right – my Hindi sucks but I can get away with mediocre expressions since 'ordinary' is the latest trend in literary circles. That's actually not bad, as it helps average people write rather interesting books in average language!

Honestly, if my book made it to the publishing world, people might call it the fluke of the century. But I don't see why not – I mean I don't need to be able to write too well to get my book published, right? Just the way you don't really need a lot of political experience to be a CM or even to be good-looking to be a model.

Me: I'll show you! (It was going to get ugly as I was too young to know that *hypocrite* is not really a cuss word but a survival skill.)

Mama: Cut it out, girls! Can't you both sit amicably even for ten minutes? Baby, behave like a grown up and Tara – we'll talk about it later; why don't you explore more options and then decide . . . also, you are just too young to even be thinking of a career.

Dadi: Look at her – she has barely learnt how to hold a pencil properly but her zabaan is too sharp already, you people have badly spoiled your girls by giving them too much freedom! Now, Simran, why do even care about what this *piddi* wants to become? *Nalayak puttar, basta bhaari!* (Stupid child with a heavy schoolbag.)

So now this pin-drop-silent classroom had turned into a fish market. I know Mama intervened just to rescue *Didi* from being scratched by the undisputed champion of cat fights, but *Dadi* – how cruel could one get? Just because I wasn't born a boy or what? Oh yes, if you watch Bollywood films, you already know *piddi* means little. And *soni kudi* means beautiful girl, which clearly we Kapoor girls are not, in my respected *Dadi's* eyes. If you don't watch them – I don't like you and you are not my friend.

And I hope by now you have got it that my killer opening line 'Life begins with murder' is from that famous 'koel bird scene' from *3 Idiots*.

Thankfully, we reached home safely; considering the traffic that night and the way my dad was driving, it was almost a miracle. The next couple of days, I felt uncomfortable because deep down I knew being an actress wasn't my cup of tea but I did want to be associated with the glamour world. But how?

I kept bringing this up with my parents who were initially a bit apprehensive but the hangover of the movie made all

Indian parents introspect. I even heard an uncle supposedly telling his eight-year-old son to do what he wanted to.

Obviously most Indian parents still don't want to take the risk of encouraging their kids to compete in 'Channel Zoomi's Oomph Factor Season 9'. But Papa, who was always accused of being unreasonable, gave in and in fact pretended to be cool about me following my dream. Just a small stipulation – go for a more 'respectable' line – instead of an actress, become a movie director! So typical, yeah? But then he is my dad – an ex-*fauji* who doesn't mind offering beer to his teenage daughter once in a while and even cheers her on if she participates in the 'Ms Punjab Rifles Beauty Pageant Night' but from inside is an orthodox Punjabi Villain Father who wants to actually shoot his daughter's bloody bastard boyfriend!

Honestly, I am not too sure why am I wasting so much time in convincing you that I had my parents' blessings, as now that I think about it, they couldn't care less!

So, no acting-shacting for me!

Which is a relief! I may be a drama queen (that's Mama's analysis during my tantrum episodes and sometimes I do surprise my own self by extreme over-exaggeration) but truly, I can't act to save my life!

When I was a kid, during school concerts I always ended up playing parts that have no real dialogues – like a flower (when I was short) or a tree (when I grew taller)

You know why?

There were two main reasons:

One, like most regular girls, I was never the utterly butterly delicious teacher's pet and –

Two, I had selective mutism – if a teacher asked me a question, my cheeks would burn and I would just freeze in front of the class (technically it's not possible to burn and freeze at the same time but then, which language except Sanskrit is foolproof?)

I always got pushed in the background like junior artists in films are.

It was fine – I wasn't that ambitions to begin with and going by my genes I did not have a good chance getting in FRONT of the camera like my latest crush (now don't jump to conclusions, OK?):

Since then, I started dreaming of becoming a great movie director and winning an Oscar, just like our very own Danny Boyle, perhaps make an even filthier film about the abandoned holy cows shitting on Indian roads, but there was another problem . . .

Nobody took me seriously

Because I just had a vague idea of what direction meant. For a long time, I wasn't really allowed to use the computer since I was still very young. But when I was finally given access I just had to do my first research project. I learnt that directors are creative people with an innate sense of building characters, situations and translating the writer's vision into a movie . . . and some more technical stuff.

Which meant directors are totally dependent on the writer's words to take the story forward, so who was more important? This was my 'A-ha' moment when I decided to write movies! I know what you are thinking, a lot of wannabees get inspired by Chetan Uncle and end up writing crap but *lend me your eyes as my story will do something to your soul that years of reading magnifique prose couldn't!*

Many years have passed . . .

I have watched the film maybe ten more times on TV and it still triggers a sense of 'career consciousness' in me. Over time my resolve has just gotten stronger. I began by writing short stories which became longer and longer over time (like this one, which I do want to cut short).

I wish I had a longer list of credentials apart from the column called *Growing-up Pains* that I contribute for my school's monthly newsletter. Hey, just like our 'item numbers', I can use these newsletters as a 'filler' in my book. However, here they will not be totally irrelevant. Or at least I will try.

Patriotic Public School

Newsletter for the month of July

Growing-up Pains

Homeschooling, anyone?

By Tara Kapoor

Sometimes when the going gets tough, I start wondering if a day will come when I will not have to go through so much of a grind in attending school, completing these never ending assignments, when I will not have to spend minimum two hours in the school bus daily, when I will be given some extra time to really 'get' these formulae. I am sure that it's not just me, but all normal students are tired of this system. But do we have a choice? Last evening, when I was rushing out for my Maths tuition, I met a kid with a cricket bat in the lift of my building. He looked kind of different - because he seemed happier and more confident than most of us. He told me he was homeschooled. I was taken aback that how could this sporty, sweet, well-mannered kid not go to school? Were his parents so irresponsible? Or did he have dyslexia like Ishaan from Tare Zameen Par? But after a long discussion with him (yes, I missed my Maths tuition yet again), I realized that this might actually be the way forward.

(continued on page 3)

Break up

By Gayatri Shah

My bed is lovely, soft and deep
But he won't just let me sleep
His messages go beep beep
Sorry this promise I can't keep
So all I do is weep weep
And weep weep

No time for PE?

By Vani Dhillon

Being the sports captain of our school, it pains me to see that we have time for everything except PE. Now for athletes like us, this is one period that we look forward to, but usually it is taken over by something 'more important'.

KINDERGARTEN DRAWING COMPITITION

Winning entries

Theme: I love Summers

My articles have been slightly controversial as I don't really write to please anyone but myself! I am yet to find out if it's a good thing but I must mention that I almost got selected as Vice President of my school's Literary Club. 'Almost' because the position instead went to Gayatri Shah whose mom is a famous poet. This weirdo does some kind of rubbish with double-meaning dialogues and all. The school assumed that she is a child prodigy because of her mom's so-called radical thoughts, but honestly, I don't think Gayatri has really taken after her. Mostly she just writes crappy love poems. It made me give up on school politics and I started underplaying myself. Still, you can't really curb talent for long . . . that's why you have this book in your hands.

So let's begin from the beginning . . .

. . . like all great Literature (or do I mean Movies?) . . .

INTRODUCING

Tara Kapoor: That's me – a chubby girl with a beautiful face (if you don't notice my braces).

Megha Deshpande: My best friend, whom I hate secretly as she is 'a girl who has everything'!

My BFF
Megha

Dolly Nanda: My second-best friend, a self-confessed Selfie Queen, whom I could have hated if she had not been so dumb.

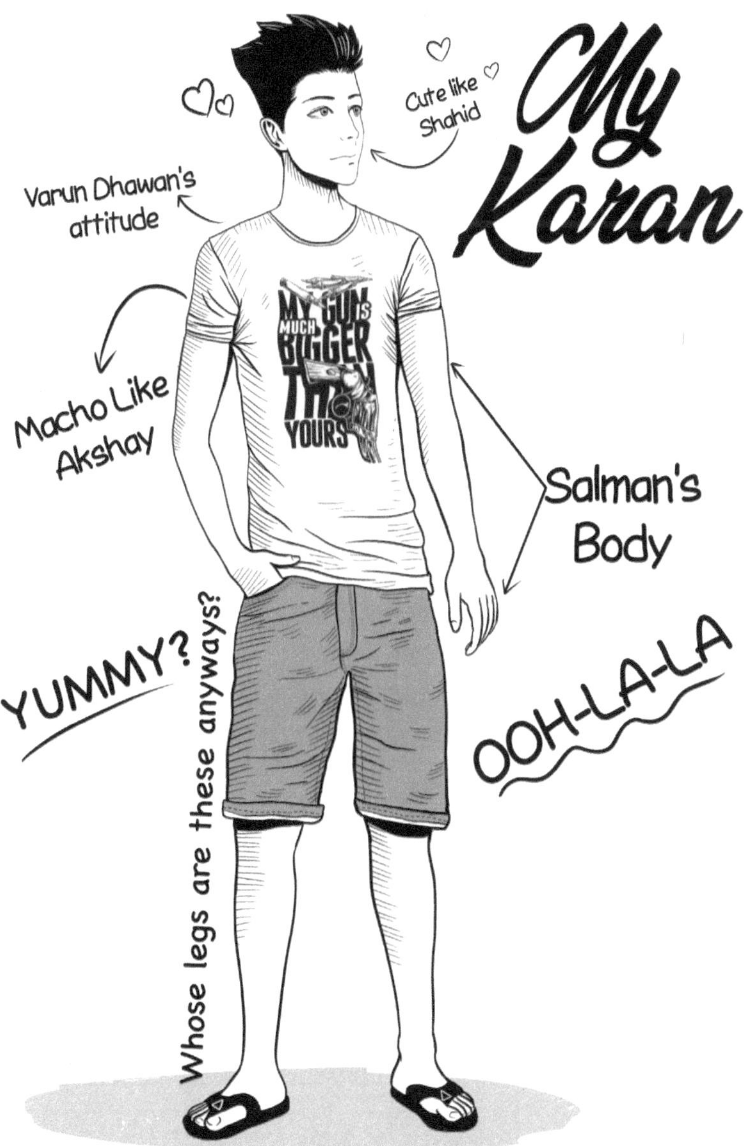

I JUST CAN'T STOP LOVING YOU

SUPPORTING CAST

Mama: A reluctant housewife. Like all women approaching menopause she remains angry and irritable most of the time... her only respite is running, which she had started probably to run away from her dull life. Now she organises these racing events in the Society that nobody wants to attend.

Papa: An ex-Army Officer who is still not over it. Now a corporate guy. Honestly, I don't have a relationship with him, as he hardly talks to us except for the monthly lectures on his disappointment with his younger daughter. Who knows what he wants from me, is it my fault if God did not make me hardworking enough?

My elder sister: Well, she's called Baby as my grandma chose a unique name for her, which the general public has a hard time remembering! She is the perfect example of what is wrong with our education system and our country in general because in reality these are the kind of people who really make it big in life! I am dead sure the moment Baby *Didi* is independent this is the first thing she will do!

Dadi must really love *Maine Pyar Kiya* and hate Mama, but to take it out on a child?

Naintara: I am introducing myself again as Mama says I have a split personality: outside of my domain (my home, dude) my reputation is of a sweet, docile sort of a girl but at home, I am a true Leo – I roar and I rule. Again it was *Dadi*, but this time round Mama put her foot down to make it more bearable – so I am officially Tara though *Dadi* still calls me 'Naayan-tara'. Really, these old people are not as harmless as they seem to be.

Dadi: My grandmom doesn't really need further introduction and thank God she is slowly losing it so her sarcasm doesn't hurt as much. She doesn't have much to do in the book but her picture is here as she claims she is the best-looking *buddhi* in the society. You decide.

(Sorry, *Dadi* – I am exaggerating just to make it interesting; we all know what a pure soul you are.)

Snoopy Dog: My brother from another mother. But he doesn't live with us anymore. The old soul had a habit of running away from home to start a family with those bitches on the road. Though nobody talks about it but it seems he contacted an STD and died. Living or dead – he will always be part of this family.

In case you are still wondering how did I manage such a brilliant casting coup as having Shahrukh Khan in my book then I have news for you. I was just fooling around. But I have my reasons and valid ones at that. One is that Mama says having a superstar to endorse my book would really help sell it, and second:

I really do love Shahrukh Khan so I had to give him something, even if it's a friendly guest appearance.

(Mr Khan – I admit that technically you did not endorse my book but you are public property, no? So your fans have every right to use your pictures, especially if it makes a difference in someone's life – namely mine.)

Even though I look quite hep, from inside I am a simple, homely girl (just the way film heroines who fag, drink and make out in public are actually very innocent and domesticated in real life).

I see a lot of cable, even the classics from my parents' generation and well... I kind of like those, especially because every character is in the frame for a purpose – everyone is significant whether it's a servant, a distant relative, or a *kabootar*. I really appeal to my generation to try the hits from '80s and '90s to realise that a Pomeranian can read and even turn things around at the climax! Nowadays my parents keep wishing for the good old Bollywood which was pure desi culture and still managed to have an international appeal (if you consider Pakistan and Bangladesh international).

I guess my genre will be clean, family-oriented films where the bare-chested bhaijaan gets turned on just by looking at his pregnant wife serving him a *garam chai ki piyaali* (kind of like *Prem uncle phir aayo*). Actually, I am not too choosy, so I can try different stuff if an interesting project is offered. TBH, I would prefer those 'rowdy' movies that are making a huge comeback.

PAISEWALLA AND SONS
PRESENT
A Bloody Violent Romantic Saga
प्यार प्यार प्यार
या फिर मार मार मार
Dhamakedaar Release this Diwali

My 'Society' (or 'Condo')

I live in one of those 'Fully sustainable lush green townships with all amenities' in Gurgaon, which has these buildings standing so close to each other that you feel claustrophobic till you get used to it.

Can you believe it's actually called 'Global World'? There is nothing global about it except that each of the towers is based on the theme of some region on the planet. It was supposed to be creative and all, but either the builders went bankrupt or the designers were lazy.

So the only thing thematic about the buildings is the entrance lobby. Like my building is called 'Arabian Nights'.

Then we have an 'American Dream' tower, and, more absurd, a 'French Kiss' tower, and an 'Italian Pasta' tower. Talk about heights of laziness – the designer probably just picked the first names that came to mind. So apart from the lobby, all floors, all lifts, all flats are exactly the same.

There are about 7 Towers x 7 Floors x 7 Apartments – that, too, fully packed – so you can imagine the number of people we bump into each day and try to avoid.

Strangely, we are close to just two other or three families here: all the rest are sort of downmarket; you should hear Dad: *they are bloody civilians – uneducated – their children have no manners.* (Sorry, neighbours, but my dad can be very rude sometimes.)

Actually, this is the best my parents could afford . . . even though I think my dad is doing really well in his job as his company keeps sending him to the US. But I also know India happens to be the most expensive country in the world and no matter how much money you earn, you can't afford to buy a decent house here – especially if you have a private school, a hospital, a five-star hotel or – God forbid – if the Metro is coming up nearby: you can just forget about that property. It doesn't matter to me but I have heard Mama cribbing about it many times . . . She is really sad about it, more so because Rubi *Maasi* just bought a plush new bungalow on Golf Course Road . . . you know, life is just not fair!

My best friend Megha lives on the same floor with her folks. Being an only daughter, her parents dote on her and give her the best upbringing possible. Unfortunately, she is always first in class, school swimming champion, on the soccer (OK, football) team and has zero per cent fat on her! A perfect butt on perfect legs. If fit is the new sexy then she sure tops the list! These sick health magazines have actually ruined the chances of girls like me to ever have a shot in life – I used to think women should be soft and rounded but how ignorant I was.

HEALTHY GALS
SLIM AND HAPPY FOR LIFE
TONE YOUR BUTT IN 10 MINUTES
Get back in shape with this 'never fail' diet
Lose BELLY FAT in a week
Just 3 YOGA SECRETS to your best body ever

Megha is still considered hot despite having an almost flat chest.

As you might have guessed, I am no princess and my life isn't a fairy tale either. I have another version of Megha at my home – my sister – except that my sister is an Ugly Betty (sorry, *Didi* – I didn't want to hurt your feelings but in this profession, I solemnly pledged to be honest, so don't take it personally; the silver lining being you might eventually get a handsome, rich guy), nor does she play any sport but yes – academically nobody can beat her! So Mama-Papa are always comparing me with either Megha or Baby *Didi*. They don't do it openly, as they happen to be New Age parents who have read ten different books on modern parenting!

To be honest – they are still experimenting.

In my house I never know what is really coming. Just when I think all is well, my dad calls out for me to have 'the talk', which basically means one thing. And then some more. Being 'irresponsible' tops the list and then I am branded with having 'no respect', 'no ambition' and 'no future at all'. I still haven't figured out what triggers it but I try to keep a safe distance from my father, as – trust me – it doesn't do any good to my self-respect. And my mom. She, too, is really unpredictable. Whenever I think it's a good time to ask for something, she brings up my whole life in front me and makes me realise that I can't have it as I don't know how to take care of my things. OK, I might have misplaced a few random items like *Didi's* markers, the TV remote, Mama's new Raybans or the gold chain *Dadi* gifted me on Diwali, but what's the big fuss about? Is it only 'things' that matter? And then she will accuse us of being too materialistic! And the chain – of course it had to go –it was too thin to be visible (Mama's words) so what difference does it make whether I wear it or not?

Dolly lives next door to me. She's what we call a poor student. Her best score has been a skimpy 72 per cent and she's even got that report card framed (I am lying). Mama says that in her days big eyes and small lips were considered beautiful but things have reversed over these years. Dolly has these small, light-brown eyes and enormous, bee-stung, naturally red lips. On a fair skin, it looks damn neat and you can't take your eyes off her oval babyish face. Till she opens her mouth. She is the typical giggly girl in spaghetti tops and short skirts (I know it's stereotyped but she does happen to be a dumb beauty) so my parents actually feel good when they see me fully covered. I overheard Papa whispering something to my Mama about Dolly's mom . . . and they say that only women gossip!

Speaking of fully covered – this is the funda – to me my body is a sacred and I don't want to expose it to the world. Dolly says if you have it, flaunt it – but I would never dress like her even if I was 15 or even 20 kg lighter!

Dolly is kind of fast. Or she just tries hard to be. Actually, if I show you what her opinions look like on my slam book, you will know what I mean. OK, let me include Megha's first . . .

These are a few of my Favorite things

Name:	Megha Deshpande
DOB:	30th December
I love:	Sports, music and intelligent guys (so hard to find)
I hate:	Mindless gossips and dumb girls (quite a few out there)
My favorite Book :	The Fountainhead
My favorite movie:	Gravity
My favorite music:	Jazz and Soft Rock
My greatest fear:	Failing
My greatest joy:	Winning
I get turned on by:	Geeks working out in the gym (oo la la)
I get turned off by:	If they stink (yuck!)
My best friend:	Tara Kapoor
My boy friend:	Still waiting for the right one.
My first crush:	Harry Styles (I am still having it)
My favourite bedroom line:	Sorry , no time !
My greatest wish:	To be a National Champion !
Any advice for me:	Be the best you can !

These are a few of my Favorite things

Name:	Dolly Nanda
DOB:	2nd April
I love:	Hot couture' and living life on the edge
I hate:	Girls who are 'J' of me
My favorite book	Betty and Veronica series
My favorite movie:	Sorry its strictly "A"
My favorite music:	Romantic Bollywood
My greatest fear:	Not having boys noticing me
My greatest joy:	Shopping for the trendiest brands
I get turned on by:	Guys who play hard to get
I get turned off by:	Guys who play too hard to get me
My best friend:	Tara and Megha
My boy friend:	You mean current or ex?
My first crush:	My cousin Suraj bhaiya
My favourite bedroom line:	Can't wait any more
My greatest wish:	To be famous
Any advice for me:	Get a life ! (I mean a 'love' life)

♥ Dolly ♥

So did you get the plot?

Never mind, let the story unfold.

November

The other day I met Dolly in our shopping complex, she was wearing practically nothing – well, almost – an off-white peasant top with a really short, 'suggestive, titillating, miniest' denim skirt. (OK, I know you got it, but it's too much, man. I mean she has to be a bit considerate of girls like me, and this is India, OK?) And these big guys were ogling at her, while she is no less – she was actually enjoying the attention. My God, some girls can be so cheap! And she is really dumb to wear this in this weather! But she has those awesome leather boots which make her legs seem even longer. Sad . . . very sad.

One of the guys staring at her was Karan- I used to think he was a decent guy but I guess all men are same!

Talking of Karan, then. I have been in love with him since I was in preschool! He has got this sort-of-golden hair that he's inherited from his *Angrez nani*. His family is one of those unapproachable 'foreign types' that everyone is in awe of. Like his mom divorced his dad and lives with her Ukrainian lover boy, right in the opposite block. An elder sister who ran away from her hostel in Panchgani to pursue an alternative career in Spirituality and now runs a 'redemption centre' in Sri Lanka with her Philippina girlfriend. Another sister who works in a spa in Bangkok. And father – don't even ask. I don't know about others but my parents hate his family to the core, especially Papa, who calls them a 'menace to our society'. I don't know how many struggles I will have to go through, against my own flesh and blood, for my love. But he is not like them. He is like us. Fine, he might be attractive – but in a regular sort of a way. Seems to be humble and approachable despite his Casanova image. My school's ex

Head Boy who is in St Stephen's. OK, so there's almost a generation gap between us but then my dad is also six years older than my mama and they seem to be doing fine despite the age difference, so I guess Karan will make a good husband for me.

This is my BIG secret that I have not even told my best friends, I am just waiting for the day when he asks me out before I make it official. But before that I have to be careful about these:

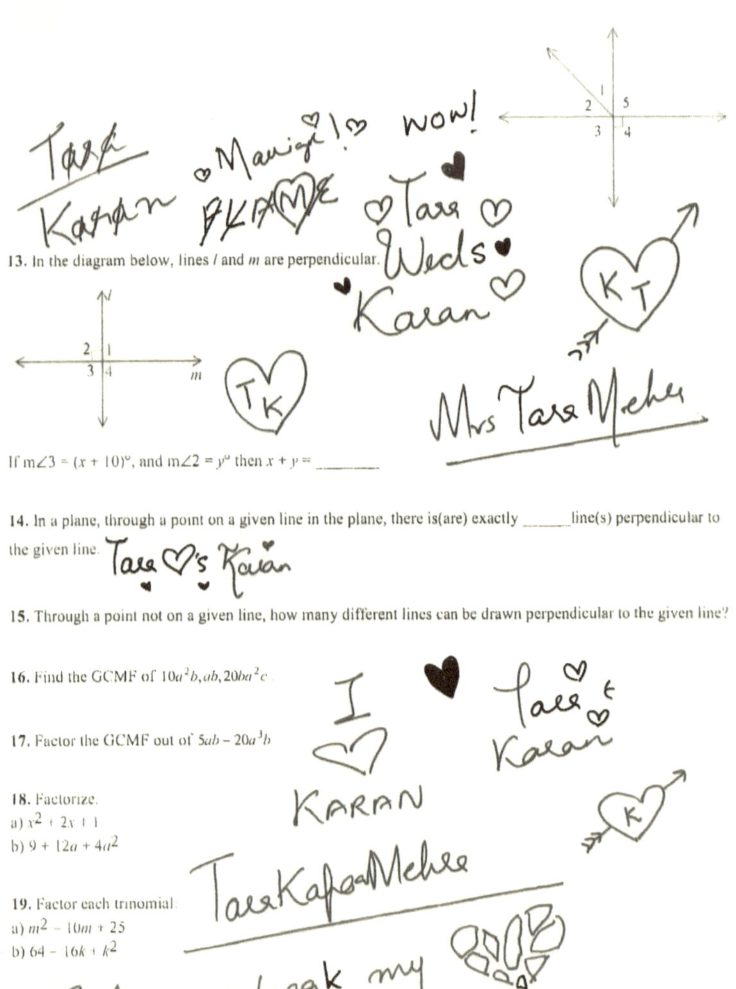

13. In the diagram below, lines *l* and *m* are perpendicular.

If m∠3 = $(x + 10)°$, and m∠2 = $y°$ then $x + y =$ _______

14. In a plane, through a point on a given line in the plane, there is(are) exactly _______ line(s) perpendicular to the given line.

15. Through a point not on a given line, how many different lines can be drawn perpendicular to the given line?

16. Find the GCMF of $10a^2b, ab, 20ba^2c$

17. Factor the GCMF out of $5ab - 20a^3b$

18. Factorize.
a) $x^2 + 2x + 1$
b) $9 + 12a + 4a^2$

19. Factor each trinomial.
a) $m^2 - 10m + 25$
b) $64 - 16k + k^2$

More on Karan . . .

What can I say . . . he is always on my mind. Believe me, one day I will make him the happiest man in the world. I promise to the holy skies above and to our thousands of *devi-devtas* to transcend him to the status of my life partner from what he is now – a 'quarter' boyfriend. Sometimes I wonder if it is God's way of letting me know how to truly live – to surrender myself to Karan's being – to be content and consider myself blessed just because I get a glimpse of him sometimes. As ultimately he is meant to be mine. Both in body and soul. Just a matter of time.

Yes. I can talk this shit too, but I do follow my Mama's diktat to always be real. So I never fake. ;-)

Coming back to the real world, just the way Kareena is so hot it's criminal, this stud should have been in jail to be protected against the likes of Dolly. The quintessential Bollywood Star Son just about to make his debut! He is a celebrity in our Society (thanks to his bloodline) and school too. You know – plays state-level cricket and has received a prize from Kambli himself! Moves around in his dad's classic BMW convertible. The girls adore him, the guys want to be like him. So where does this leave me? All I have to do is get his attention.

But how?

To begin with I have to lose these extra fifteen kilos and I will end up weighing exactly the same as Dolly. But I will never compromise on my modesty – I will never wear short dresses except in private   for his eyes only. OK, maybe

I'll do it on my eighteenth-birthday surprise party that he'll throw for me on a terrace, with heart-shaped balloons, stuffed toys, chocolates and gifts all over the place (like in the most provocative song – *Mere Rang Mein* – of my *dadi's* favourite film). I don't want to be so cruel as to make him wait till marriage and surely he won't have the patience for it, either. Actually, times have changed so don't expect me to cover up and all like Suman! (Readers: watch it on YouTube or ask the older generation because I can't explain.)

Anyway, I have been planning to do it for the last few months (maybe years) but have not lost even one kilo despite giving up ice-cream! I even refused to attend a birthday party at McDonald's because I am so addicted to Happy Meals! Mama says I need to grow out of it but then these days they are giving away such nice toys that it's impossible to go for regular-size meals.

Coming back to Karan . . .

When I saw him staring at Dolly, I gave him a dirty look – you know the one that says, 'never-expected-this-from-you' but he gave it back to me – the look that says, 'do-I-know-you?' OK, I know I don't yet have the right to stop him from looking at other girls and it might even be a natural 'boy' thing to do; but Karan, come on – Dolly is MY friend! Not only that, he also came to talk to us . . . (read Dolly).

Though we live in the same society and he used to be in my school, we never hung out together as he never really noticed us girls before . . . I guess the age gap was bothering him too.

But these little girls have grown up now . . . well almost

He came and said Hi to us, and began some casual talk with Dolly. Anyway, I tried to ignore them by looking elsewhere but I had to strain my ears to listen . . . just then he took her hand and started 'reading' her palm. He was whispering about 'future husband' and 'love life' and 'two babies'!!! . . . No, No, No!!! And this despo – she turned red and couldn't stop giggling at his PJs . . . This went on for a few minutes. I was losing my patience and decided to stop it before they went too far.

I interrupted them, saying, 'Dolly, don't you remember we have this surprise Maths test tomorrow and if you flunk again you are dead?' (Honestly, I wish I had actually said that but all I did was just pull her arm and said bye to Karan; fine I was being a bad person, but then . . . whatever.)

After a while I decided to give her a piece of my mind. I said, 'Are you insane? Don't you know he is much older and you know guys want only one thing. He is only interested in your looks' and blah blah . . . Dolly seemed puzzled and was actually pleased that he wants that 'one thing' from her. Oh God, some girls will do anything to get a guy!

I came home all grumpy to face more grump

Mama-Papa were having a serious discussion. I just hoped it was not about my last term's results. So I quietly walked past them pretending to be zoned out but tried to listen through the door of my room. I heard them saying something about Baby *Didi* – her academic career – the holy town of Kota! It didn't sound interesting so I just decided to do something more productive – like go on Facebook.

And it broke my heart

I mean they just spoke for the first time, just half an hour back and they are friends already? I knew Dolly was an airhead but how could she be so mean? How could she not know that I loved him too?? Jesus, why did you do this to me? I just prayed and prayed that Karan starts hating her!

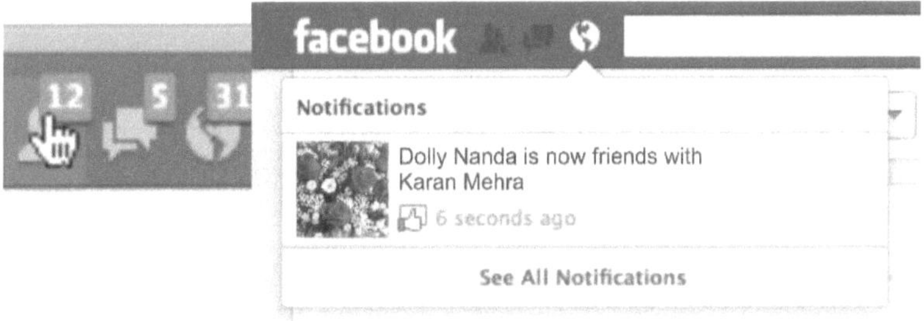

But instead . . .

He asked her out. Today, in school, Dolly was irritatingly giggly so I had to beg her to let me know what was going on. I knew it was inevitable but I was secretly hoping that God would be on my side. I then found out that he had asked her out on a date! I mean, OK, we are fourteen but to go on a date with some random guy? What will her parents think?

But I should have known better. You see, Karan's dad and Dolly's mom are both from the creative field. Means they are broad-minded. That's why my dad feels the way he does. Karan's dad is a fashion designer who is best known for his fling with a Russian item girl who might be a contestant in the Big Boss house next season. Dolly's mama is the hottest looking aunty in our society – an ex Ms Delhi. Dolly once told me her mama has a tattoo on her navel; since that day I have been dying to have a look but unfortunately I don't have X-ray vision. Now she has her own finishing school. Means she trains girls to be more ladylike, walk and laugh in a certain manner and then if all goes well, land an NRI for a husband if the girl is 'homely' or a modelling assignment if the girl is career-minded.

Karan's dad and Dolly's mama are friends – actually, rumours are that they are 'more than friends' . . . Now this is all adult talk, so I'll just skip it except that our maid Sweetie claims she saw them kissing in the lift! Oh well, this is top secret and Mama told me I should not be bothered but what was really bothering me now was that my own marriage was at stake. I had to take some serious steps. But first, time for another 'filler'.

Patriotic Public School

Newsletter for the month of September

Class VII student wins National Junior Level Debate competition

Resham Singh has again done us proud by bringing home this prestigious award, for the event held in Agra last Thursday. The sensitive topic being **'Are we free to push Freedom of Speech?'** She spoke against it, highlighting how fortunate we are to be born in this country where we have the right to exercise this gift, even when some self-proclaimed youth icons are misusing this privilege to get famous. Having Freedom of Speech does not protect one from the consequences of saying something, whether it is being mocked for being ridiculous or punished for being seditious. Resham concluded reiterating the fact that Hate speech is NOT Free speech and irresponsible freedom could actually be deadly to society.

थक गया हू

हमारे शैलू की कविता

थक गया हू यारी का हाथ बढ़ा के
पर मुझे कोई चुनता ही नही
थक गया हू पुकार पुकार के
पर मुझे कोई सुनता ही नही
थक गया हू सो सो के
पर ख़्वाब है के बुनता ही नही
थक गया हू खो खो के
पर मुझे कोई ढूंढता ही नही

Growing-up pains

Why no lip-gloss in school?

By Tara Kapoor

To my teachers and friends – you know me, do I really look the sort who cares two hoots about make up? But if you think about it, it is a burning issue for us girls, something even more important than being able to use cell phones in school. I have a question to ask – why are we always told to dress neatly and smartly for school? Isn't it about looking presentable? Then why is some touch up not allowed when it enhances our features and make us feel more confident?

Just for Fun

But there were other issues back home

When I came back from school, I heard my parents again talking something about Baby *Didi* . . . She was in Class XII, preparing for her Boards, and was never seen or heard outside her room – she studies 24 x 7. She was also supposed to appear for the Great IIT Entrance exams so there was extra pressure on her but, surprisingly, she did not seem to mind! She had no life apart from school and coaching classes and had only one friend, Charu Didi, who was a geek like her. Both were competing for the same thing – top position in school in the Boards and a higher rank than the other in the IIT Entrance exams . . . but they didn't mind helping each other out in their studies – I guess they were real best friends and will always be, unlike mine, who decided to ditch me for a boy!

So when I came home

Though they were discussing Baby *Di*, as soon as they saw me their topic changed. My mama asked me about this term's results, which were due, and how had I done. Frankly, I did not remember as my mind was too preoccupied with Dolly and Karan; so I think I said I'd done pretty well and would let them know. This seemed to satisfy them and they continued with their favourite topic: Baby *Di*.

So I logged on again

At the cost of being branded a psycho, I will reveal my other identity on Facebook . . . I know it sounds wrong, but then who would ever know? While I am still young, I have every right to experiment. I don't know where I heard it but as of now – this is where I can be what I want to be . . .

Trust me, I have taken selfies from every possible angle to make my double chin go away but it just doesn't happen. So after a lot of research, this is what my Profile picture looks like:

Name:	Isabelle
Age:	18
Interested in:	Men
Relationship Status:	It's complicated
Music:	Hard Rock
Movies:	Hollywood and French
Email:	isabelle98@femail.com

I just added my 4311th friend!

Here, I am a celebrity in my own right. So much more popular than Megha or Dolly. And that Karan – I think he does not deserve a person like me.

Today my friend Rocko, 22, was online, so here is the 'transcript' of our chat (yes, I can sound like an adult too).

Rocko: hey there

Isabelle: wassup Rocks?

Rocko: nothing much just leaving for disc in 10 mins

Isabelle: good for u

Rocko: hey where r u from?

Isabelle: US of A, my folks are NRIs, my dad's in India on a project

Rocko: India, where? I am in India too

Isabelle: Delhi

Rocko: holy shit, me too! Where in Delhi?

Isabelle: you know, Defence Colony

Rocko: i am from Vasant Kunj so we r quite close . . . let's go clubbing

Isabelle: we will see . . .

Rocko: hey girl don't mind gotta go. bye

Before we go on you need to have a look at his profile picture!

ROCKO
HE IS SURELY NOT MADE IN INDIA!!!
I know nobody looks as good as their Profile picture but in this case I was hoping he's close!!!

This is not the first time

On Facebook, I have been asked out many times . . . but Rocko seems to be a cool guy. At least he doesn't start with 'what colour are your panties?' The only issue is he is twenty-two – much, much older than me . . . but he is helping me take my mind off Karan.

Just then Mama entered my room

I did not hear the door open and would have been caught today had I not seen her reflection on my monitor. I quickly closed the window and got saved.

It seems she wanted to have some mother–daughter quality time with me. I had been dreading this moment for ages. Not because this is the first time we were having 'the ladies' talk' – it was maybe the hundredth. You see, I am fourteen but still have not got my 'chums' . . . and Mama's concern is having an effect on me too. Almost all the girls in my class, including Megha, have started. But it has not yet happened to me. TBH, my friends have shared all the gory details with me and I am not exactly looking forward to it. Then there is this bra issue . . . I know the only reason I need to wear one is because I am plump around that area and NOT because they are really growing bigger. But then I can brag about it to Megha and Dolly, who were acting so American when their mamas took them lingerie shopping! I knew my mama would probably just hand me down Baby *Didi's* stuff without even bothering about my size! I wish I were an only daughter. It would have been fun growing up!

But as of now I am not even sure if I want to grow up

I know grownups can do whatever they want to but I know sooner or later I will end up looking like Baby *Didi* – I don't want to be rude but she is well . . . Fugly! Thick glasses and two caterpillars for eyebrows. In fact, Mama has been insisting on her getting contact lenses but she happens to have super-sensitive eyes that flutter like a scared butterfly if anyone tries to touch them. That's why she has never worn eyeliner or got her eyebrows shaped and is perhaps stuck with those glasses for life!

I fail to understand why my parents are so obsessed with her (maybe even I am a bit obsessed because I think I have already brought her into the conversation many times already). So here are some facts: the only makeup she does is Parachute coconut oil for hair and skin and Vaseline for her chapped lips and heels. And Odomos is the only moisturiser she has ever used. And some figures: her lowest percentage has been an 87 two years back when she got malaria (despite the moisturiser). Her vision is -6.5, which she sacrificed to speed-read more than 700 words a minute.

Over the years she has mellowed down; now we hardly fight. She is very polite, does Sarasvati puja every morning and whenever she gets time helps Mama around the house. If I ever go to her with a Maths problem she tutors me with full commitment and genuine sisterly affection . . . in other words she has become very, very boring and I am haunted by the thought of ever being like her, even if she tops the school, the state or the country for that matter. More so because she doesn't even have a boyfriend and I surely don't want to be single when I am her age!

But then you can't fight genes and everybody says I am a junior version of her! Please God, anyone but Baby *Didi*!

Unless, of course, I lose this weight and become sexy as I am meant to be!

Speaking of 'sexy'

December

I don't know what's with Dolly these days – looking more 'full bodied' than before. I think she has put on a couple of kilos around her bust and butt, which is really frustrating for me . . . especially now that Karan and she are officially going around. I am sure if I had a boyfriend like Karan I would have been really motivated to look better . . . I don't know. God, why can't I get over this guy . . . well, I just know what I need to do

So I logged on . . .

I have seen the entire series of Friends and know that after a bitter break-up people tend to go on a rebound. So it was destined to be. When I saw Rocko was online I sent him a message:

Isabelle: hi Rocko

Rocko: hi Issi baby!

Isabelle: don't baby me ok?

Rocko: why? aren't we friends?

Isabelle: yeah i guess so. how come u have just 420 friends?

Rocko: i am choosy, anyway how r u today?

Isabelle: down in the dumps

Rocko: why?

Isabelle: this guy I really liked – he is going around with my best friend!!!

Rocko: ☹☹☹

Isabelle: imagine, my own best friend – how could she do this to me??!

Rocko: did she know you had the hots for him?

Isabelle: well, I never told her but she should have guessed

Rocko: life's a bitch baby – ur own people turn against u and then it bites u where it hurts the most

Isabelle: ya, I wanna get over him! Now!

Rocko: u r at the right place baby…count me as ur friend… will be always there for u!

Isabelle: u r a great guy Rocko – u have a GF?

Rocko: no, still have not met the 'right' one

Isabelle: lol u'r kidding, right?!

Rocko: I mean I have not met a girl who understands me

Isabelle: try me

Rocko: u r so sweet Issi baby, I want a girl who is mature and sensitive like u

Isabelle: u'r pulling my leg!

Rocko: no I mean it, since we started chatting I have been thinking about u…I really want to meet you…

At this point this was getting too much for me to handle. I was blushing hotly and couldn't think straight. Also, I did not want to rush into another relationship so I just signed out.

Sweet dreams are made of these . . .

I am chatting with Rocko almost all the time and he is sure helping me get on with my life after Karan

The best thing about me and Rocko is that we have real conversations; we talk about deep stuff too like what all is wrong with this world and what we need to change. We also discuss lighter topics like movies and my favourite Wimpy Kid series. We talk about our aspirations and our passion for writing. Except that he is into serious kind of work and my style is more functional and easy to get. Sometimes I wish he wasn't so much older and good looking, maybe then he would have accepted me the way I am. But this is the dream world that I have created for myself, where I am this sensuous, creative girl who is capable of stimulating guys intellectually too. **Somebody, stop me!**

I really wanted to tell someone about it but things were kind of strained between me and Dolly. She doesn't have a clue about my feelings so I have been kind of avoiding her . . . rather, she has been avoiding me and everything else in her life.- She is either hanging out with Karan, or whatsapping him or talking to him on her cell! This damn technology! But then the same technology was helping me enter into a beautiful relationship myself . . .

I thought of going back to my official best friend – Megha.

But my old pal Megha has no time for me now . . . another consequence of overzealous parents.

More on Megha – my first friend

Megha and I have been together since Class II. She was a really chilled-out girl and I had my first sleepover at her house.

We were almost romantically involved – I don't know what's with little girls, the kind of letters and poems that get exchanged between them – it really makes you wonder if things are all that straight! Particularly considering the harmless 'house-house' and 'doctor-doctor' games we both always played whenever our parents were not around! Thank God I am over that phase but I still have preserved all the letters and cards she has given me.

And what a lucky girl she is – her parents are both high flyers. I heard both are 'Board' members in some big multinational. Being super achievers, they want Megha to follow their footsteps and be really successful in life. Therefore, since the last couple of years, Megha is on a very strict schedule:

Timetable for the month of December

Day	6:00 am	7:30 am- 2:30 pm	4:00 pm	6:00 pm
Mon	Maths Tuition	School	Swimming	Homework
Tue		School	Tennis lesson	Homework
Wed	Chem Tuition	School	Football	Homework
Thu		School	Maths drill	Homework
Fri	Physics Tuition	Student council	Creative writing	Toastmasters club
Sat			Animal rights centre meet	Homework

Note: *Interschool Tennis championship on 11th*
         Mama's birthday on 19th, Christmas partyin the compound on 25th
         Extra classes in school during winter break 10 am- 12 noon

Not only this . . .

Megha is also actively involved in school government – she is a Super Prefect. I must tell you about my school. It's called Patriotic Public School and is run by a bunch of ex- Army Officers! Our parents think it will inculcate a sense of 'honour, responsibility and discipline' in us.

I am not sure if a school can change anybody because its only claim to fame is having the revolutionary TV personality Raina Gupta as an alumnus. A crusader in her own right- she has brought many a scam into the public domain. She is in her thirties, not married, and every time I see her on TV, I get goose bumps. The best thing about her is that despite her persona she tries not to intimidate anyone. She does not grill politicians for the heck of it and asks only relevant, logical questions. She is soft spoken but is very strong headed and an inspiration to all smart girls. I want to be like her when I grow up in every way, except her relationship status. Sometimes I wonder, how could such a personality be a pass out of this school?

Our Princi is a retired Colonel from the Education Corps but is in fact every bit a civilian. Despite him having these big bushy moustaches, nobody takes him seriously. (How can we, he is at the most five feet four inches tall.) He is obviously shit-scared of his wife – Vice Principal Ma'am who is a monster in disguise. It's impossible to imagine her having another life apart from this school, which she runs like an Army base camp. (Except for the fashion shows – ever wondered why most Ms Indias have an Army background?)

So like the Army

My school has lots and lots of ranks. We have the usual Head Boy and Head Girl and their 'Vices'. Then all the students of the school are grouped into four houses (yeah, 'house' is a funny word to create division amongst the students). These houses have their representative colours, Captains and Vice Captains, and the organisational structure goes on and on . . . not to forget the clubs, which have their own presidents and subordinates. It feeds the egos of the teachers who are House In-charge(s) and the kids reporting to them, equally well. Since a quarter of the school holds a rank, howsoever insignificant (like Hall Monitor or Stationary Store Assistant or even Blackboard Keeper), the number of complaining parents also gets reduced.

Since we were still in Class IX . . .

The best a student can manage is being a Super Prefect or the Vice President of a club, like the Literary Club. I missed out on getting the post but I am somewhere in the hierarchy – (but really way down, as I am just a writer for our newsletter). Megha holds the important position of Vice President of the Sports Club, so I too get my share of respect since we are – or rather, used to be – almost inseparable at school, I never felt bored as I had this really smart girl for company who used to laugh at my jokes like mad.

But that was then and this is now

Since last year her parents have been on her case like crazy. OK, she might be doing pretty well in life but a girl needs to have some space too! She has to balance so many responsibilities on her delicate shoulders . . . though since she is a swimmer I am sure she has quite well-developed muscles on them! Anyways – bottom line – she has no time for me anymore. I don't get to hang out with her outside of school, and even in school, she's just too busy with a load of stuff.

I need her again

I have got to share my new love life with someone, I need her to listen to me and relish the juicy details . . . you know, I kind of want her back but maybe one of these days she will realise what she is missing out in life by not hanging around with me anymore. I mean, how serious can you be? This dame's got to have some fun, man!

I decided to go to her house and have a frank girl-to-girl talk

The problem was, when? If you see her schedule, you can tell I fit nowhere . . . maybe this Sunday when she spends quality time at home, I could squeeze in half an hour; maybe I should make an appointment. So I borrowed *Didi's* cell to WhatsApp her on her new iPhone 6 (did I really have to mention this?). Thank God for these chat applications – it would have been awkward to call up someone after this long, and actually talk. I just hope I remember to delete the chat.

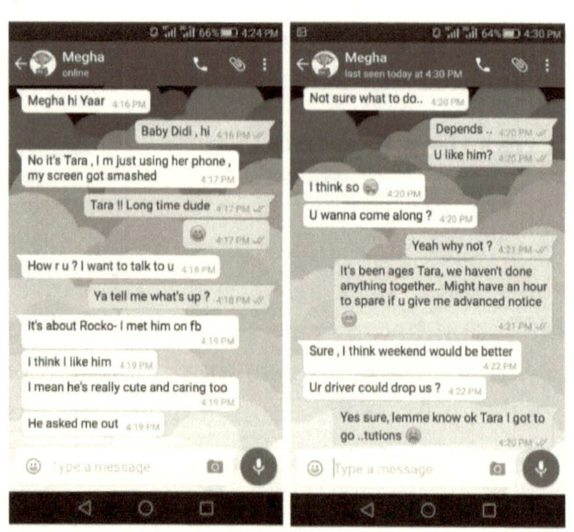

To hell with her

An hour to spare? Who is she anyway?! Cool down, Tara, have to fix this date.

But have things ever been easy for me? I just hope my phone gets repaired without Mama having to spend a lot, otherwise I will be branded 'has no value for Dad's hard-earned money' for life. And this laptop of mine, an antique which was used by Baby Didi for three years (yes, that's what I am – a second-hander) takes centuries to boot and then almost every time, can't find network connection. Keep trying, Tara, don't give up

hope . . .

So after fifteen minutes of fidgeting with this machine, here I am again with my Rocko:

Isabelle: hi Rocko, hru?

Rocko: hi babes

Isabelle: what's up?

Rocko: sad without u! ☹☹☹

Isabelle: lol ☺☺☺

Rocko: btw when r we meeting?

Isabelle: but aren't we going too fast?

Rocko: it's been a month! gotta meet now

Isabelle: well...

Rocko: come on babes u can do it

Isabelle: ok...where and when?

Rocko: someplace romantic? ♥♥♥

Isabelle: *(Thank you God, this can't be happening to me!)* McDonalds?

Rocko: ROFL

Isabelle: why? Too cheap, u wanna take me out someplace more expensive?

Rocko: sort of…ok first meeting ur call, then I decide. ok?

Isabelle: Rocko, I have to tell u something though, promise me u won't get upset?

Rocko: try me

Isabelle: it's not my real name

Rocko: lol

Isabelle: u r not mad at me?

Rocko: why? it's all right

(I was so touched I had tears in my eyes, he sure knew how to treat a girl.)

Isabelle: so will u still meet me?

Rocko: as long as u r a girl, I will lmao *(what's that?)*

(I wanted to tell him my real age as well but maybe he would be really hurt so I decided to postpone it; but what's with him today, what's lmao? So I was looking it up on Google at the same time, just to make sure it wasn't an indecent comment – aahh . . . 'laughing my ass out'.)

Isabelle: ok let me know which McDonalds and when…

Rocko: ok will send u a msg…so TTYL…

Isabelle: hey, don't u wanna know my real name?

Rocko: doesn't matter girl...let's keep the surprise element alive...tell me when we meet.

hey, take down my cell no 919812349900...give me yours

(Ufff . . . My Rocko, where were you all my life and what's TTYL?! Just forget it.)

But the problem was . . .

I did not have enough time to lose any weight. So he will reject me as soon as he sees me! Oh God, have healthy girls like me no right to fall in love?

Maybe I should just prepare him – so as soon as I got my phone back (of course, I have no value for my dad's hard earned money – it's another story that he just sits in an air-conditioned office the whole time 'net-working' – whatever the heck it means). I Whatsapped him

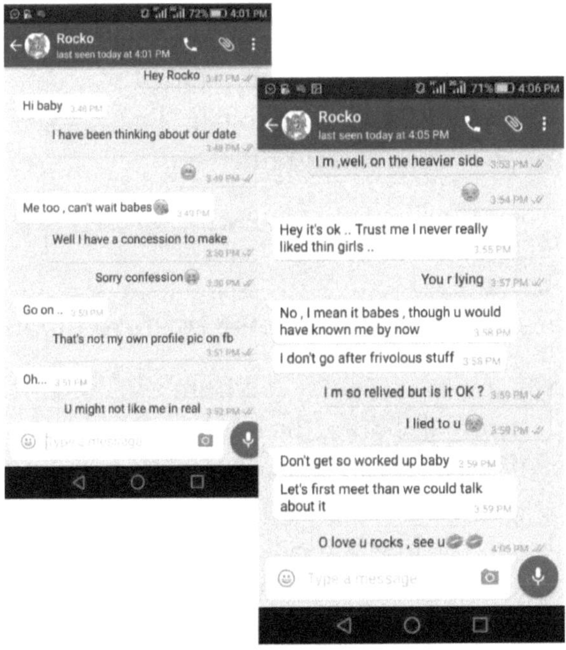

So problem solved for now . . .

As I was preparing for my big date, I also had to tie up with Megha to come with me . . . at least she could console me if it didn't work out between Rocko and me . . . should I message her? Well, I really want to see her so I'll give her a surprise visit: busy or not, here I come!

And sure enough, she is a true friend

Though it was kind of awkward when I went to her house after a year or so (last time was on her landmark birthday bash when she entered her teens – I am really tempted to tell you that it was an 'Instagram-themed party'! Her parents are so good, really) . . . I mean we meet practically every day in school, but she is in her own zone. Thank God we connected like nothing had happened . . . actually nothing did happen except for her schedule. But then maybe it was time to show her how to lead a normal life, like me.

When I told her more about Rocko and that we might be in love, she was as excited as me and started planning the date at once without even referring to her 'Things to do' list! Oh thank God, we are in this together!

So after spending a happy hour with Megha, I went home in a good mood.

But there was something else in store for me . . .

Apparently my mama got a call from the school about my marks . . . before declaring the results officially they decided to discuss my report with my parents. I got a rotten 78 per cent, that's all! My mama was like, 'Tara, after all those tuitions, is this the best you can do? What will happen when you have board exams to take? When will you get serious in life? It's not a joke, OK . . .' Blah blah blah . . .

Sounds cheesy but when you are in love . . .

You get the strength to bear anything so I just stood there and let them vent out their frustrations. To be honest, I did not want to feel sorry about it. You see, after a long time I was actually happy and I did not want anyone or anything to spoil it for me so I just apologised, promised that I would do better and went into my room with a real sad face – after all I had to give them some satisfaction . . . who says I can't act?

I was feeling quite connected to Rocko now; in fact, it was even OK with me if we never met, as deep down I did not want to get exposed and ruin a beautiful friendship. Despite his cool dude looks, he sounded very sorted out and mature. Except that his favourite pastime was lazing around on the sofa watching the Tom and Jerry Classic collection with nuggets and cola for company. (OK, this might not sound mature but if you analyse it, it meant he was man enough to admit it.) He has a spiritual side to him too, which actually sounds quite logical. Though it's my book, I'll share a part of his blog:

'Why are we so miserable? Is it because a majority of people don't do what God intended them to do? Each of us has some inherent talent, which was gifted to us by God to make things easier for us and to run this world without chaos. But we have made it difficult for own selves by not listening to our calling and by being too influenced by what others might want us to do or be.

'If all of us follow our own natural path, the world will be a much happier and more loving place. It is our own frustrations that give rise to hatred and jealousies for others, who we think are doing better than us. All of us are just competing to come first in this never-ending rat race. We are running so fast that though our heart tells us to stop and think, we can't. We are too insecure to let any other run past us. Even if the prize comes at the cost of our forgotten dreams, we still want it; even if we forget ourselves in the bargain, we still want it; even if we are all losers in the end, we still want it.

'We have made it so difficult for God to give us happiness and still we blame Him for our miseries. Why? After all, we asked for it.'

Isn't he something?

But that evening I watched a repeat of the Internet episode of Gumraahhh on TV.

When things are too good to be true they usually are . . .

I watched this programme, which has that cute host who keeps telling kids to beware of the dangers, of the big bad wolves in the bushes . . . and I knew this friendship was a big mistake! Maybe Rocko is actually a psycho or worse, a rapist or a serial killer! I mean was I mad or something to think I had found true love on the Net??!!

But it does happen . . .

. . . to other people. I know that Sonu Didi (so who's she? She is Ruby Masi's daughter. And who's Ruby Masi? The one who has a plush bungalow on Golf Course Road, remember?), not only found her true love on the Net, they are now actually married and have a balloon for a baby!!

The other day they came over to our house and Mama and Dadi were going gaga over it. Hey, babies have the right to be round, but not me? Not fair!

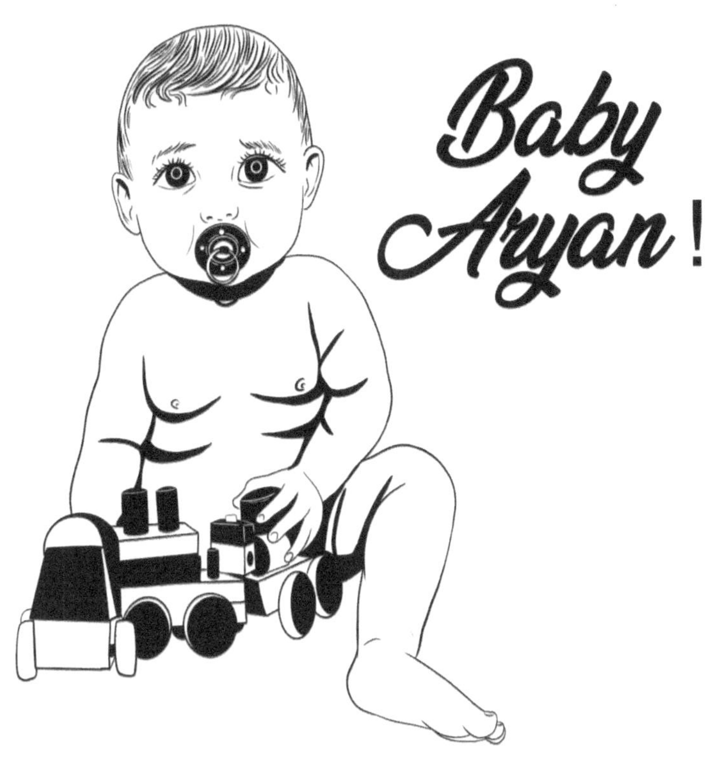

Why this Kolaveri Kolaveri Kolaveri di?

But then why was I getting so paranoid, maybe Rocko is a really nice guy and is exactly how he sounds on the Net – except that I feel his real name is not Rocko . . . and he always wanted to meet in someplace private and romantic! Maybe he just wants that one thing from me . . . but my heart refuses to believe that he is evil . . . he is not only a great looker, he is also sensitive, and so damn intelligent . . . how is that even possible . . . . OMG there was so much confusion.

But one has got to learn to take some risks in life and I decided to carry on with my plans of meeting him. My only worry was that Rocko might find Megha more attractive . . . well, too late!

Ishq waala love?

Wasn't it romantic? It was a Sunday but I woke up even before 8 am with butterflies in my stomach reminding me of what lay ahead . . . maybe a handshake, maybe even a kiss? I got up from my bed just the way thin girls in movies do (except for the bad breath and messed up hair), with pink teddy bears and Barbie dolls on my pillows; the setting was just perfect! Surely the rest of the day would also be straight out of the movies . . .

It's rocking – yaara kabhi ishq to karo

For the first time, I found myself singing in the shower . . . I kept rehearsing what I was going to say to him but then decided to just play it cool. I mean, I didn't want to look like the 'always available' types. I got dressed and told Mama that Megha and I were going to McDonald's as we wanted to catch up . . . my parents were really pleased as they did not approve of Dolly in the first place and were glad I started 'playing' with that 'decent girl' Megha again. Megha also told her Mama she needed the driver for an outing with me. Likewise, her mama smelled nothing fishy about it so off we went. In principle we were not lying . . . just a few small distortions in the facts . . .

Tu kahan, kahan, kahan, kahan, ye bata

We had been waiting nearly half an hour for him to arrive. There was just a bunch of kids hanging around. He had told me he would be wearing a black Lacoste T-shirt with light-blue faded Levi's jeans and white Puma shoes. I kept straining my eyes to spot the brands but I wasn't able to find this combination. I was supposed come as The Lady in Red but decided to change my look at the last moment as it wasn't looking all that great on me. And it turned out to be a really wise move.

Tujhe dekha to yeh jana sanam

Pyar hota hai deewana sanam!! I swear. I saw a fatso with the same combination of black, light blue and white, with a Footlong in one hand and a cola in the other, giving even Jughead some tough competition; but wait, he looked familiar – oh God, this can't be!

But I didn't want to jump to any conclusions, so called up Rocko from my cell to double check!

Kaise bataun . . .?

Rocko, my handsome 22-year-old stud was actually Rohan Gupta, a guy from my school! He was in Class X, considered a geek who had no interest in girls. This drip even played chess, was a member of the Literary Club who was originally offered the position of President, which he declined saying that he was only there for the love of writing! He is the one who writes sad poems in Hindi under the pen name Shailu. Rohan, Rocko, Shailu – God knows how many other avatars he has. He was beginning to freak me out. Imagine – this sweet, innocent, philosophical kid was some sort of Internet criminal!

The indigestible part being he was so crazy about food that he couldn't even wait for me!

I looked at Megha, disconnected the call, and

Bhaag bhaag DK Bose, bhaag bhaag!

We ran and ran till we reached the parking lot where her driver was waiting for us. Thank God I have a rich friend with a plush air-conditioned car or I would have died of heartburn! And then we carried on about how stupid I was to think that a hot guy would fall for me and we should never trust anyone on the Internet and not chat with strangers blah blah . . . I made her promise that she would never ever spill my secret to anyone . . .

But we were not the only ones in the car . . .

Megha's Driver Uncle, a faithful of their family for a decade, her self-appointed bodyguard (stop thinking about

Salman Khan and read on), was listening to all the juicy details but I was sure he got nothing as we were speaking frantically in the kind of English which sure was beyond his comprehension. But that smart ass picked the buzz words like 'date', 'Internet' and 'mistake', which were repeated on and on . . .

So the next thing was Megha's mama waiting for us to rip us apart. Apparently this man had called up Megha's mama and blurted out everything to his Madam while we were still in the lift . . . these grownups really get a kick out of humiliating us kids!

Guess it was time to face some real music

'Girls, don't think we don't know what all is going on in your lives . . . we have been your age and understand that there could be physical attractions; after all the body is changing and you are becoming young women . . . didn't we teach you that it's very dangerous to talk to strangers? Even if it's on the Net it can have lethal consequences, then who will take responsibility of your actions? One wrong step and you will regret it for the rest of your lives! God, where did we go wrong?'

And she started to cry . . . and so did Megha, who gave me a dirty look as if it was all my fault!

It was too much for me to take so I just headed back home . . .

And I should have known better than to actually trust Megha's mother! When I came home, my parents were already waiting to pounce on me.

I had no option but to tell them everything – including my fake identity on Facebook, Karan, Dolly and what happened today . . . surprisingly, they did not scold me – maybe just looked at me with sheer contempt. I guess they needed time to digest what they had just heard and then decide how to punish me, so I just went back to my room and had a full bout of crying.

Oh God, I have let down everybody!

For the first time, I felt guilty about this whole episode. My parents would have never imagined that their roly-poly cutie pie was a cheapo! Not only was I cheap – I was also foolish to get into a relationship with someone I had not even seen . . . Oh my God, I had been pouring my heart out to this weirdo! I had lost Karan to Dolly; now even Megha would probably break up with me . . . worse, I have still not started preparing for the term's exams . . . oh God, I didn't ever want this!

I had almost finished crying when I heard Mama entering my room. I tried but I wasn't able to think straight and come up with excuses for my erratic behaviour.

And what happened next, almost changed my opinion about my mother.

Mama: Tara, can we talk? How are you feeling? Here, I got your favourite *adrak wali chai* with extra sugar.

Me: You are not angry, Mama? . . . I am really sorry . . .

Mama: And so am I . . . you see, I am sorry I did not give you the time you deserved, that your papa and I were always preoccupied with your Didi's academics and forgot we had another daughter who needs us too.

Me: What? Mama . . . I don't get it.

Mama: You see, it's your weight problem that is leading to so many insecurities in your mind . . . that's why you created this alter ego on Facebook . . . I understand all that because I have gone through this myself when I was younger and I still don't have a perfect body despite these half-marathons. But you know what, I learnt early that if I wanted others to accept me then I've got to accept myself first as I am and not try to be someone else . . . so just try loving yourself more, Tara.

Me: Easier said than done, Mama . . .

Mama: Remember, Tara, being thin will not change the person inside you.

Me: It will make me better looking, though.

Mama: But will it make you a better person?

Me: I guess not . . . but I want to lead a normal life, Mom, like a normal girl, like Dolly! See how popular is she with the guys.

Mama: Oh, so maybe that's the 'new normal'! Tara, you are not Dolly and I wouldn't trade you with anyone in this world. You are smart. Can't you see that?

Me: Being smart is not good enough, Mom . . . you don't know how it feels when I am alone in the trial room, trying to fit into something trendy. Or when I have to keep pulling down my T-shirt to cover my humongous bumps while my friends show up in tank tops and shorts. Or that till now not even one guy I know has shown any interest in me. Or when I look at these fashion models and wonder why has God been so cruel to me . . .

Mama: Tara, you see their perfect bodies but you don't see the hard work and time spent in the gym to achieve those bodies. Nothing comes easy in this world, Tara. If you want to lose weight so badly you've got to sweat it out. Or learn to accept what you have.

Me: Dolly doesn't go to a gym, Mom, she plays no sports, she is simply blessed. Oh, how I hate her!

Mama: Tara, you will not understand it now, but one day you will, I assure you.

Me: Let's see, Mama, but I am truly sorry . . .

Mama: Honestly, I am a little disappointed that you went ahead for that date . . . you were lucky you got saved!

Me: Lucky? That my Prince Charming turned out to be a frog?

Mama: No, because your frog turned out to be Prince Charming. What if he happened to be an old guy in his forties? What if he tried to get physical? These things do happen in the real world, Tara, face it. You are not a kid anymore but you are still very vulnerable . . .

Me: Yeah, I guess you are right; it did strike me, but I thought really good things and really bad things only happen to others. For average girls like me, life is plain boring . . . *Bach gaye* that Rohan did not see me or I would have been the laughing stock of school.

Mama: No, he wouldn't tell anyone as he was as involved as you were, and he too was playing with fire . . . try to get me his mama's number, I need to speak to her.

Me: Oh noooooooooo! Mama, don't do that to me!

Mama: But I have got to put an end to this.

Me: I have an idea . . . talk to the school Principal to organise some sort of workshop to warn kids . . . keep it general, please, I don't want anyone to think that I have anything to do with it. Or maybe as a parent you could just contribute an article about it in the newsletter. I know it's allowed.

Mama: Oh Tara, I am so proud of you! I always knew you were very smart . . . but why are you so anti Rohan? I heard he is some sort of an intellectual? Maybe you both can be friends?

Me: Yuck! Just the thought is gross! No girl at school would ever want to be seen with him, do you know what he looks like?

Mama: Oh, never knew you were a racist too!

Me: I am not but my own friends would probably break up with me if I included a loser like Rohan in my friends' list!

Mama: Oh yeah? Just because he is fat? Nobody is perfect, Tara, and he is definitely doing pretty well for himself − a topper, a state-level chess player, a writer . . . and he is not worth you? What if somebody felt the same about you?

Me: Maybe somebody already does but this is life, Mama - it's not fair!

Mama: Life is unfair. That's why it is beautiful. I guess you will learn with time . . . you know I don't want to push you

Me: Yeah, so let's not talk about Rohan any more, Mama, promise?

Mama: Okay, but remind me about the article I have to write, OK?

Me: Yeah, OK.

Mama: Also, this weekend we are going to get you some nice bras and all! Just me and you, mother−daughter time . . .

And she hugged me − after ages, I think. After our 'chai pe charcha' I felt so much lighter. And about Rocko, sorry − Rohan − then I am a racist. The system is like that, and I am not ready to change it. As yet.

But I had still not learnt my lesson . . .

What a nerve. I was the one who always felt conscious

about my weight, and Rohan? Hats off to his confidence! So I was back to square one. Karan would have never taken advantage of a girl like this. God, why am I thinking about him – is it yet another rebound?

Then I made a pact with myself to stop thinking of that jerk Karan, that airhead Dolly or that football Rocko anymore. What's done is done. I had other important things waiting for me at school as well as home..

Like my mama

Her so-called article was the usual five rules for Internet safety we all know but don't usually follow. And guess what, it got printed right next to 'Shailu's' award-winning poem. Though it's a very sensitive issue, he actually ended up getting a lot of attention from girls. Including me. Because he made me cry. Once again.

It's pathetic, what my life has come to – like a jigsaw puzzle whose pieces I am desperately trying to fit. I know Karan has no idea that he has ruined my life – in fact I bet I don't even exist for him except as Dolly's 'fat' friend. Megha, who was once my better half will stay away from me now. Dolly couldn't care less – she has Karan all to herself. Rocko – he doesn't exist. Literally.

So what do I have – my laptop and my cell phone for company and an unlimited supply of chips and cola for comfort.

Also this dark cloud of depression is hovering everywhere ever since this little girl, nearly a preschooler, got molested. I am too sad to write anything so I will leave you with the newsletter I was talking about. You will see why I still don't hate Rocko, despite what he did to me.

Patriotic Public School

Newsletter for the month of December

Internet Safety and You- 5 Rules to Follow:

1. Promise you will go only on those websites that are age appropriate

2. Use passwords that other people cannot guess easily

3. Don't go on dating sites and never go meet your 'purely online' friends.

4. Avoid scams about winning lotteries/prizes.

5. Never display your personal information (cell number, address, etc.)

वो क्यो रो रही थी ???

कल जब चाचा ने पास बुलाया था
गोद मे बिठा के मेरा गाल सहलाया था
मां , क्यो तुने मुझे चिल्ला के अंदर बुला लिया था ?

Friend School से जल्दी गई , सुना है , पेट मे उसके दर्द उठा था
हमारे P.T. Teacher का तो मान बहोत था!!
मां , फिर क्यो पुलिस ने उन्हे arrest किया था ?

School bus वाले हमारे driver uncle
देने लगे मुझे काफ़ी महंगीवाली chocolate कल...
मां , क्यो तुने खुद मुझे रोज school छोडने का, फैसला लिया था ?

ये क्या हो गया है तुझे मां आजकल ?
मुझे लेके तुम क्यो डरी डरी रहती हो ?
और इतने सवाल करती रहती हो...!!
" किसने दी chocolate? , " क्यो हो गई Late ?"
" ये निशान कैसे ? " .... "किसीने , 'कही ' छूआ तो नही ? "
मां , तुम्हे कुछ हुआ तो नही ?

ये सारी बातें छोडो मां ,
आजकी बस बात सुनो मां....

हमारी Principal madam कही चली गई है !!!
School के सामने बह रहा लोगों का झरना है
हर एक political party का वहा धरना है
मेरी समझ मे कुछ नही आ रहा है...

और हां,
School के gate पर , मेरी 'उस' सहेली के papa,
अपना सर पटक रहे थे !!!
और उसकी मां फुट-फुट के रो रही थी !!!
पता नही , वो क्यो फुट-फुट के रो रही थी...
मां , क्या तुम्हे पता है के, वो क्यो रो रही थी ?
चुप क्यो हो मां , बताओ ना , वो क्यो रो रही थी ???

Anyway, I was talking about Mama

Since our last talk, she had loosened up. She wasn't even shouting at me anymore. Something was up, but what? Maybe these guys had decided to send me away to boarding school to fix me but then I've been threatened with being sent to a hostel since I was three years old and now know better: that my mama fussed over us so much that she could not bear the separation. So what was it?

I know my mama used to be an important person earlier; sometime back I saw some old business cards with a fancy title and all, lying around in her drawer. Who knows, if she had not given up her job, probably she could have been even more successful than Megha's mama. This was ten years back and things change . . .

I have seen her doing a lot of stuff

Apart from cribbing about Sweetie and taking care of the house, I also know that she is some sort of an artist. She says when she was younger she could not follow her dream of being one and instead did an MBA. (Like most Indian students – no matter where they come from – arts, commerce or engineering – an MBA is compulsory! I swear, when will people dare to think beyond the IIMs?)

So, obviously, she dutifully got into the corporate world. Her folks were college professors and in those days 'Art' was not a real career unlike now when over-enthusiastic parents push their reluctant little Picassos into drawing lessons.

But I think she did not find office politics very exciting so she gave it up and became a full-time housewife.

I felt I needed to find out what was up with her, I owed it to her. So I went ahead to have a talk about her for a change. Have you ever realised that nobody thinks of mothers as real people who also have feelings? Well, after our talk, I did.

Me: So, Mama, what's up? You look very happy.

Mama: Yeah, Tara, I am – you know, I'm going have an art exhibition in a couple of months!

Me: Oh! What do you mean?

Mama: What does an art exhibition mean?

Me: When did this happen?

Mama: Well, I have been thinking about it since the last year or so but wasn't sure if I could do it.

Me: Means you are going to display your stuff? Wow! We will be famous!

Mama: We? Yeah, if everything goes well. You know, I wasn't going to do it but your dad motivated me to try it out. I wasn't sure if the stuff I do would actually sell. Your dad tried to convince me to stop thinking about it from a commercial angle. But I couldn't help it, coming from a marketing background. Moreover, I did not want to fail.

Me: Fail and you, Mama? I heard you were a top student and had a great job? Why did you give it up?

Mama: Well . . . when your dad left the army and took up this job in a private company, it was almost like he was starting from scratch . . . being an HR consultant, he had so much travelling to do, visiting all the company offices wherever they were. We hardly got to see him except on weekends. I was with a start-up and mine was a tough job, too. You were just a baby and clearly suffering, always down with the usual cough, cold and fever . . . and I used to get home late. It was getting tough for me to manage everything by myself plus the guilt had taken a heavy toll on me. It all started with my forgetting my computer password, our flat number, even Baby's real name . . . and before I knew it, your dad took me to a shrink.

Me: Oh, really?

Mama: Yeah . . . then I had a long talk with your dad and your *dadi*, who had come over to take care of you girls. However, she couldn't stay for long as your *dada* was still alive but was very sick himself. I know she sounds mean sometimes but she helped us a lot. But I realised I was shit at multitasking. We agreed that somebody has to take a backseat, and being your mother, it had to be me. Don't ask me why because I can't explain. I was going to take a sabbatical.

Me: Then why didn't you go back to work when I got older?

Mama: I guess it was not really meant to be . . . I got so caught up in running my home that I did not realise that time was flying and I lost out on many opportunities. I did try a couple of times but by then it was too late . . . the reality is that I got lazy, but sooner or later, I knew, I had to return to my first love – art. But I am still not sure if I would do well as an artist.

Me: But you are fabulous!

Mama: Yeah, here's the deal –fabulous stuff does not sell so easily. I am an uncomplicated, practical person and not a philosopher or a psychologist! I do stuff that involves a lot of skill, technique and looks great to the eye . . . and not something that is too deep to understand.

Me: Oh . . . I think I am getting it. But it's OK, Mama, Dad is right. Like Rancho said – don't run after success – run after excellence; then success will automatically follow!

Mama: Tara, I under estimated you – you are so mature for your age! Thanks, I feel on top of the world!

Me: Go ahead and have that exhibition, Mama – I am sure you will do great!

Not only did I feel super after counselling my own mother, I understood one thing – that adults have even more 'complicated' complexes!

So I was growing up in the true sense. Until . . .

They announced at school that Classes IX and XI were going to get their own farewell nights, except that here it would be called **'Prom Night'** (*I know what you are thinking*). So this year even we will get to party. This demand for parties for IX and XI had been going on for ages but this year, finally, the school administration gave in. Usually such events are planned for before the exams but the school is sick of parents complaining that kids can't really prioritise what's more important and they lose focus on studies.

My school has this knack of making a Project out of everything and then spending inordinate amounts of time in preparations!

Maybe kids are not really meant to grow up! The whole school was on some sort of adrenalin rush! I mean it's just a damn school function, after all, and to be honest, I was happy that was not going to be called 'Farewell'. The students (except Class XII) just get promoted to higher classes and do not really leave the school!

But I was part of this whole corrupt system and got influenced too. I had to be, as my pals Megha and Dolly were both raring to go, and were totally obsessed about it, like what they would wear, who would be Prom Queen, and so on . . . I wasn't really competing for that title as I was busy thinking of my academic score that I had to work on. I had promised my mom I was going to work really hard. OK, I confess: deep down I was secretly praying that something miraculous happens and I get that crown.

If you don't know how it works, then this is for you . . .

**Students are invited to the event of the year
the Prom Party**

There will be fun activities and some grooving too Come
beautiful and handsome to celebrate those magical moments

Exciting games and new titles:

Miss and Master of class | Miss and Master All rounder
Miss and Master Brains

Chief Guest:
Our Alumna Raina Gupta -- Popular TV Journalist and activist
Crowning would be done by our alumni and now celebrity guests:
Mr. Karan Mehra & Ms. Sonali Das

Dress Code:
Smart and decent Formals

Timings 7:00 pm onwards
Dates: 26th of March Class IX | 30th of March Class XI

What was that again?

OMG! Crowning would be done by whom? Oh no, why did Karan have to be the only male ex-student doing well in life! Actually, he is still in college but he just happens to be more famous than any of his batch-mates; needless to mention he's the Princi's nephew too. God, this means he is coming for my class's Prom Night! And he is going to see me in a sari or an evening gown! Oh God! This can't happen to me! God, why??!! Why did you do this to me? Of all the girls out there, why was I the one who was always referred as 'being on the healthy side'? I hate it, I hate being healthy! God! Do something!

But maybe I was being too hard on myself

So what if he would be there? I could just carry on as if nothing happened between us except for my one-sided love. Sad but true. Maybe he wouldn't even notice me as his eyes would be on Dolly all the time! But how could I give up so easily?

I decided that I would not be a quitter!

I will fight tooth and nail for the title of Prom Queen even if I have to die for it! This is my one big opportunity to grab Karan's attention and I am not going to blow it! All I have to do is lose 15 kg in the next three months, which is not so difficult, after all – I will just give up eating! How hot I will look. Imagine, if in a cylinder the radius is reduced by 25 per cent and the height is increased by two per cent, what will happen to the curved surface area? God, I badly want to be thin this time, I am really committed, so don't give up on me! And guess what, the timing could not have been better – New Year's round the corner and I can start from first January! Oh, this is divine intervention!

So how do I begin?

I didn't have any game plan, so I looked it up on Google . . . I couldn't find any decent three-month diet plans (except a '3-month wedding day plan', which was a bit embarrassing to do plus I had to eat grilled crabs for dinner; come on, who eats that shit in North India except those on Page 3?)

I did find some regimens of shorter duration. So after a lot of research on the Net, I concluded that if I alternate between a *7 Days' Little Black Dress Plan*, followed by a *2 Weeks' Beach Body Plan* and so on, it would lead to a loss of minimum 18 kilos by the end of three months (had to keep a margin of three kilos for Seema *Didi's* big fat Punjabi wedding end of February).

Tara's New Year Resolution:

To lose 15 kilos by 25th March

Hey, maybe I should take notes in case I decide to write a book on it later . . . it will be for a noble cause to help girls like me; needless to add, there'll be media coverage and all – I am going to be famous!

Day 1: Only fruits but no mangoes or bananas

Day 2: Only raw vegetables/salad except potato

Day 3: Go bananas (nothing else)

Day 4: Milky way (nothing except milk shakes- so get creative)

Day 5: No breakfast. Only vegetables juices through the day

Day 6: Treat day: Fruits and any one meal of boiled rice and dal

Day 7: Fruit smoothie for breakfast and salad for lunch, no dinner

By the end of the first week of Jan, I am going to fit into a black dress. Which I don't have. Instead I could try that tight, black see-through T-shirt? Ummm . . . sexy.

Week 1	Week 2
Breakfast: one fruit or corn flakes **Snack:** 4 almonds **Lunch:** Soup and boiled vegetables **Snack:** One unsweetened biscuit **Dinner:** 1 boiled egg	**Breakfast:** 1 tomato or 1 cucumber **Snack:** 2 walnuts **Lunch:** boiled rice/ 1 Roti with a cup of vegetables/dal **Snack:** Toast with margarine **Dinner:** Small cup of milk or yogurt

By the third week of Jan, I should be ready for the beach! But there is no beach around and it's January! Maybe my new red bra and panty set in my shower will do for now. Ummm . . . Sexier.

I am sure in the coming two–three months I could convince Mama to buy me a black dress but from where would I get that bikini?

Well, I looked for this diary which Dolly gave me on my last birthday, and found it under a pile of old school note-books. I thought it looked too kiddish so never used it – until now.

25th Dec

Good morning, Diary.

Merry Christmas! *What an auspicious day to start writing my new Weight Loss Book. As I take the first step, I must learn to enjoy the journey and not just be overtaken by the destination! Yes! What a profound thought — the journey is more important than the destination — wonder why nobody thought of it before?!*

Tonight there are Christmas celebrations happening in the Party Hall. The whole society is going to be there but I am not too sure I want to go, as frankly I have nothing to wear! Baby Didi is not going either as she is really annoyed because she was asked to come as Santa!

I can't pretend to be happy when I am not . . . but then I am starting my diet from 1st Jan so this means I just have this week to freak out! I have to go to this party, I heard they have got goodies from 'Carolina's Cakes and Pies'! Can't afford to miss it! Maybe I can find something from Baby Didi's wardrobe. The silver lining is that it's Winter so who can go wrong with the classic combination of a white top, black trousers and a red jacket?

26th Dec

1:00 am

Thank you, Santa — everything was perfect — as usual.

At the last minute Baby Didi decided to go and stole my 'classic combination' idea! So as usual I had nothing to wear!

There was a Couples' Game and guess what – no guy wanted to pair up with me so I couldn't participate, even though it was about Bollywood and I could have easily nailed it!

The cakes and pies from Carolina never made it to the party venue due to the traffic jams, so the wise aunties from our society decided to treat us to homemade namkeen and laddoos!

Karan and Dolly couldn't take their hands off each other – close dancing and all – such shamelessness! Everybody was watching you, guys, take it easy!

They announced **'Star Couple of the Evening'** *– and no prizes for guessing who won.*

1st Jan

9:30 pm

Dear Diary,

Happy New Year. *Unfortunately, my first day was a flop. I couldn't do it properly as Mama had planned a family brunch at a new upcoming dhaba-style Punjabi restaurant at Pandara Road.*

Who can resist Yakhni Chicken, Kadhai Paneer, Mutton Chops and Butter Naaaaaaaaaaaaan??!!

I feel terrible. I really have to make it work, I can't afford to fail this time!

4th Jan

9:45 pm

I did it! Three days of crash dieting!! I didn't know I have so much willpower!

Is it just me or are my jeans already fitting better? I am so proud of myself . . . it's not easy but totally worth it!

So at the end of 3 months I will be a brand-new Tara — slim and trim. Then maybe I won't even need to run after Karan — I will get any guy I want. Yahooooooooo!!

7th Jan

10:15 pm

Dear Diary,

I have been following this diet for a week now. And man, it's tough! When I woke up today I wasn't able to move my body . . . I felt so lethargic . . . My stomach was making all sorts of rumbling noises and my body begged me to eat . . . but I ignored all such obstacles (like a true-blue Indian student) and went ahead with my daily plan. I pushed myself to go to school, but man, was it tough!

During assembly I couldn't stand and almost fainted . . . I knew I had to eat. I headed straight for the school cafeteria and thought of ordering something light like a salad but it wasn't on the menu. The schools serve only grub like fries, burgers and samosas . . . I tried to go back without eating but then it was impossible for me to ignore the smell of hot samosas. I planned on just one but by the time I finished I realised I had actually eaten four . . . suddenly all this high-calorie food was making me nauseous and I went straight to the girl's toilet and vomited.

When I was done, a thought hit me — I wasn't feeling sick — in fact, I was feeling better after the puking. I actually offloaded all the samosas straight to the pot! My body got no fat from this junk! It meant that I could actually eat all the food I wanted to and then get rid of it! Why did I not think of this before?? This will be a game changer!

13th Jan

11:30 pm

Dear Diary,

I don't know if it's the large bonfire in this chilly winter night or having Karan coming over to say hello to me during the celebrations in our society that is making me feel so deliciously warm and longing for . . . you know what . . .

Just 2 kilos less and I already feel the difference . . . yeah, because Karan had never even noticed me before so why did he specially come over to wish me Happy Lohri and offer me some popcorn, too? But shit, I want to kick myself for not having a conversation with him, imagine what it could have led to if I had the bloody guts to open my mouth:

Karan: *Hey, hi there, Tara.*

Me: *Hi, ah haan . . . Karan?*

Karan: *You know me right? We have met a couple of times before.*

Me: *Oh yes . . . I remember. How are you?*

Karan: *I'm OK, same as ever, but you look . . . changed?*

Me: *Oh . . . hope it's for the better.*

Karan: *You look spectacular . . . and this fire . . . this weather . . . I didn't realise how beautiful you are.*

Me: *Sorry, Karan, don't forget I am Dolly's friend . . .*

Karan: *Oh that? I am not really sure about it, she is just a pretty face and I like girls who are also intelligent – just like you, Tara . . .*

Me: *Stop it, Karan, I am not comfortable discussing this*

Karan: *Will you go out with me? Will you at least think about it?*

Me: *You are moving too fast.*

Karan: *I have to . . . There is something about you . . . Can we ever be together?*

Me: *Not while you are still with Dolly . . . sorry, Karan, you have to choose and I don't compromise, OK? I don't want to be the reason behind anyone's breakup.*

Karan: *No, you are not . . .this has been going on for the last few days. She does not understand me, Tara . . . we are not compatible, have no communication – and I have a strong feeling about you and me . . .*

Me: *Sorry, Karan. It's not the right time to even talk about it.*

Karan: *But Tara . . . I think I love you!*

Me: *I am leaving right now. Goodnight.*

Karan runs after me till we reach a spot where no one is watching. He tries to hold my hand but I resist. He has this tender yet fiercely passionate look on his face that makes me go weak in the knees and before I know it, I melt into his strong arms. And then Tara and Karan have their first kiss.

Wow! And it could be reality. Soon.

16th Jan

10:00 pm

Dear Diary,

I am doing great and have already lost 3½ kilos. Today Gayatri celebrated her birthday at school. The pizza smelled like heaven so I had to try a small Margarita but then who cares? After the party I excused myself to go to the toilet. Oh, I wish I had started this much earlier — Karan would have surely proposed to me this Valentine's. But all is not lost as I have another chance on Prom Night.

If I continue like this, I would even be lighter than Megha and Dolly by March-end. Then with my sense of humour and a brand-new body, nobody can stop me from winning the title, and Karan along with it! So Skinny jeans up and stilettos down (PJ).

Tu haan kar ya na kar, tu hai mera Karan.

22nd Jan

11 pm

I am happy but my body does not seem to be . . . Mama is so busy organising her exhibition she has not really noticed that I am looking better! TBH, for some strange reason I am not looking better even though I have lost so much weight . . . maybe I need to lose more . . . but why am I feeling so lazy and in pain? I am supposed to be getting fitter, no?

STOP HAUNTING ME!

25th Jan

9:15 pm

Dear Diary,

I was a mess at school today. It's not just my body . . . I am feeling kind of unstable . . . hopeless and anxious. Why am I having these bouts of crying? I was dumb as a zombie. Could not figure out simple linear equations in Maths period today. All I was thinking about was my diet regime, Karan and that prom. I am obsessed with food, even though I am starving by choice.

I am spooked by these numbers on the weighing machine.

Despite that, I had a whole chicken burger all to myself during lunch break and since then was feeling awfully guilty . . . Come on, why do they tempt us with this kind of food at school? I did not even get the time to take a trip to the bathroom. Maybe I will offload myself now . . . I am soooooooooooo tired. Thank God! No school tomorrow! It's Republic Day!

31st Jan

8:30 pm

Mama looks worried about me. She thinks it's the beginning of puberty! Is it? Maybe the mood swings are an indication that I am going to get more girly . . . which is a good sign . . . so I will just carry on with my diet.

Mama is also getting all geared up for her big day — 10th Feb. I want to be excited for her and not burden her with my problems. Even Baby Didi, who is busier than the President of USA, is supporting my mom so much that I have started feeling bad about not being actively involved. But Mom asked me to just chill and concentrate only on my studies as exams are just round the corner.

Baby Didi is encouraged to help Mom with some odd jobs (like calling up Society aunties about the event) in her free time, which is at the most 15–20 minutes a day! In the creativity area she is zilch but she is good at this and it takes off some of the pressure from her Boards and IIT Entrance!

I don't know what's up with my sister! I mean there's a limit to how much a person can slog! She really does believe that hard work is the key to success!

This time even I really do want to focus on my exams.

2nd Feb

9:30 pm

Dear Diary,

Just look at me! I hate how I look in the mirror! This balloon of a face, these tires around my waist, these pillars for legs! How did I end up being so gross? Can you believe it, till now I have lost 6 kg but it just doesn't show. I am practically living on liquids . . . but my body is failing me. Big time.

Heer toh badi sad...hai oye

I don't think I have ever cried so much in my life, even when Snoopy died. Snoopy, where are you? I miss you so much, your slobbery kisses, your hungry eyes, our splashing in the puddles, the way you listened to me . . . my baby, hope you are happy wherever you are. Can't you come back? I'm so alone without you.

I hardly come out of my room. I have told Mama that I need to be served food in my room as I am preparing for exams and do not want any disturbance. But I don't touch it; instead I just flush it down the toilet! Dadi is sensing something queer is going on so she made me eat dinner in front of her. No problem, coz I am going to vomit it out now. There is no way anyone can find out what I am up to . . . OK, then – got to go now.

4th Feb

12 midnight

Is my mind failing me too? As I can bet I saw Snoopy standing next to my bed, wagging his tail and with the same puppy eyes begging for an extra treat. Snoopy, I wasn't serious about it when I asked you to come back. Shoo – those old horny bitches are waiting for you in heaven.

6th Feb

9:00 pm

This evening Mama again asked me if I was feeling alright. I gave her the bullshit again about losing this puppy fat since my chums could be round the corner. It was kind of lame but she couldn't have guessed my game plan in her wildest dreams. Maybe I'll break the record of losing maximum weight in the minimum possible time and surely the weight loss book is going to make me a star. Then of course that

Karan won't be able to ignore me!

Speaking of Karan and Dolly – I hardly ever get to see Dolly these days, even at school. I am really dying to tell my achievement to someone but Dolly is being very difficult to deal with. The other day she got suspended for being downright rude to Chopra Ma'am. What is her problem, the most wanted girl in our school? Attitude.

Megha is again back to her busy lifestyle. So I don't have any close friends, which is kind of lonely but then who cares- you got to sacrifice something in order to get something in life!

I learnt this from my mom who is all charged up as she has her exhibition in a couple of days. Now that they are giving free drinks, hopefully people will turn out to look at her stuff, otherwise she would take it out on us.

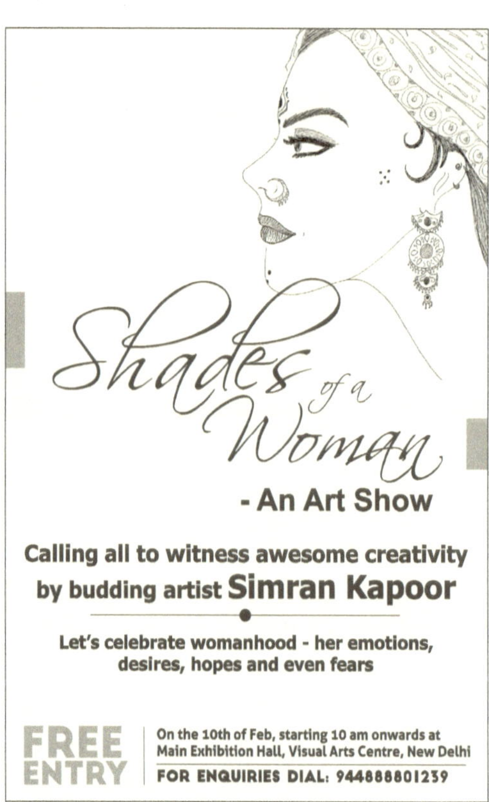

9th Feb

11:45 pm

Dear Diary,

I know it's very late but this was the strangest day of my life . . . when I went to school, I learnt the Prom Night was preponed and it was today. Hey, I wasn't prepared for this – I have a lot of weight to lose but the Princi insisted that I change into a bikini for the swimsuit round. What were these guys up to?

Was this some kind of a joke?

Anyway, Megha and Dolly were both wearing swimsuits and got me a red one, Baywatch style, to put on . . . everything was very confusing . . . I put on that red swimsuit and despite my weight, I looked like a hottie! They made me stand on an XL-Size weighing machine (remember – 'biggest loser'?) and pose for the cameras. The whole school was there, they were all cheering me on . . . I was embarrassed yet super pleased. Guess what – I won the crown! I was smiling so hard that my cheeks were beginning to hurt. Can you believe it, Karan finally proposed to me in front of the whole school but before I could say yes, I felt a weird taste in my mouth! Oh God, this can't be – I was puking in public! I wasn't able to stop myself and soon it was flooding with my vomit – the whole venue, furniture, students, teachers – all drenched in this foul, slimy liquid . . . only Dolly was laughing like mad

What a disaster! I was so ashamed but went on and on puking until I started screaming . . . I screamed and screamed!!

*This wasn't real – it was a **nightmare**! I don't want this ever again, God! But I can still taste something sour in my mouth . . . Oh no, this time I really have to do it!*

10th Feb

11:00 pm

Dear Diary,

It was a big day for our family. Even though it was a weekend, we all woke up early just to get prepared for the event. In fact, the three of us did not have much to contribute except just be there for Mom, who was a nervous wreck. My mom left for the venue early morning and the rest of us were supposed to join later.

I slept real late last night and couldn't get up despite the snooze alarms. Then Didi pushed me to the bathroom to get ready and bang that's the last thing I remember before finding myself in the hospital!

What the hell just happened? Did we meet with an accident on our way to the exhibition? My head was spinning and everything was so confusing. There weren't any bloodstained bandages on me, so what was I doing here?

I saw my family standing beside my bed trying to look calm but clearly something was wrong. I didn't even have the strength to open my mouth to ask anything so I just waited for someone to tell me the truth. Then the doctor came in along with Sister (not Baby Didi, stupid – a nurse) who got me some food. It was the usual hospital stuff – a couple of cucumber slices, a boiled egg and a bowl of clear soup. And I said something which let out my dirty dark secret. I said I wasn't going to eat since I was on a diet. The doctor looked at my parents and took them out to have a talk . . . and then these grownups – they did their own calculations, made me confess and finally it was all out in the open.

Why were they looking so worried? It seems I am suffering from an eating disorder called Bulimia. At first it didn't make sense but then they gave me some sort of a write-up downloaded from the Net to read. When I finished it, I knew it was me.

'Bulimia is an illness in which a person gets obsessed about losing weight, indulges in binge eating and then uses methods of purging like vomiting and laxatives to prevent weight gain.'

Am I mentally sick ?

Except I did not use laxatives! Maybe I should have —- to speed up the process.

Further:

'People with bulimia often eat large amounts of high-calorie foods, usually in secret. People can feel a lack of control over their eating during these episodes. Bulimia is a serious health problem, which if not cured early on, can be detrimental.'

So there was no point being in denial anymore.

In short, these episodes of vomiting had caused my body to dehydrate and so I passed out in the bathroom. So that's how I was here.

Thankfully, the doctor said my Bulimia was pretty much manageable because it had not been a long time since I discovered 'offloading'. Also it depended on the severity of the symptoms and I did not need any medication. It was totally curable with some TLC from my family . . . and, well, some therapy.

A word of caution before we go further:

NEVER DO THOSE DIETS

IF YOU WANNA LIVE.

TRUST ME.

My story is not meant to diagnose or treat any food disorder. If you think you have any of the symptoms, **talk to your parents** *and seek medical advice immediately.*

So diary, I cannot stick to my resolution. Goodbye, diary, as I can't take it anymore. And I really need some rest! Oh shit, today was my mom's exhibition and I ruined it for my family! I don't deserve their tender love and care.

But this is India – the land of *Hum saath saath hain* and Star Parivaar Awards!

Next day onwards, my family treated me like royalty – even better than when I had won the Best Essay Writing competition in school last year! How could I say that this family doesn't get along? We do care about each other but usually do not know how to show it- just like most other families. Unfortunately, it takes an event like this one to bring us closer. Anyway, I took time off from school for a whole week to recuperate and what a vacation I had! My dad became an even kinder version of Alok Nath and to the women at home I was their new mother-in-law! My mom got me my favourite comics and my sister smuggled in *Kya Kool Hain Hum* and *The Dirty Picture* for us to watch while my parents went grocery shopping! TBH, this was not my first time. A couple of years back, at Sonu *Didi's* wedding, when all the uncles and aunties had gone to the boy's (read groom's) house for the shagun ceremony, our older cousins had somehow managed to sneak in a couple of uncensored DVDs (*Jungle Instincts, Babes in Water* and *Honeymoon Train*). Just to feel they had the upper hand, we younger kids were forbidden to join them but then it led to so much bickering and fighting that they just gave in, else precious minutes would have been lost in settling this dispute. Anyway, if I described all that we saw, this book would get an 'A' certificate. But the funniest part was Baby *Didi*, who started crying as Ms. High Morals couldn't accept the fact that she too had animal instincts like us lesser mortals!

Baby *Didi* has loosened up over the years and doesn't mind an occasional slip herself. So here we were, going through a life-changing experience. Because when we saw main lead, our eyes popped out! Baby *Didi* had arranged a special screening with a projector and all to give a movie-theatre-like experience! I could not believe how much she was enjoying herself and then it hit me! In fact, it hit the two of us at the same time as we both looked at each other with the same 'in awe' expression!

You see the heroine was not a Size Zero – she was FAT! (Sorry Ms Balan, but in *this* movie you were.) And never before in the history of Indian cinema had a woman looked nearly as hot as a porn star. *Clarification*: First, I am just trying to sound adult – the only porn star I possibly know is Ms Sunday Leone and second, there can never be a comparison. Third, Ms Balan looked good to the general public like me and not the high-society snobs out there who are perpetually on a detox diet!

You might think I am biased but believe me, I KNOW because there is not one Hindi movie I haven't seen and if the TV channels ever need a new face for a film critic – I am the (wo)man for the job!

Coming back to the point – fat women are sexy! Oh What a revelation! Happy Valentine's Day, Tara!

I forgive you, God, for making me fat! (Guess it's a case of sour grapes but better to be fat and happy than try to be thin and be unhappy.)

So no more dieting or vomiting for me! I don't even have to exercise. Fat is in! I mean, I had some clue about it as some international magazines have banned pencil-thin models but didn't really believe it! This was great news and I was going to share it with my mom! So she does not have to sweat it out in the gym . . . No wonder even the Size Zero Ms Kapoor, who started it all, is looking more voluptuous now! (Well, she might again lose these extra 1.9 kilos by the time the book is out, as consistency is not one of her strong points.)

Yet again I got it wrong! My mom told me that exercising is actually a great way to get healthy. You feel more energetic, confident and feel good about your body – nothing wrong in that! But moderation is the key and yes, I did not really have to go to the gym as of now. I could just control my junk food intake and play a sport or even walk around the complex for an hour a day and that's it.

Mom says when she was my age the kids would never stay home – they were always hanging out, walking, cycling or playing some outdoor games with weird names like Staapu, Pithu, and all. They did not have an iPad! My dad's time was even stranger – they had NOTHING – except a black-and-white TV which always had news playing and a telephone with a spiral wire attached to it which no one was allowed to use except my *Dada*. No entertainment at all!

When my dad shouts at me for being so thankless for this 'easy life we are blessed with', I always wonder – is it our fault if they had to struggle and we don't? That we have these fancy gadgets and they just had a carrom board? Who knows, my own kids could have something even better – like a robot to do the homework and attend PT in school on their behalf?

With all this going on, I almost forgot about the exhibition

I came to know that because of my hospitalisation, *Didi* and Papa missed it too. But it seems it was a huge success and Mom even got interviewed by the local newspaper! Almost all her paintings got sold out! Oh thank God, Mom would be really pleased with herself for making 'saleable' stuff!

Oh, it feels so nice to be happy again!

My psychologist is a very gentle lady, absolutely non-judgemental. I have realised that I need to accept myself – that I will have my good days and bad, that I need to know myself, my emotional ups and downs and then build on that. I don't have to accept the bad part and give up on myself- I could always improve but it's all right to let go sometimes as perfection is not possible. And that no matter how hard you try, some people in the world are not going to love you- I have heard this before but I only got it now in the real sense.

I wanted to impress my friends with my new-found philosophy (or was it psychology?) of life but . . .

Unfortunately, the only company I have in school is Gayatri, as all the girls have their own groups and she is not welcome anywhere. I think it's either or all of the following four reasons:

| Other girls are plain jealous since teachers are partial towards her, or

| Other girls feel intimidated since her mom is famous, or

| Gayatri is too ahead of her times, or

| She looks like this?

I have no idea how the collective mind of girls operates, really! I don't know why we got along, I guess we were both unconventional in our own different ways. I didn't mind it either but still missed normal girls like Dolly and Megha.

The funda with women is that we are very forgiving . . . so when Dolly came to see me I remembered a quote I had read, it's kind of spooky and not original but here it goes:

'Keep a fair-sized cemetery in your backyard, in which to bury the faults of your friends.'

I was feeling very philosophical about everything anyway so I decided to let go of my anger against Dolly. I know she probably does not deserve it but . . . well . . . it's not so easy being honest to yourself. Deep down I knew it wasn't her fault if guys found her hot. Some girls have all the luck in the world but Dolly did not seem to think so. And then she blurted out her story.

What?? They broke up?

'Everything was going fine, we were having so much fun just being with each other. Nothing else mattered to me except Karan, and I was forever obsessing about how and where to meet him. We kissed maybe a hundred times and it felt awesome! You know my mom, how she is very chilled out. So she knew I was seeing him. When I told Mom about the kissing part she told me it might not be a good idea and I needed to control my feelings! After a while Karan started to insist on more – he said he wanted to take our relationship to the next level. I am fourteen and knew exactly what he meant but I wasn't sure if my mom would approve.

'Remember the Christmas party, Tara, it was so beautiful when we won 'The Star Couple of the Evening' prize; you know, I felt so close to him emotionally. After the party Karan took me to his home as his dad was away partying. He started touching me everywhere. I wasn't sure how he would react if I refused or whether I truly wanted to refuse. It was confusing, exhilarating but scary at the same time. Tara, you won't believe he almost forced me to go all the way. Before we went overboard, I came to my senses and escaped from there.

'It was my bad that I went ahead and spilled out everything to Mom, and my God, she freaked out! She immediately called up Karan's dad and gave him hell about raising such a shameless animal! You won't believe how Karan's dad reacted – he grounded Karan and made sure he broke up with me . . .

'I don't know Tara, I miss him so much . . . and I have seen my cousin having a breakdown after a bitter breakup . . . so maybe I am next . . . but my mom says I will get over it and have to carry on with my life . . . maybe she is right . . . I do need to slow down and think hard before getting into any relationship in the future . . . and to be honest, it's not that terrible. At least I can start acting normal again, at least you and I both are back together! But Karan – I am going to have to keep him at arm's length or my mom will create another ruckus in my life.'

So *ladke ka character dheela hai?!*

After listening to Dolly's story, I was relieved that it did not work out between that horny Karan and me, as I am dead against sex before marriage!

I was also thinking of Megha

I went over to her house on a Sunday . . . and as usual found her playing a board game with her mom and dad.

We are a happy Family

Oh, the quintessential Indian upper-class happy family – always lovey-dovey! And my home – I can't remember the last time the four of us were together in the same room and did not end up bickering.

I thought I should just leave but they asked me to stay. We headed for her room and settled down on her bed. Initially it was kind of weird as I was going to talk to her for the first time after the Rocko incident. My God, what was I thinking – this was going to be awkward! And sure enough, as soon as we settled down, she teased me about Rohan and I wanted to just kill her! But then we both burst out laughing! No matter how desperate I am I would never go out with a guy like him! Anyway, one thing led to another and . . .

What? Who's breaking up now?

'You know, Tara, my mom and dad are probably going to get a divorce. I knew things weren't all good between them but was kind of avoiding having these thoughts . . . My mom and dad both are very ambitious, always travelling around the world, they hardly got to see each other except on weekends. They got so busy in their careers that they sort of drifted apart . . . but I have to give them credit: they never had any ugly scenes at home. So I was actually taken aback when they had a family conference and told me that they were seeing a marriage counsellor, and that there was a possibility of a divorce.

'You know, Tara, you are really lucky your parents dote on each other. I know your parents are really romantic – I saw them having a candle-light lunch this Valentine's Day.'

So my parents had not really gone grocery shopping on Valentine's Day. (Is this worth even mentioning?) I could not imagine my parents acting all mushy so I changed the topic to Megha's parents who were not so close anymore. Megha went on:

'You know why was I always on a tight schedule? So I could be kept out of it! Probably they thought I would be too busy to notice the lost love between them . . . I kind of knew it wasn't all hunky dory. But I could have never imagined that it was perhaps leading to a divorce! I can't handle it, Tara. I would die if my parents separated!'

I didn't know how to deal with a divorce

What was I supposed to do? I had no practical advice to give so I just let her cry and decided to keep my mouth shut or I would have said something really stupid. Like maybe 'it's for the best' or 'hope they find true love outside'. Actually it was kind of embarrassing to discuss our parents' relationships . . . and I had my own developmental milestones to cross.

Like using the toilet normally

I was back to eating but I had lost out on time. We were just one-and-a-half months away from the big night at school!

But I wasn't the same stupid Tara anymore. I was stronger and more confident. I wasn't ever going to go on a diet, thin or fat!

I don't know why I keep using this evil word – I am not really fat. I mean I weigh about 60 kilos with almost a normal-range BMI; I am just heavy for my age. Secondly most girls in my school are at the most 40–45 kilos so it makes me look more rounded than I am. OK, the boys in my school tease me, and yes, it makes me mad! How I hate them – I am sure those bullies will rot in hell!

Just look at my mom, she is my weight and only slightly taller but the aunties in our society keep complimenting her on her great figure! I guess grownups can get away with murder!

To hell with that waste of time!

There wasn't anything I could do so I decided to just let it be – like the other girls in my class. I am not going to lose any more sleep over that party!

I don't know if it's only my school or if the teachers did it deliberately. This year it's after the exams. I think they don't want us to spend more time than is necessary on planning our clothes, jewellery and make up while also figuring out quadratic equations.

But then it kind of rubs off on you. So while my life was back on track I was still really confused between a sari or an evening gown! I mean, I did not want to end up looking like an aunty in a sari but did not really have the figure to carry off an evening gown! I wish I did not give so much attention to this beauty pageant.

Then I thought of taking Baby *Didi's* advice

I mean, she also has her own farewell night to plan but some suggestions wouldn't do any harm. And guess what – she was going to boycott the event! I mean, at last there is something exciting happening in our school and she's not going to go? Didn't she know she is a top contender for the 'Ms Brains' title?

But she said she has the Boards and then the IIT exam to worry about so she's not going to let a stupid event ruin her chances of making it. Already she had lost valuable time because of Mom's exhibition and no, she couldn't afford to be anywhere except in her room, slogging away!

Baby *Didi*: And what's with these titles? Will they mean anything ten years from now?

Well, seems she is too stressed out and doesn't know what she is saying so I just let her be with her beloved mock tests for company!

Maybe she was right

I wasn't taking Boards but I had to get a grip on my studies. I wanted Mom and Dad to feel proud of me for once. And I wanted to prove myself to my *dadi* also who called me a 'psycho case' in front of everybody! So I got busy with my books too.

Meanwhile in school, temperatures were soaring. My exams would begin in early March and we would celebrate their culmination with Prom Night! How logical!

Dolly is kind of behaving really weird. OK, so she was facing her first post-breakup trauma. I don't know why women are so emotional – can you believe she actually said this:

'Maybe I should have just given in to Karan. I love him so much and I just hate my mom – she ruined everything for me!'

I tried to give her some valuable advice – like *Bajirao ne Mastani se sirf ayyashi ki hai, mohabbat nahi!* Maybe she just needed another distraction – why couldn't she get busy studying for her exams? Then we both saw a flyer on the notice board of our building:

LET'S TALK ABOUT SEX

A WORKSHOP STRICTLY FOR TEENAGE GIRLS

Feeling Attracted to someone?

Don't want to lose him by saying No?

Want to do the right thing?

Then this session is for you.

Inviting all adolescent girls to take part in a presentation by Dr. Neela Lal, a leading Psychologist and Consultant, about the dilemma facing teenagers in urban India:

TO DO OR NOT TO DO
The Presentation will be followed by Question-Answer round

Date: 26th Feb
Timings: 4 pm onwards
Venue: Party Hall

Parents are advised not to attend but need to register their daughters for the event.

**For enquiries please call 92367846112
or log on to our website www.Inditeeniweeniissues.com**

Wow! A Sex Education class right here in our society!

Dolly and I were thrilled! Even though we sort of knew that it was actually going to be a Moral Science class, but at least they were going to talk about sex and might even show some graphics, which was good enough for us – for the time being.

It's not that I couldn't have found all this on the Net but my parents have some sort of software installed that stops me from viewing any 'illicit content'.

And worse, Mom gives me these surprise visits in my room to check on me!

Another problem – my mom isn't exactly broad minded. I was dead sure Mom would say no.

But I underestimated her

As soon as I came home my mom told me about the workshop and insisted that I attend. She was even going to persuade Dolly and Megha's mothers to let them go too! So my mom was finally getting the hang of being a New Age parent!

However, at school, there was some sort of an emergency declared.

Even though teachers and students alike were pretending to be serious about completing their 'portions' (of the syllabus) they were actually more interested in making preparations for the so-many events planned back to back!

Thankfully I wasn't one of the chosen ones

We all know that in each class there is a bunch of students who are involved in EVERYTHING! They are the media-savvy kids – get selected to play MCs, take part in dance items, make lengthy speeches and wear the Organising Committee Member badge with utmost pride! On the big day you can see them running around, ordering others, looking hassled and on the verge of a breakdown. Still, they are super-confident, not necessarily good looking but definitely charismatic. They are born leaders and will do anything to remain in their teachers' good books . . . and like I said – I wasn't one of them – so I could take it easy.

Unlike my best friends

Megha, who had the lethal combination of beauty and brains, was appointed the MC for the Farewell Party we were giving to our seniors. Dolly was asked to choreograph a fashion show. Of course, she's got it easy – has her mom to guide her. Dolly aims to make it big in the beauty business. To give her credit, she probably will as she is quite good at the whole beauty thing – not that I think much of it but Mama keeps telling me to believe in 'dignity of labour' and that 'even modelling is a respectable profession these days'. (Not my words – as I know girls from regular middle class 'simple' (particularly army families) have been modelling for absolutely ages.) Hey, I don't want to sound like an aunty but these days any girl who is thin and tall wants to be a model – and surprisingly, unlike my parents, people don't seem to mind. Well . . . I will restrain myself from commenting further. OK, guys – call me narrow-minded but I got it from my father!

So everybody got busy until we remembered that we had a workshop to attend!

I had not really forgotten about it, in fact I was secretly looking forward to it. That day we all got together at my house where Mama, in order to act cool, started talking, throwing in some slang language of her times. Come on, Mom – we know everything so don't embarrass us any further! *Didi*, as usual, wasn't going as she had 'better things to do'.

So when we reached the Party Hall

We saw about fifty girls of various shapes and sizes chatting away . . . all of them were supposed to be from my society but I had never seen some of them before in my life . . . Hey, who was that? I couldn't believe that Baby *Didi's* best friend Charu *Didi* was amongst all us curious cats. She was such a studious sort that it was difficult to imagine her ever giving sex a thought. Baby *Didi* is going to have a good laugh when she hears of this. There was so much noise in the background that nobody heard the doc telling us to shut up and then it was suddenly followed by that uncanny collective silence that usually suddenly occurs in the middle of gatherings.

There were three middle-aged, sari-clad women sitting in chairs facing us. They were going to lecture us on sex. I wish they did some profiling before giving out jobs to people. They should have got at least one reasonably hot young woman who could have given us some tips. But, dude, this is not America where they make out in public!

One of the three rose and stepped forward.

'Hello, young ladies,' she said and smiled. 'I am Dr Lal. I did my PhD in Psychology from USA. (*Then why are you dressed like this ma'am?*) When I came back to my country I discovered that though in some schools Sex Education is mandatory, teachers are not yet comfortable discussing sex; indeed, I am sure even your parents might not have guided you seriously on it. But a word of caution before we go on – this is not a 'Pondy' workshop. (*Laughter. So what was I doing here?*) We are aware that you all know the basics. But what we want to do today is help you deal with the dilemma you might face in the future and, frankly, some of you might even be too familiar with it.

'The dilemma is whether to say yes or no. While this is your personal choice, you must be warned that saying yes to sex before you are ready can be damaging – just because you have attained puberty doesn't mean you have a right to destroy your bodies. And it's not just physical – you will probably end up being emotionally scarred for life. So, girls, even if you are not convinced as yet – say loudly: NO to sex! Come on – No to sex!'

I wasn't in the mood for another lecture

Frankly, I did not exactly come here to listen to her sermon. And the other girls were beginning to look slightly bored too. The doctor kind of sensed the restlessness and quickly opened her file which was basically a bunch of PowerPoint slides with lots and lots of anti-sex talk to hammer down deep in our brains. OK, so it did make some sense even if we were listening to her half-heartedly . . . yes, she had a point. So let me show you these handouts which were distributed at the end.

Puberty: Its got to happen

Whether you like it or not--your body is changing. The hormones which were sleeping suddenly are on rush and going haywire. So what really happens:

- **Breasts get enlarged**
- **Pubic hair appears**
- **The body is growing**
- **Acne crops up**

Teenagers as Sexual Beings

- Teenage is a critical period to develop values and attitudes towards sex.
- Learn what you can--curiosity is natural
- Try talking to people you trust-- your parents, teachers or your doctor
- Mixed signs and communication gap causes lot of confusion in the teenagers minds
- Sex is not a bad thing but it can turn ugly

Are you ready for it ?

- There are no easy answers
- Teenage is not the time to handle this responsibility
- You may be physically ready but not emotionally
- Even the body may not be too happy--you could get STI's (Sexually transmitted infections)
- And worse...

When it turns ugly..

- You might end up being seriously ill like acquiring HIV
- You might even get pregnant !
- If there is no respect and you jumped into it -- you will be heartbroken
- SO say No to sex but if you really cant help it - Play it Safe

Abstinence is cool

- If you are attracted to someone but want to say No:
- Just say NO Firmly
- If he pushes you when you are kissing, stop it there--don't give mixed signals
- Your reasons could be personal, cultural or religious--but stick to them and he has to respect how you feel

Your body is yours only

- Even if you have done it before doesn't mean you have to do it again and again

- Don't underplay your feelings--have conviction

- If he says you don't love him because you are not doing it with him--don't give in

- If he pushes you--get more firm

- If he tries to force himself on you just move away or hit him and run

I don't know if that doctor regretted adding the last line in her presentation as what followed later was a cyclone of questions, some of which were dangerous, never heard or seen before and some utterly irrelevant. Obviously, there were no personal questions; it was all about a friend or a cousin. Example:

Girl 1:   A close friend of mine has a crush on her brother's friend who is going around with his sister's friend who happens to be the best friend of my close friend. She is planning to risk this best friendship . . . what should she do?

Girl 2:   My friend is going around with her *rakhi* brother who says he will fight the world for the sake of their love. My friend is really worried as she has crossed the limits with him (*starts crying*) . . . what should she do?

Girl 3:   My cousin has a friend (*oh yeah, sure*) who is not interested in sex at all. She has no feelings and considers it dirty. How can I tell her to loosen up?

Girl 4:   A friend of mine . . . you know . . . has . . . well . . . done everything! Or almost. And this is all she thinks of all the time . . . her grades are falling, her parents seem worried . . . but all she wants to do is . . . you know . . . it . . . Actually they have so much in common, like they're meant for each other, it's not her fault . . . what do you say?

And guess who was the source of the 'question of the day'? None other than Charu Didi! It was kind of hard to believe that she had the guts to reveal her own story in public:

Charu *Didi*: So this friend (*again?*) is very plain looking, considered an intellectual by her family. (*Come on, Charu Didi, you don't have to describe yourself.*) She is dead serious about her studies and career. But since last year she has been going around with a senior from her school whom she used to go to for Maths tuitions. The guy is also a topper, not good looking but very caring and gentle in bed. (*What??!!!!!*) They have a deal to keep it strictly physical and not lose touch with reality you know, both are very ambitious and their parents have high expectations from them, so they don't want to get emotionally involved. Lately she has started to feel guilty and off track but she doesn't want to end it as she says that when she is with him, making out, it's the only time she feels alive. Frankly, I am not sure if she is doing the wrong thing . . . but am confused . . . she does not love him, though . . . but she likes him a lot. I . . . she maybe needs help?

Dr Lal: Well . . . It's a very complex situation. I really want to see your friend and help her sort out this problem as it's in appropriate to talk about her issue in this forum. Please visit me along with her as soon as possible.

I didn't know if I was supposed to feel sorry for Charu *Didi* or join the gossipmongers after this seminar. I wasn't ready to accept it that an average-looking geek could make out before she turned adult. But I did not disclose it to Baby *Didi* afterwards as she would have been really sad about her best friend's life. But then, maybe she knew already . . . Whatever it was, I wasn't going to bring up this touchy topic with her, ever.

Wonders of wonders. The lecture was customised for Dolly – she was listening intently and seemed to be taking it real seriously. After the question–answer round, the Doctor divided us into groups and we were asked to conclude the presentation with the five most relevant points that we were totally convinced about. The team with the best points would be getting a special prize!

Oh, the smell of competition . . .

We girls thrive on beating each other at any cost – it doesn't matter in what. So all of us just got down to work. After some heated arguments about what points to include here is what my group's list looked like, which was kind of neat:

1. Remember, bust size varies from girl to girl and there is no point in comparing it with your friends

2. The body grows during puberty, so don't be afraid of the weight gain

3. Having sex is a big deal

4.   It can be dangerous – you might even get a baby

5.   If a boy cannot wait – he is not worth you, so dump him

But guess what? We didn't win.

Another group which had older girls wrote down some tough English and got the first prize!

1.   Abstinence is the only 100 per cent protection from STDs or unwanted pregnancies

2.   Intercourse is not the only way to show intimacy

Points 3, 4 and 5 I don't even remember.

I mean, even the doctor's presentation was much simpler!

But in the end I took it sportingly as the prize happened to be a book which all the girls in that group had to share – and I was sure nobody was going to read it anyway!

So what were you expecting Tara, a Playboy?

So after this seminar, I was really looking forward to something more interesting, like Seema *Didi's* wedding that I had factored in while I was making my diet plans.

Great, it was on a Friday so I could attend it without much tension about the revision tests starting next week. We all know why we attend weddings. Primarily for the free food that we could never dream of being able to afford anywhere else. I mean wedding food's not about having these small Chinese or *chaat* counters anymore. The *pandaals* were like a global village with a Mediterranean Corner, a huge Nawabi Clay Oven, a Japanese Seafood section, an Oriental Treasures display, an Intercontinental Hall – the last full of lobster, beefsteak and some unappetising meat in oyster sauce! Any normal person could not even try a bite each from these hundreds of multi-cuisine items. Despite lacs and lacs spent, our evening wasn't really fun as I ended up vomiting (this time I had a legitimate reason: a second helping of Lebanese *keema*) on the way back and Papa kept cribbing about the wastage at weddings. And all this was from a family that never eats out, to save money. So all their savings blown up in one evening, feeding people who will spend the next few years complaining about the ill-treatment and humiliation they got from the girl's side.

I guess it happens only in India.

Now back to studies

So we were all back to our routine – cramming, cramming and more cramming!

Why is being a student so tough?

I just don't buy this concept of these being 'the best years of life'.

Actually this is that time of life when I have no freedom. No money. No clubbing-shlubbing. No *daru-sharu*. No hot body-shody. No love life. No respect.

Baby *Didi* is older and she has one more 'NO' in her list. No time. At all.

My mom is much older but she has none of the above plus even more responsibilities.

Dadi. Freedom – yes. Money – yes. Parties – yes. (OK, those are actually laughter yoga sessions in the park.) *Daru–sharu* – yes. (Remember, I come from an Army background, we are liberal, OK?) Love life – a big yes. (Everyone knows about her *chakkar* with a long-retired Brigadier Uncle who lives in the Caribbean Tower of our society.) Respect – yes. (Dude, she is old, does anyone have a choice?)

So which are the 'best years of life'? I rest my case.

Anyway, coming back to studies, the funniest part is that with our curriculum, the odd-numbered classes are tougher than the next even-numbered, e.g., Class VII is tougher than VIII, Class IX is tougher than X, and so on. The guys who designed it must be sadists of the highest order! And if you don't believe me, ask any kid who is in an odd-numbered class!

Will I be able to complete everything in time? I've got to brush up my act, and do it fast!

Students who needed some extra support got into a 'Fast-track exam preparation course', which our very own Aggarwal Sir started after school and sure enough, I was the first one who was forced to get enrolled.

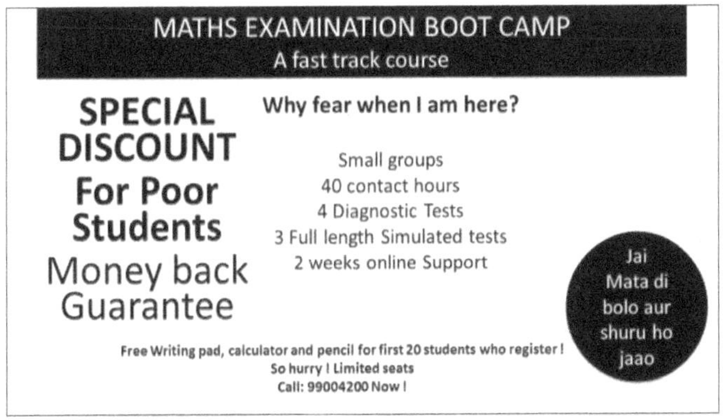

Maths was my weak area – I just hate Algebra, the formulas make absolutely no sense to me. I mean what I can't visualise, I don't get. And Trigonometry? Have a heart! Unless we decide to become Maths professors, how will doing this kind of Maths ever help us in any occupation? Papa says all this manipulation of figures led to the financial crisis, so why are we even doing this? When will grownups learn? Last year when my final exams got over, I shredded my Maths books in a million pieces! Baby *Didi* witnessed this incident and narrated every detail to my parents, especially about the guilty pleasure on my face! My mom lectured me on how knowledge is sacred and books should be worshipped. Yes, I have to agree with her – Indian students can't get away with an act of rebellion against *'Padhai'*! Either you treat it with respect or your own life goes for a toss.

I am just waiting to be done with Class X, after which I am going to have a choice on what I study. But then, it depends on how much you scored and not what you are really interested in . . . like Baby *Didi* – this IIT ambition is her life for the time-being, as most definitely she will be pushed to bell the CAT after her Engineering! Unfortunately, she has no real talents (except a remarkable memory) so this is the only shot she has got.

My only consolation was that it was even worse for Baby *Didi* as she had double the work – Boards then IIT-JEE!! Thank God I am still young!

TBH, if this is the best then the rest of my life is going to get even more complicated than Mahesh Bhatt flicks. Oh, I forgot – the newsletter! Tomorrow is the last date to submit my article and I haven't even thought of a topic. Oh yes, of course . . . What else?

Patriotic Public School

Newsletter for the month of March

It doesn't matter if you are a high achiever or an average like me, we all go through it. And while it is easy to listen to advice from parents, we all know this is not really the time to 'keep calm and study.' I am not competent enough to give you tips for topping the exams but I do know a thing or two about managing the nerves.

l   Dance on Bollywood fast beat numbers

l   Take a walk outside

l   Read a funny book during your breaks

बच्चो की जान लोगे ?

Dear Parents ,ऐसा लगता है

तुम्हे फर्क नहीं पड़ता के हमें क्या बनना है
ऐसा लगता है हम खुद के लिए नहीं
बस आप के लिए पढ़ते है
हमारा, और कितना एहसान लोगे
क्या तुम बच्चो की जान लोगे ?

देख तो लो के हम
रट्टा लगा रहे है के Logic
के Teachers कर रहे है कोई Magic
क्या जाने हम हर साल,अगली Class में कैसे बढ़ते है
हमारी कच्ची नींव से कब तक अंजान रहोगे
क्या तुम बच्चो की जान लोगे ?

शायद ऐसा हो के
तुम्हे दिखाना है कमाल
बना कर हमें corporate मज़दूर या हमाल
इसीलिए practice कराने हम पे रोज़, भारी भरकम बस्ते लादते हो.....
क्यों हमपे अपने अधूरे सपने लादते हो ?
यु...ऐसे...कब तक हमारा इम्तेहान लोगे ?
लगता है तुम...सच्ची मुच्ची, बच्चो की जान लोगे

Oh God, is it March already?

Baby *Didi* ended up having slight fever the night before her Boards started. She took it really badly and there was a lot of tension in our house . . . my mom tried to reason with her but who can explain it to this warrior princess who could not face even the slightest of obstacles on her path to victory? Anyway, I did not want to get influenced as well so I just minded my own business.

Which was poking into others' business

I did not plan it but while *Didi* was in the bathroom, I got hold of her diary hidden in her cupboard, under a pile of clothes when I was looking for something interesting to wear. I tried to restrain myself but then I am human too, so I peeped into it only because it was hard to believe that Baby *Didi* could write a diary. I mean who does that anymore? (Well, I did it too but then it was for a different cause altogether.) When I read parts of it, I almost had a stroke. The breaking news being that Charu *Didi's* seminar story was not her own, but actually a friend's. No points guessing who the friend was. Baby *Didi*. Yes, you heard it right, my own Baby *Didi* was involved with a guy, with no strings attached, like no commitment, nothing! It was purely physical! How could this be? This was my sister, the Ugly Betty, the boring, stick-in-the-mud type. How could she do this to herself? It was a shocker that I wished had never happened. But it had probably been happening for a year or two! It was worse than being hospitalised with bulimia, it was like a stab in the back, of trust broken, of being deceived by someone I considered pure, untouchable, sacred . . . why *Didi*, why are you doing this to yourself? No matter how cool it may sound, it's NOT RIGHT. I can't explain it, but it's not.

15th July

This evening something happened, which I never ever thought would to a girl like me. While solving a tough equation I noticed him staring at me. Then he took my pen from my hand, put it down and took my hands in his own. I was taken aback, as honestly I had no such inclination. But I did not resist, so he moved closer and kissed me. It was just a peck on the cheek but how wonderful it felt.

20th Sept

Why was I even there? I had no more to learn from him but couldn't help going back to him to revise again. He says we must not lose focus, that we are not in any relationship, that we just like to be with each other and should not have any long-term plans as we don't want any extra baggage. I sort of agree with him as I never longed for a guy like him to be my boyfriend – I wanted someone charming, full of life and funny, and he is just a boring, average-looking serious guy who wears glasses. Just like me.

20th Feb

We hardly meet but when we do we can't resist each other. I think we went too far today but I want it again.

25th May

He won't talk to me as he thinks he did not make it to IIT because of us. I am really nervous myself because next year it might be me. Maybe I need to distance myself from him.

15th Sept

Ufff . . . I did it again! What a feeling . . . Happy Birthday to me.

1st Jan

What a New Year! He is avoiding me, maybe will break up with me, says we both need to concentrate on our exams. I am not surprised but relieved. I must not get carried away. From now on it's only me and my books.

What was I supposed to do?

I needed time to think as no matter how smart I considered myself, I did not have any references to take ideas from. Oh yes, the movie *Cocktail* . . . we are friends, we have sex but nothing more will ever happen! But they were maybe in their thirties and in America! But then it's become so common in Hindi films these days, but for God's sake those are just fiction! This is India. We are still school girls. And this is my sister. I couldn't stop crying, I was too disappointed, or rather, ashamed of *Didi*. I was wondering how far she went. Oh God, I hate her. I wish she would just die! What if Mama found out?

And I got caught

Baby *Didi* had her shower and as soon as she entered her room, she knew that I knew. I was crying and she picked up the diary, which had slipped out of my hands onto the floor. She seemed rather calm for such a situation, though I was out of control. What followed was a conversation I am still trying to erase from my head, as honestly I still have not understood her motives. But I now understand what stress can do to you.

Baby *Didi*: You OK?

Me: Does it matter? I never expected this from you.

Baby *Didi*: Oh the burden! Now you too? Get the hell out of my room and dare you touch my diary again!

Me: You bloody bitch, you let us down, all of us . . . why, how could you?

Baby *Didi*: Mind your tongue, Tara, don't forget I am older than you, show some respect.

Me: Oh really? You deserve no respect! I despise you! You stink, man!

Baby *Didi*: Either get out or calm down and listen to what I have to say.

Me: You get out of this house, we don't want you here!

Baby *Didi*: Stop being so dramatic, OK? Anyway, I am not going to be here for long. So deal with it like a mature person.

Me: Look who's talking. Really, Baby, I still cannot believe that you were the main lead of Charu *Didi's* story! Having an affair that is strictly physical? Oh shit, what do you think this is? It's India and we are still answerable to our parents, if Mama gets even a wee bit hint of this, you'll be dead meat.

Baby *Didi*: So now I have to take this 'sanskar' shit from you, Tara. I told you get out or listen.

Me: OK. Go on, but don't think I will change my opinion about you.

Baby *Didi*: Balls to you! Do you think I don't know about your Rocko episode? I still have your WhatsApp chat with Megha about that date, OK?

Me: Oh, you've known about him all along?

Baby *Didi*: Yes, but did I ever embarrass you by bringing it up? Anyway, now that you are here, I guess you should know my side of the story. Since last year or more, I have been seeing Sunny, remember him? Sukhdeep Bhalla? School topper from last year. I used to go to him with Maths problems and he was always patient with me. He made me feel special for the first time - not for my brains, but in a feminine sort of a way. We were both almost burnt out and going through hell. Honestly, I had no time to even think how little I liked my life with these exams, mock tests, drills, Papa's expectations. I was doing everything dutifully but I badly needed an outlet. Charu was going through the same and I wonder why we ever made an attempt to discuss anything except studies. What started as some casual kissing with him led to a lot more but we don't love each other, OK? This year is critical for both of us and we have actually not met since the last two months or so. Frankly I don't miss it except when I need a break.

Me: What do you want me to say – great, *Didi*, at least you are not doing drugs! Don't you get it? It's not done!

Baby *Didi*:   Well, I am almost eighteen and know exactly what I am doing. It's hard to accept but you have to. But it's not going to last, anyway. He sure will crack IIT this year. He is averaging eighty four hours a week so I can bet my life on it. And I am trying my best. If I make it, there is little chance we will get the same institute and if I fail, I am packing my bags and going to Kota. So it's already ended, OK? Though we haven't made it too official, I guess there was nothing in the first place.

Me: I don't buy any of this, *Didi*, if you think it's no big deal then you are lying to yourself. Don't you think it's wrong?

Baby *Didi*: Yes, it is, and I will tell you what else is wrong. Mama- Papa emotionally blackmailing me constantly to make it to IIT is wrong. That I can't remember the last time I went out with my friends is wrong. That none of my friends go out anyway is wrong. That I have lost my childhood, my innocence to the demands of this brutal, fucking competitive world is wrong. That I have never had teddy bears or Barbie dolls to play with is wrong. That I put on weight by the day as I get no exercise at all is wrong. That I will probably kill myself if I don't make it is wrong!

Baby *Didi* was losing control and had started crying and I realised that my anger was turning into pity. I did not have the guts to ask her how far she had gone with him but somehow it was insignificant.

Me: Didi, what should I do? Do you need to talk to Mama about it.

Baby *Didi*: Forget it, Tara, this is just a weak moment. And I have no more time to waste. I still have to revise these questions.

Me: But you need help. You said you will probably kill yourself if you don't make it. Didi, don't you realise how serious it is? That it's a real situation?

Baby *Didi*: I cannot allow myself the luxury of taking out the time to discuss my problems with anyone, Tara. Now get out of here and leave me alone. I have an exam to take tomorrow.

Everyone give way! Here come THE EXAMS!

This is the time of the year where all kids have to prove how responsible they are about their lives. When all of us – 'topper', 'has potential', 'average' or 'just no hope' – become great planners and executors. Our days and nights were divided into chapters from the books we had to conquer, we were desperate to find those extra notes from the tuitions that were long forgotten. If only I had been more attentive in class. Maar, maar, maar, ratta maar.

The next few days were full of, well, everything!

We were all on a roller-coaster of emotions – nervousness, excitement, disappointment, but there was not a second of relief. Not until the last day. But for poor Baby *Didi*- the ride went on and on till the competitive exams. We couldn't wait for these finals to get over – and get some sleep!

But when it did happen, we were too excited to rest. Every Indian student has at least twelve such precious moments in life.

Call it bliss, nirvana or pure ecstasy – but this is the feeling which makes it all worth it:

We don't need no education!

So this is what FREEDOM means! When we realise that there will be no more timetables, date-sheets or sample tests. If only it was always like this. But grown-ups don't call life a battlefield for nothing! What they don't know is that perhaps it's too early to push us kids into attaining martyrdom. As some of us haven't even learnt to use a gun, sorry, a pen properly.

Tonight is the night

Right after lunch we all met in Dolly's house where her yummy mummy was waiting to get us styled for the party! Oh, what a woman and what a toned body she has! At last I had a nice look at her tattoo! Mom says she has gone under the knife on her stomach but it's just a case of sour grapes! Aunty may be a bit irritating –- like, she'll not address her daughter by name, instead call her 'Sweetiepie' or 'Gorgeous' or 'Princess' or whatever but she is not that bad a person.

Dolly told me today that women in this society are jealous of her and are spreading false stories about her mom and Karan's dad. I did not have the nerve to tell her that I had also heard this news some time back so I pretended to be shocked and disgusted at the women who are jealous. (Sorry, Mama, but you are in the list too. But I've got to give you some credit, as on a closer look, I realised she *has* got her nose fixed, too – it's way too small for an Indian face, and yes! Yes, her lips are a bit too big.) Anyway, I don't want to admit it, but that tattoo was making me drool. Sorry, Aunty, but you want it, no?

Actually when I started this book I thought I'll use pictures of only important characters- but she is what cheap guys call eye candy so it would be unfair on my part not to include her as well. So she is the third character after my *dadi* and baby Aryan who are in this book just because they are cute. And then they say looks don't matter. And hips don't lie.

I believe in manicures, I believe in overdressing, I believe in primping at leisure and wearing lipstick.

– Audrey Hepburn

Aunty had our dresses neatly arranged with accessories and all. I had chosen to wear a sari for obvious reasons . . . if only I had longer hair and had Sabyasachi as my designer, the crown would have been mine!

Getting professional help is not such a bad thing!

We couldn't help admiring ourselves in the mirror. I didn't want to compare but Dolly was nothing short of a bombshell! Even Megha was a diva in her strapless blouse. You see, Aunty knew she had broad, well-defined shoulders, so wanted to accentuate her strong points! Actually, it wasn't even a blouse – just a piece of cloth wrapped round her bust like Tamanna wore in *Bahubali*. About me – I could not recognise myself! So having Dolly as a friend again was a good idea! (Sorry, Mom, I know I sound manipulative sometimes.) If only I could hide this pang of envy I couldn't help feeling for my two best pals!

All set for the Stage

When in doubt – put more makeup

So here is how the function went:

I don't know if I want to waste a lot of paper on describing the agenda so I'll give you the highlights.

Karan was there. He was in formals – a black tuxedo with a red tie . . . the girls couldn't stop swooning over him.

I got to see my idol – Raina Gupta. The firebrand journalist was right in front of us. She was dressed in an elegant off-white printed cotton sari. That's the thing about brainy women – they have personality. Wish I could be like her.

RESPECT !

And yeah, all the girls were looking nice except for Rags (Ragini Anand – another weirdo in my class) who decided to turn up in black. Not a black sari or a black gown – but black jeans with black T-shirt!

I mean just because your mom runs an NGO for women, doesn't mean you show your protest like this. The teachers looked miffed but did not have the guts to throw her out! The only girl rooting for her was Gayatri, who herself turned up in school uniform. Gosh, some people will do anything for attention. Well, Rags has to understand that this is school and fashion is an integral part of life – so what if they made all of us walk around on the ramp in front of the self-proclaimed judges who kept scribbling something whenever a girl walk past them . . . yeah, we were being given numbers based upon how glamorous we looked or how gracefully we carried ourselves . . . yeah, maybe it was slightly demeaning but then I don't have Rags's courage to rebel against the system!

Juniors had done a super job

I never knew there was so much talent in our school and you can't really expect such young kids to plan anything. But they put up a couple of acts which were quite entertaining:

- Comedy Circus

- A medley of old Hindi numbers

- A short skit – *Leave Me Alone*

This short skit was written by my secret lover. It was played in last year's Annual Day and I was curious to know what was so great about it. I managed to get my hands on the manuscript so here you are . . . I really recommend it.

Dad, leave me alone

The setting is a typical living room of a middle-class family with ordinary furniture, a TV and a vase with plastic flowers on the centre table.

Opening Act: *Mother and Father are sitting on the sofa discussing something when they are interrupted by the sound of the doorbell.*

Ting Tong!

Mother opens the door.

A plump lady with a loud personality enters.

Lady: Oh, hello Chhoti! Glad to find you home

Mother: How are you, *Didi?* Welcome, please come in . . . but first, please accept my congratulations

(The women hug, the man looks on indifferently.)

Lady: Oh yes . . . so you heard, the loudmouths in our family, ha ha ha!

Mother: You must be really proud. How does Manu beta feel, to be in the top hundred rankers of the IIT-JEE?

Lady: Well, I don't want to brag but we were expecting this. Manu is a very hard-working boy, you know . . . though he is a bit disappointed with his rank. You know how he is – a perfectionist. Hee hee.

Mother: Oh yes, I am sure he will get the institute of his choice . . . Actually, I was wondering if he could guide Roshini – she too will be trying next year.

Lady: But of course . . . but you know how busy he is. I will talk to him to take out some time for his little sister. No problem, ha ha ha!

Father: So what is he opting for? Electronics?

Lady: How do I know, Sharma Saab is into these technicalities, all I know is that my son is a topper. I worked very hard on him, and finally I can relax. God has been very kind to us – lacs of students don't make it. Anyway, I've got to go. Here, I got some chocolates for Roshini.

Mother: Oh, you shouldn't have! Anyway, goodbye . . . say my congrats to Jeejaji also.

Lady walks out.

Father: What a show off, this sister of yours!

Mother: What do you mean? Don't you realise what mothers go through bringing up their kids and she has done a great job, I must say!

Father: Oh yes, the credit is entirely hers!

Mother: Oh, men can be so jealous!

Roshini enters, an ordinary, studious looking girl, holding a racket in her hands.

Roshini: Hi Mom, hi Pop . . . Hey, did Maasi come? Wow, my favourite chocolates!

Roshini unpacks the box and starts eating. Mother and father stare at her as if she isn't allowed to even touch them.

Roshini: What happened, who died?

Mother: Mind your language, girl. Do you know Manu Bhaiya topped his IIT-JEE?

Roshini: Yeah, I heard – I called him last night – good for him.

Mother: So what do you have to say? You are appearing for your Boards next year and you remember how you did this year?

Roshini: I remember Mom, but it seems you have forgotten that I had a nervous breakdown the day my exams ended. And that doesn't matter to you?

Mother: It doesn't matter to us? After all that we have done for you? You have the nerve to let us down with a measly 81 per cent and instead of feeling sorry about it, you are trying to blame it on us?

Roshini: Do you guys realise that I had to work my butt off for this measly 81 per cent? And yes, I am sorry, for I cannot do any better and frankly you have to accept this fact!

Mother: Accept what fact? The fact that I have sacrificed my career for you! And that your father works like a dog to provide you kids with the best education, and you say you can't do better? Oh God, what did I do wrong? I guess I am not as lucky as *Didi*.

Roshini: Dad, I am not Manu, I can't get better marks and I know even if my life depended on it, I won't be able to crack the IIT-JEE. Please, I am sorrybut I have my limitations; is it so difficult to understand? You guys made me choose Non-Med when I clearly do not have the aptitude for it, you know I have always struggled. Why can't you see this?

Father: What do you mean – you will not appear for the entrance? My daughter is a quitter?

Roshini: God, stop being so hysterical! I don't want to do it, that's all. I just don't want to do it. (*Starts to cry*)

Father: You are giving up without even trying? I can't believe this is my own flesh and blood!

Roshini: Again, stop making me feel so guilty! You work like a dog not just for our education – it's your career too, remember? And that flat you want to buy, and that vacation in Malaysia, and Mom's diamond ring. Please don't make me go on or it will be very tough for you to hear!

Father: (*Sarcastically*) Go on, daughter – how very proud of you we are today . . . thank you for making us see the light . . .

Mother: (*Shouting*) This is what happens when you encourage your kids to use their own minds! So, Roshini's dad, are you satisfied now?

Roshini: Why are you guys fighting? All I am saying is that I don't want to be an engineer. I cannot be, even if I tried. There's more to life than studies!

Father: Oh, now you are saying we are not bothered about your all-round development? Who pays for your badminton, karate classes, art lessons?

Roshini: Dad, I am not so good at any of these things. I just have to do it as other kids are doing it too. Frankly, I didn't even ask for it

Father: So what do you want to be? A nursery-school teacher? A housewife?

Roshini: Yeah, why not? What's wrong in being a housewife, your wife is one! Money is not everything, Dad. Frankly I don't know what I want – maybe I would want to be an activist – or join the Police, I feel for my country and its people, but I am not sure which direction to take. I need you guys to help me find out.

Father: So you are not even sure what you want to do in life?

Roshini: Right now, I am not and that's why I need your support. Help me discover my strengths, my desires . . . can you believe it? I don't even know what I am good at or if I am good at anything at all!

Father: Give me some time, I need to digest it.

Roshini: Dad, it's not such a big deal. There are many other professions that could be equally satisfying. I don't know yet, but I am going to find out. So please don't ask me to pursue this engineering. I might take up Commerce or even Arts. Please accept it.

(Long silence)

Father: OK, kid, take your time. Who knows, you could do even better than Manu!

Roshini: Thanks, Dad, for understanding me but please – I don't want to compete with anyone. You know, when I had that breakdown, I had a lot of time to think, lying in the hospital bed. I want to be left alone to think. Please, that's all I want. And I promise you I won't let you down.

Mother: OK. We understand. We might be old fashioned but I hope you realise we only have your best interests in mind.

Roshini: Of course, Mom – I know. Thank you, guys.

(Family hugs)

When the skit ended there was a stillness in the auditorium for what seemed like a long time. I guess all of us were lost in our own worlds – our homes, our parents and these neverending expectations. So – what now?

Wonders of wonders

Our chief guest Raina Gupta walked up to the stage and here is what she had to say:

'Hello kids, what you just saw is a true story. It's slightly dramatised, as in reality parents don't give in so easily. I know because I am the Roshini from the skit. And those were exactly like my parents. How does Rohan have this information? Because he is my kid brother. A talented young man who has the guts to want to be a writer one day. He did not want his school to know about me but I feel he is his own person even without my help.'

Oh wow, she is Rohan's big sister? Isn't she too old? Maybe a stepsister? Or cousin? Or adopted? Well, it's their personal matter, so as my *dadi* would say – *Saanu ki? Bhaad main jaayain.* (Meaning, why should we care? Let them go to hell!) What to do guys, we are like this only. ;-)

'This was fifteen years back and if I had not rebelled, I wouldn't have been standing here before you, giving you a motivational speech. (*Laughter*) You are all growing up and you need to take some time off to look deep inside you. Because there is a fire burning in each one of us. At first you might not feel the heat but go deeper and enlighten yourselves.

'Don't give up – it's your life and you need to know what you are good at, what you want to do but most importantly what you don't want to do. But stay grounded – your profession is not what you are. Try being a good person first. Anyway, I won't bore you more as the night is still young (laughter) but here is something that was written by your very own Rohan, and in English for a change.' (*He sure got a lot of publicity that night. Good PR job, sister.*)

'I can't be a doctor coz the sight of blood nauseates me,

Can't be an engineer coz machines don't fascinate me,

Can't be an MBA coz business doesn't excite me,

Can't be a teacher coz children irritate me,

Can't be an accountant coz numbers are my enemies,

Can't be a politician coz manipulation is not in me,

Can't even be a cricketer coz I get a pain in my knee,

I can't be anything you like, so please forgive me.

Till I know what I can be, just let me be me.'

We were too stunned to react but then Rags got up and started clapping, so all of us joined in.

Honestly, I wasn't too comfortable with this heavy stuff and badly needed something lighter. Just in time Vice Princi took the stage.

Vice Princi: Thank you, Roshini, oops, Raina. I have had the privilege to see this before and even though it's the story of our lives, it makes us all feel and think differently each time. So, students, what's next?

This was getting even heavier to bear because now they were going to declare the finalists.

My heart was pounding out of my blouse. I knew I had a slim chance but you never know – today might be my lucky day. One of the judges – our English teacher, Mrs Chopra, came on stage and here is what she had to say:

'Before I declare the results I want to thank Class VIII for putting up a wonderful show. Maybe some of you will be great event managers one day. Oh, here I go again, kids –

tonight you could just forget about your exams or career, you have the school's permission! Secondly, we might be choosing just five girls and five boys as finalists – but all of you are winners!'

Don't know how all of us are winners but anyway, here is the main part.

Both Dolly and Megha were among the finalists. **I did not make it**. And who cares about the others in the list? The fact is my best friends were up there on the stage and I wasn't! Why was it so difficult to believe? Was I expecting to be standing on the stage as one of the five best-looking girls in my class? Has God ever been kind to me? What a loser!

Next we had the question–answer round with the most FAQs in beauty contests around the world, like:

⎸ If you could change one event in history what would it be and why?

⎸ If you were the Education Minister of your country, what steps would you take to improve the system?

⎸ If you won the title today, what is the first thing will you do?

Come-on guys!! What can a Ninth Grader do anyway, except party?

I was beginning to feel disgusted but then there was a big surprise.

Vice Principal Ma'am now came forward.

'Children, our school's mission statement is to provide the best possible education and at the same time nurture talent and leadership qualities in our students to help them make their country a better place, even for future generations.

(Hey, when did that happen? Maybe it's a new advertising gimmick!)

'Yours is not a military school but we always try to inculcate the patriotic values of our great Indian Army. I wish Principal Sir was here but he is too busy with the OROP rallies. We all are so proud of him. *(Oh God, I underestimated him! Way to go sir, we are with you!)*

'So, before we declare the results, for the first time we want to give a special jury award to one who has relentlessly carried on the responsibilities of being an ideal student of our great school. One who has never been afraid to speak out the truth. She made us see things in a new light and I am delighted to present this award to the most unpretentious student here.'

Come again?

'So any guesses who it is going to be?'

There was a moment of silence but then some random names came up from the audience – kids who were prefects or hall monitors or teachers' pets.

'And the winner of the Raina Gupta Award for Outstanding Contribution goes to –

'Tara Kapoor!'

Hey, what did I do? Oh yes, my column *Growing-up Pains*! I think that did it!!

I did not know I had such an avid fan following! I used to think grownups wouldn't appreciate my writing as many a time I had been a bit too undiplomatic about our school and had even made fun of some teachers indirectly. But how very wrong I was!

When I went up onstage, the prize was handed over to me by Ms Gupta. Such a charismatic woman, emanating enormous strength of mind, yet with the kindest smile in the world. I couldn't stop staring. If I was a boy I would have called her an 'Intellectual *Tota*'! Karan, who was also up on the stage, shook hands and congratulated me – and guess what – his touch did nothing to me! I was indifferent to him by now as I did not need attention from any stud to make me feel special.

It was my very own moment of glory!

I would have bragged about it even more but I am going to practise staying humble as I don't really remember everything that was said about my articles. But yes – thank you. school – it was about time you acknowledged it! And for giving us the 'Freedom of Speech' that we all take for granted.

Oh, how I hate public speaking!

My face turned red and my legs were trembling so much that I was scared I wouldn't be able to carry this weight any longer. I was asked to say 'something' but as usual I was tongue-tied. Come on, I wasn't expecting this – I was actually secretly hoping to be crowned the Prom Queen – then I remembered the speech I had prepared . . . but maybe it wasn't suitable here . . . all these confusing thoughts were making me really nervous, so thank God, Vice Princi bailed me out by starting to announce the remaining titles:

| Master and Miss Brains

| Master and Miss All Rounder

And finally the most coveted:

| Prom King and Queen Class IX

What to do? My friends were born to achieve

The Miss All Rounder went to Megha. Frankly, she could have nailed each of the three titles but our teachers decided to play safe to escape the complaints of angry parents the next morning.

And guess who got the title of the Prom Queen?

The manner in which our 'could-be' Miss India Dolly was crowned would put all reigning beauty queens of the world to shame. Oh shit – my friend was truly a knockout. I've got to admit it – she did deserve to win! I noticed Karan couldn't keep his eyes off her and I have a feeling they will get back together again soon. Hey, it doesn't matter to me now! **Thank you God, I am finally, finally over him!!** *Utar gaya ye Fitoor mera*

In anticipation of the results, Dolly's mom had planned a surprise party for us at her place. So when we got there, our families were waiting for us with bouquets of flowers and gifts.

The arrangements were average (*didn't really matter*) but the fooooooooooooooooood!! That was the icing on the cake. Mona Aunty did not follow any one cuisine as there was Spaghetti Bolognese, there was Honey Crispy Gobhi, there was Sesame Fried Chicken in Lemon Butter Sauce, there were Szechwan Prawn Noodles and of course no Punjabi party is complete without Butter *Chikkan*. To top it all there was a fusion of Angoori Rabdi with Fried Ice Cream for dessert.

Now I realise how empty the lives of these skinny models and movie stars must be if they can't even afford to have French Fries on their next holiday in Paris.

Megha's parents were so proud of her – they were looking even closer as a family now. She gave me the good news later – her parents were thinking of reconciling and were open to giving their marriage a second chance. Oh, thank God! I was so happy for her! As for Dolly – I am just waiting for the day she will give me the news about her and Karan. My own family kept hugging and kissing me, which was kind of embarrassing but I didn't want them to stop, either.

I don't understand why, but the 'three winners' were asked to give a short speech. Since Dolly and Megha were game for it, I had to face it too and as usual my mind went blank. I think I underestimated Dolly and her speech made me re-evaluate my judgment about her. She may not be good in studies but she is certainly not dumb.

Dolly: Well, I never expected this (*sure*) but I am really thankful to my school for choosing me the Prom Queen. Don't you think 'Princess' should have been more appropriate? This 'Queen' tag is oh-so-boring and sounds like an old lady from England! (*Laughter*) But seriously, the credit goes to my mom who always made me proud of having a beautiful face and figure. (*Laughter.*) She always told me to never apologise for being who I am, that it's OK to be just an average student as my destiny lies somewhere else, that I should never compare myself to my smarter friends Megha and Tara, as I am my own person and intelligent in my own way . . . Thanks, Mom, you mean so much to me!

Applause

Megha: Thank you, Dolly. We all know how unique you are. Frankly, I knew I was going to get the Ms All Rounder title, and my parents have worked for not only this night but for all the future awards and titles I may achieve. Thanks, Mama, Papa, for making me a winner. But I am tired now and all I want is to go on a vacation with you both; nothing exotic, even Nani's house in Ambala will do, where there are no schedules, no 'to do' lists and no hurrying from one place to another . . . that's all I want. I do want to congratulate my friends Tara and Dolly for getting their own prizes. I am really proud of you guys, especially Tara, for never mincing your words and always speaking your mind. I guess I have a lot to learn from you. Thanks, guys. Thanks, Aunty for your efforts – I really appreciate it.

More applause

Oh God, I'll never be able to beat that . . . especially Megha's emotional angle. Why didn't they give some advance notice? Tara, get over it, it's just a casual party. Just go ahead and face it ! Just be yourself!

Me: Hi everyone, I will start with a confession: I was praying to win the Prom Queen title – but yes, I was just being naïve. No matter how hard I tried, I could never look half as good as Dolly, and yes, she is worth it. And a lot more. But what I got was even better . . . at least for me, as it was not about this one night but the work that I had done for past couple of years. I want to thank my mama for encouraging me to write and have an opinion. She made me realise that even if life is not fair, we have to be fair to life. That we are not supposed to have all the answers as yet. I want to thank Baby *Didi* for always being there for me; and *Didi*, even if I don't understand you sometimes, I love you with all my heart. And Mona *Aunty, police mat bulana, abhi to party shuru hui hai. (Laughter.)* I am so damn impressed with myself, not just for winning an award but also being able to fight my fear of public speaking. I may not eventually win that debate competition in school, but just to be able to speak in front of all of you is an achievement for me. Truly, this night has changed my life!

Even more applause

Of course, there is something else I forgot to tell. Dolly's older brother Sandy Bhaiya had also landed from Mumbai for this special occasion and now I really know what drop-dead gorgeous means!! I never noticed him before but I could have eaten him up as he was our desi version of that One Direction star himself – luscious brown hair, deep blue-green eyes, dimples around those full lips . . . a shy smile . . . total firang! I was spellbound and almost in love again.

But then I had to control my emotions – mostly because he had eyes and smiles only for my dearest friend Megha!!

A few months since then . . . all is well . . . (?)

I have learnt so much about myself and life in general. My biggest achievement has been that I stopped feeling sorry for myself.

Didi and I joined those martial arts classes in the neighbourhood. One, it's a fun way to exercise and two, I am learning self-defence, which Papa says is actually crucial for all girls in today's times. Weight loss or not, for a change I agree with him. On second thoughts, why only girls, all kids should get this training. Compulsorily.

Mama is now a full-time artist and is working on her first project for an upcoming five-star hotel near our society. She seems more excited than I've ever seen her.

'Excited' *se yaad aaya* – Snoopy came back! (Remember the STD story?) So the mongrel who gave it to him delivered some puppies just next to our society gate. Some got adopted and some were destined to be slumdogs. But Bruno got picked up by *Dadi* because she was 'one hundred and ninety-nine percent' sure it was our *Marhoom* Snoopy's *aakhri nishaani*.

I am back to eating like before – is it because I like food more than I like being thin?

Dolly's clothes are getting shorter by the day (she really believes in and lives the principle that Less is More) and I have learnt to accept that it's a democracy and she has a right to wear whatever she wants to. Would I, if I had her kind of figure?

Also, it did not bother me a bit when Dolly got back with Karan. It was meant to be. He promised her he wouldn't ever push her till she felt ready. What if she says she is ready now?

Megha and Sandy *Bhaiya* also were slowly forming a new friendship. I am not sure if it will lead to anything as Megha thinks long-distance relationships don't work . . . How does she know?

Now that Karan is out of my life, I wonder how is it even possible to so deeply love a person for whom you don't even exist? Does love come so cheap?

Tara Kapoor got a friend request from Rohan Gupta! Why did I accept it and wasn't over-reacting anymore?

Baby Didi did not make it through to IIT though she topped the school in her Boards. Surprisingly she did not kill herself but Papa was devastated. Why wasn't it good enough?

I guess the fast-track Maths course really worked because my percentage jumped to an Eighty eight! Mama looked proud but Papa said now that I am in Tenth, I needed to work harder this year! Why can't some people ever be satisfied?

Sometimes I wonder if I had not got that prize on Prom Night, would I have got my confidence back?

For all complex questions – there are answers. Simple, straight and probably wrong. But I am still growing up and in no hurry to find out.

**I conclude by clapping my hands as I am happy
and I know it!**

Finally – *Achhe Din!*

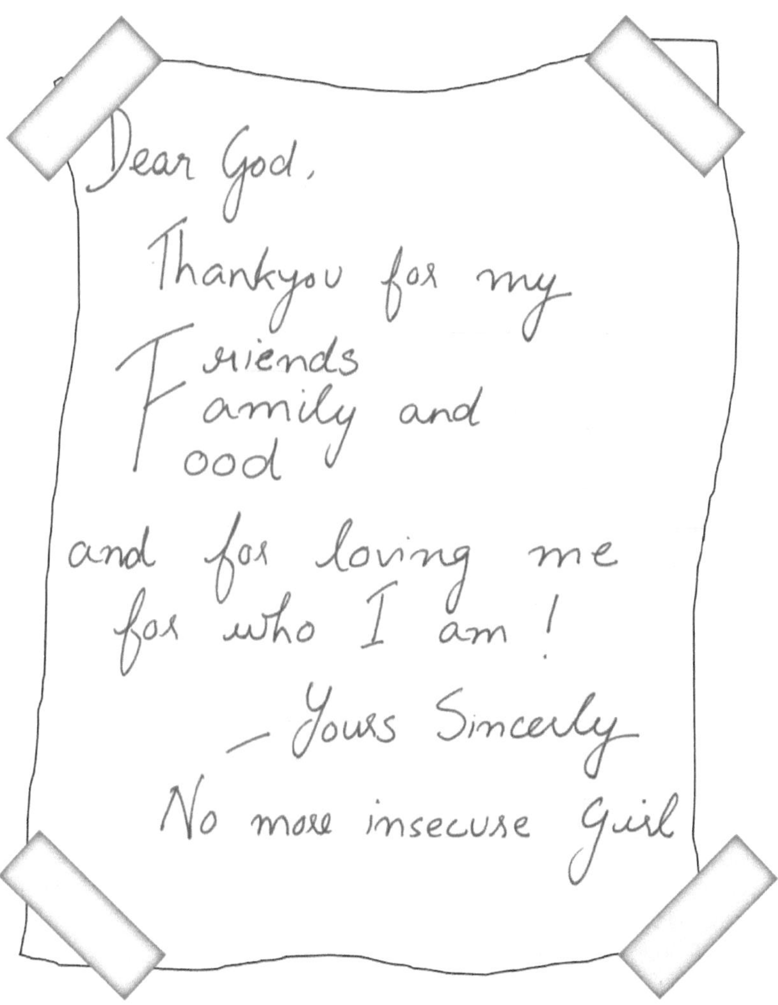

PS: Thanks, guys and before you go – enjoy the latest edition of my school's newsletter. Yes, just like the leading national newspapers, the school also has to resort to 'those cheap tactics' to get maximum readership! But think about it, we are all guilty of it, isn't it?

Patriotic Public School

Newsletter for the month of August

Ex Student wins the Bikini Round in Ms India Competition

Sonali Sen makes history by winning the very coveted title of Ms Perfect 10. We all remember that she visited the school last time on Prom Night and crowned the Prom Queen. Ms. Sen is not only beautiful from outside but with her voluntary work for women empowerment she has proved to be a true Patriotic School product. In her latest tweet she said, "Feeling on top of the world, those millions of crunches were so worth it."

A message from the Vice Principal :

Dear Students,
It has been reported that some girls are crossing all limits of decency by wearing skirts as much as three inches above the knees. The school policy about inappropriate dressing has been communicated to you many times. However, I have to warn you of dire consequences if the school's directions are not adhered to. The administration plans to complain to your parents if repeated offences are made so kindly refrain from doing anything that spoils the name of our reputed institution.

Growing-up Pains

Moms – unpaid workers?
By Tara Kapoor

Haven't you heard this many times – that the lady of the house is a cook, a driver, a maid, an accountant, a nurse, etc., etc.? And how thankless her job is? That imagine how much money she would make if she did all this outside? The sad thing is that I hear my friends quoting this so proudly. Is a mom's worth measured only by the taste of her food or how clean she keeps the house? What happens if you have a maid or two doing most of the work? Does it make this 'housewife' any less important? What if she just sits around reading, painting, knitting or doing absolutely nothing (meditating – in my own mom's words)? She still is your mother, whether she decides to cook or not. Or goes to work or not. And she has no obligation to impress her family by making her own life so tough. So friends, forget this cleaner, cook business and learn to appreciate this woman who should not have to give justification for her existence. And let her live. Guilt free.

Before you totally go –
A million Likes for the girls...

Who have unkempt hair and braces on their teeth. Who prefer chatting to talking, get scolded by parents for being careless, lazy and *dheeth*.

Who study for their exams at the last minute, who go to bed really late. Who gorge on the pizza instead of the salad on their plates.

Who choose flats over those peep-toes which are not all that great.

And obviously who never get asked out on a date.

Who go to malls just for the *chole-bhature* in the food court and but choose not to burn it by playing any sport.

Aren't we all in the same boat?

Who are not popular but still have a big heart, unnoticed by boys but still very smart.

A million Likes for the girls who trip over things, are moody, weird and sometimes blue.

A million Likes for the **girls like me and you!**

ACKNOWLEDGEMENTS

Like an ideal Indian daughter, I begin by expressing sincere gratitude to my mother who was so fond of feeding *ande*-bread to her three daughters that we could never follow our dreams of winning any beauty contest, not even a Miss Ambala. Instead, we ended up following every diet in the world but were never able to stick to any for more than a day! So, in a way, she is the indirect reason why I wrote this book – because weight is the favourite, rather, only topic of discussion in the Kumar household.

To my father, who is the most positive man in the world (actually, thanks to him I hardly ever got to know more than a handful of men). Colonel Saab hated the male species so much that even our dogs were bitches ;-) But I still thank him, as he also brought us up into these bold, aggressive, confident women, attracting and eventually marrying these completely opposite, polite and most amenable gentlemen in the Punjabi community!

One of them pulled me out of my comfort zone and inspired me to write a book: my husband, who has always kept me grounded – even on a pedestal. Thank you.

Thanks to my beautiful sisters for usually being so funny and kind. And sometimes very difficult to deal with too! I hope one day you will read this book.

Thanks to my children for choosing to be born in my house! And making it so challenging and still so worthwhile.

A word of gratitude to my friends and some important people in my life; again I am not taking any names, but you know I am talking about you. (Yes, I am trying to be smart.)

And now some names – first and foremost, thanks to Uzair at Leadstart for giving me more creative freedom than I could have asked for. To my wonderful editor Padmini for her attention to detail and for being ever so accommodating. To my friend Shailesh for letting me use his Hindi poems. To my designer Ashwini & designer Sachan for understanding so well what I really wanted.

PART-2
TEEN
RILOGY
MEGHA

Monisha K Gumber
DYING
A story of grit and determination and passion?
Nah! It's a story of a nervous girl with a screwed up mind who gets her life back
To Live
A Novel with pictures

For Siddhi – the love of my life

and

my BFFs

Bhavna Doegar and Namita Zutshi

If you haven't read *Sick of Being Healthy . . . you must read this!*

Although I am hoping you have read it, even if you haven't, I will not take it personally.

The novel you have in your hands right now is a sequel to my first book about Tara, a plump, fourteen-year-old girl with a great sense of humour and personality. But she didn't much like being fat and thought that she would never be able to get the guy of her dreams Karan because of the way she looked. Yes, she was cute and all but she had a major complex about her weight.

The fact that this guy fell in love with her prettier and much thinner friend Dolly, pushes her deep into the dark world of a food disorder. To lose the extra kilos, she goes on a crash diet and makes herself vomit after almost every meal. Yes, she loses some weight but she loses a lot more. Like her happiness and self-esteem. She ends up being depressed and lands up in hospital. Basically the story is about how she rises above her issues and emerges a winner in the end.

Does she get Karan's attention? Well, for that you should read that book and anyway it's not so important here.

Because this one, the second in the series, is the story of Tara's best friend, Megha. It's been a year or so since Class IX, so the girls have grown up, too. Megha, the swimming champion and school topper is going to go through a lot more hell than Tara did. She ends up learning a lot more too. Some rules about success and failures and relationships. Rules about being true to yourself and doing the right thing. Rules about acceptance and hope. And the rule about never giving up.

This is Megha's story. And like Tara, she deserves to be heard too.

But before that an important disclaimer:

This is based on my imagination, is a work of fiction and should be treated as such even though it is loosely inspired and based on lives of a couple of girls who serve in the Indian Army or/and are sports champions. The point to be noted is that there are a lot of swimming championships happening under different bodies/federations. I have taken some liberties in describing the events and dates, and at the same time tried to be authentic and technically correct. Also for the sake of simplicity I might not have described the details of the gruesome selections and preparations that go behind these competitions. Still, I hope I have been able to do justice to the struggles of our girls in sports who work harder than most. Apart from that they usually have the same old issues their friends face, which I have talked about.

The book is in honour of the girls who play. And play well. Whatever their field may be.

I balanced all,
    brought all to mind,
The years to come
    seemed waste of breath,
A waste of breath
    the years behind
In balance with this life,
    this death.

— William Butler Yeats

Prologue

10:30 pm, end of May, St. Teresa Medical care

Gurgaon, India

This can't be happening . . . it seems I have failed yet again.

I am able to think, so it means I am not dead yet. But I am not able to open my eyes, I am not able to speak so does it mean I am dead? Oh wow, now it's time to go through the tunnel I have heard so much about and merge into that white light at the end of it. Now is the time to be one with the universe, to feel a magnificent energy, to feel that bliss, that infinite love

But all I am able to feel is this damn headache. And a lot of drowsiness. I guess this must be the end. Goodbye, cruel world. Sorry, Mama and Papa.

I drifted into a deep sleep. I started to feel lighter and floated in the clouds above. Finally, I was in the 'other realm' I had been fantasising about – the place with no school, no exams and no swimming competitions. And no Sandy. Here I would get my answers. Here I would find peace. Here I would be happy. And left alone.'Oh, Megha, why did you do this to us? Why, Megha, why?' I heard Mama cry. Papa was talking to someone – probably a doctor. Which meant I was still awake. And alive. Only, I could not move. I tried to make sense of the voices but I did not have the strength to concentrate.

Give it up, Megha, just give it up.

Part 1

My life . . . before I died

I've missed more than 9000 shots in my career. I've lost almost 300 games. Twenty-six times, I've been trusted to take the game winning shot and missed. I've failed over and over again in my life. And that is why I succeed.

– Michael Jordan,
famous professional basketball player

Three years ago

'Ladies and gentlemen, welcome to the District-Level Sub-Junior Girls' 50-metres Freestyle race. This year is a tough one, with the two current favourites, Deepali and Megha, fighting for the gold. Deepali, the defending champion, is not ready to give up her title but the home crowd is rooting for Megha – can't help noticing the expression on Megha's face – she doesn't care if everyone is cheering her on – all she is focused on is winning. Can she do it? In just a few moments, we will know . . . One – two – three – Go! All the girls are fighting it out but clearly Megha and Deepali have raced ahead of them. Deepali is leading her way through but Megha is finding her form too. Can she defeat the champion? Both are neck and neck . . . Deepali seems faster and there is no stopping her . . . Hey! She slows down! Look at Megha – suddenly overtaking Deepali, she hits it. A remarkable victory! A new record!'

I looked up to thank God, and then my eyes searched for Mama and Papa. Oh, how proud they would be of me today. Thank God, I did it; the countless hours practising in the pool were so worth it. For the last two years, this had been my dream – to defeat Deepali. And finally I did it.

On our way back home:

Papa: Oh Megha, I am so happy! This medal that was eluding you for the last two years – it's all yours now!

Me: Yes, Papa, I still can't believe it. Honestly, I did not expect to win.

Mama: Megha, you did not win. Deepali lost.

Me: What do you mean, Mama?

Mama:	You know what I mean – something happened, I am not sure what. But I want to know – why did she slow down at the last moment?
Papa:	Hey, come on, Seema, give your daughter some credit. Who cares what happened, the fact is that Megha won and that's what matters. And she broke a record!
Mama:	I am not going to take it easy and neither should you, Megha . . . you could have done better. It doesn't matter that you won – because you did not give a tough fight. But anyway, congratulations.
Papa:	Don't listen to your mom, Megha, let's celebrate tonight.

Teary-eyed, I looked at the medal dangling from my neck, and felt really angry. *So Mama thinks I did not win, despite breaking a record, she is more interested in knowing what made Deepali lose. How mean . . . I hate her! But she is my mother . . . I'm sorry, God, for even thinking like this . . . But what if she is right? Maybe I would have got a silver again if Deepali had not slowed down . . . I guess I really could have done better.*

Since then that's what I heard after every competition, whether it was an interstate swimming championship, my academic ranking in class or even an informal game of Scrabble at home – I could have done better.

Over the next few years I actually started doing better. I was the undisputed champion in swimming, first in class each time and never ever lost a game of Scrabble again.

But to my mama, I still could have done better.

So when Tara's book got released, I was compelled to write one myself. Mama forced me to do it: if an average Tara could do it, why couldn't a top achiever like me? But I was hesitant. I had nothing to tell. And who would like to read the same old shit about 'pressures of being an Indian student'? But since then, a lot started happening in my boring life and I guess that is why you have this book in your hands.

So now that you have the background, I will start with my story. Before I introduce the main characters, please note that since last year we all have grown, specially Tara and Dolly with their longer hair. We have been neighbours since ages, are now mature, more aware and sensible teenagers (you wish)!

Megha:
Well, the whole story is about my evolution so I am having a hard time condensing it in a couple of lines. But since I have to do it, then I am one of those kids who are branded as celebrities in school. Topper in studies, great in sports, nice to look at, popular, natural leaders – the works. The kids who appear friendly but don't really mix with the commoners. That's me . . .

Tara: My best friend who, too, has become kind of a star since her book *Sick of Being Healthy* was released. I actually like her but lately she has acquired an attitude. The so-called sweet, innocent Tara is popular now with both boys and girls at school. Yes, success doesn't suit her kind of girl. I want her old version back – a regular girl who was always available for me. And looked up to me.

Dolly: My second-best friend, a wannabe model who always and literally always has her nose stuck in her cell phone. What can I say about her, except that she is pretty but that's her only claim to fame? Well . . . she did win the Prom Queen Title last year, but in all modesty it was because I had already won the Ms All-Rounder title and in my school, they like to give everyone a chance. Coming back to Dolly – yes, she is hot.

Mama: A no-nonsense, corporate type and in charge of every breath I take. A feminist. A fighter. A winner. Yes, Papa stands no chance. And neither does the world that she wishes to conquer. I wish I could be like her . . . but do I really?

Papa: A feminine and softer version of Mama. Yes, a no-nonsense, corporate type too. But he doesn't care about fighting or winning. All he wants is to do a good job and have a peaceful family life. I would rather be like him, but that would be a big mistake. Or so says my mom.

Nani:

The only sane person in our family. Used to be quite a woman in her younger days. Lost her army-officer husband in the 1971 war while she was still pregnant with Mama, her only child, whom she brought up singlehandedly, working as a teacher and eventually running a school for special children. Awarded by the government for her service to society. But now, in my mama's words, all she wants to do is 'Eat, Pray, Love'. She is seventy-plus, so can you blame her?

Coach Uncle: Well, he makes his entry much later but he is an important part of my life. An army officer, a renowned International champion and a part-time coach to me. Wait for him – he is worth it.

Sandy: My boyfriend or rather, ex. Well, it's complicated. Our relationship and the guy himself. All I know is that he looks like a rock star and that is how I got attracted to him in the first place. Remember our Prom Night last year?

Flashback – Last year March, the party in Dolly's house on the Prom night: WHERE IT ALL STARTED

'Thank you, Dolly. We all know how unique you are. Frankly, I knew I was going to get the Ms All-Rounder title, and my parents have worked for not only this night but for all the future awards and titles I may achieve. Thanks, Mama, Papa, for making me a winner. But I am tired now and all I want is to go on a vacation with you both; nothing exotic, even Nani's house in Ambala will do, where there are no schedules, no 'to do' lists and no hurrying from one place to another . . . that's all I want. I do want to congratulate my friends Tara and Dolly for getting their own prizes. I am really proud of you guys, especially Tara, for never mincing your words and always speaking your mind. I guess I have a lot to learn from you. Thanks, guys. Thanks, Aunty, for your efforts – I really appreciate it.'

As I finished, I looked at Mama's face and I knew I'd made a big mistake. I should have thought before blurting out about being tired and having a vacation in Nani's house. But then Tara got up to give her own 'Thank you speech', which would make it even tougher for me that night. Because I think she spoke better than me. And Mama won't approve, even if it was a stupid speech at a stupid party! Well, to hell with everyone. I won, right? Ms All-Rounder! That was me!

I thought of focusing on something more interesting. Like Dolly's big brother whom I caught checking me out every now and then.

So here is when we met for the first time.

Dolly's mother had planned a 'surprise' party for the three winners – actually she planned for two. Because no one really expected Tara to get her own prize. Even though we were all happy for her, I could still sense everyone trying to accept it – that of all people Tara got an Outstanding Contribution award for her articles in newsletters. I don't want to sound mean, but honestly, what's the big deal about writing crappy stuff meant for kids? Not that she started a revolution or something! Anyway, Dolly got busy with her cell phone and Tara with her butter chicken so when the parents got into a group discussion about the 'Meaning of Life', the coast was clear. From the corner of my eye, I saw him approaching me. Well, not that I am into boys and all but when someone looks like Harry Styles, it would be dumb to not play along.

Sandy: Hi there, Meghna . . . Congratulations.

Me: It's Megha.

Sandy: Oh, I'm sorry. I am not too good with names, you see. So how does it feel to win the Ms All-Rounder? Quite something, man!

Me: Actually, no one is surprised, *Bhaiya*.

Sandy: *Bhaiya*? Hey, I am not that old. I just turned twenty-two. Dolly doesn't call me *bhaiya* and you must be her age, right?

(He laughed and his pearly white teeth and curly brown hair cast a spell on me, but then, in all these years, I had learnt to handle pressure very well.)

Me: Yes, I guess so. So what do you do, Sandy? You live in Mumbai, right? Are you here on vacation?

Sandy: Yeah, I am taking a break. Between shooting for the first few shows of this new series that is coming up on Pariwaarik channel, *Kaali Shaktiyon Waali Saas Meri* – you know, right?

Me: *(Rolling my eyes)* Honestly, I don't.

Sandy: Oh, come on, you must watch it – it will give you a different perspective. *(He laughed*

Me: Even my mom doesn't watch it, and I am sure
                     my Nani doesn't either; who watches this stuff
                     anyway? And what do you have to do with it?

Sandy: This is my first break. I have a role in it. Well,
                     not the lead but I play the heroine's secret
                     lover who himself does black magic and all.
                     Right now, it's not big, but if people like it, I
                     will get more screen space. You know they are
                     constantly innovating and rewriting the story.

Me: Yeah, they might kill you before you return as
                     an evil serpent to take your revenge from the
                     kaali saas. (I laughed.)

Sandy: Who knows . . . anyway I gotta go. *(He sounded
                     offended.)*

As he walked off, I wondered if I had said something that hurt
him, but then he himself had started off by making fun of these
serials. Anyway, as I said, I wasn't into boys anyway so to hell
with him.

Oh, what a night it was. I kept reliving the moment when I got
my title. I tried to feel excited about it, but somehow it wasn't
happening. It had to be me, I was an ace student, was in the
school's football team, a sure-shot national swimming champion,
good looking, smart . . . honestly I had no competition. But why
wasn't it giving me a kick anymore? I won, right? So why wasn't
I feeling great?

Was it Sandy? Or was it Mama and Papa?

My parents. Married for twenty years. Met at BITS Pillani when
Mama was this beautiful *hatti-katti*, confident *Punjaban* who
had her life completely planned out and my Papa was a simple,

shy, 'single *haddi*' Maharashtrian who had no idea why he was studying engineering. Mama got attracted to him as he was the only boy who didn't stalk her around. He seemed lost, anyway, so she decided to take him under her wing and teach him a thing or two about ambition and success. Completely bewildered by a girl who seemed so sure of what she wanted in life, he gave in and eventually they fell in love. It wasn't so easy to convince their families but then you don't argue with kids who are top rankers in CAT. So as soon as they both got their MBA degrees, they tied the knot, believing that they would be living happily ever after.

Except that at first opposites attract but later, opposites attack.

All my life, I considered myself the luckiest girl around, or so my friends always told me. Being the only child, they gave me the best upbringing possible, or so my parents told me.

But if you asked me, I really don't know. I would like to think that I am really lucky to have parents like mine and some really cool friends but there are times when I feel really sad and nervous. I don't know what triggers it, but sometimes I have this weird feeling – of a tight knot in the pit of my stomach, which is . . . well . . . the worst feeling in the world. But I have learnt to ignore it as I don't want to be ungrateful, especially after Mama showed me a video about starving kids in Third World countries, who live amidst heart-wrenching poverty. So why fuss about these 'knotty' feelings? Who cares? And who has the time anyway?

Coming back to my parents, then – these days it's not so good between them anymore. Especially since my mom got involved with this guy – now don't get me wrong. It's purely platonic. And spiritual.

Since the last year or so, I have seen Mama attending a lot of these meditation sessions led by Guru Dasa-Kisna, a prodigy of the famous late Shriman Swami Gyani Saab. Initially Papa was forced to join in too, but he soon gave up. You see, he is too simple a person to believe in this spiritual rubbish. He makes fun of Mama, too, which she does not take too well.

Since Mama's guru *ghantaal* (as Papa calls him) moved into a flat in our society, the place is abuzz with thousands of visitors in orange, who are seeking redemption from their past lives by releasing themselves from all material desires. Do you think it is even possible to tame these high flyers who claim to have had enough of this rat race and are looking for 'real happiness'?

Unfortunately, Mama is the classic example of the above and I bet she leads the group, as being a leader is her most favourite habit.

Anyway, Class X had started with a bang but everyone knew that these few weeks before the summer vacations are not to be taken too seriously. I had been promoted to President of the Sports Club in our school. Tuitions had started and despite the homework, the pressures had not really started building up. I knew the real deal would be after the holidays – that's when it all starts – the drama of Boards and all. Right now, it hadn't really sunk in completely.

As for me, since I had topped Class IX and had won some important prizes, Mama gave me some time off. To take a hard look within myself. As if that wasn't hard work in itself!

So summer vacations were the perfect time for her to push me into yet another hobby. Spirituality.

The other day she dragged me along to attend a session meant for teenagers. Now the reason I went was simply because I could not bear another lecture from her about her knowing what is best for me and the sacrifices she has made to bring me up. I was sure that this baba's sermon would be more bearable. I just hoped that I didn't bump into someone familiar there as this was the last thing I wanted people to find me doing.

And guess what – he was there too. But unlike me he wasn't embarrassed at all.

So when you see a handsome hunk in orange singing bhajans with an American accent – you can't be blamed for joining the spiritual movement.

When Sandy opened his eyes, they met mine for an instant and I could sense the confusion as if he was trying to remember if he knew me. Then he smiled. And those dimples. And it was the beginning of the end for me. My end.

And then Guruji interrupted those warm fuzzy feelings...

'Friends . . . aahhhhh . . . today I see some young people and feel your pure energy . . . your being here . . . how divine. Now stay still and just listen to what I have to say . . . release your mind from your day-to-day thoughts and don't analyse . . . just sit comfortably and be free . . .' Guruji intoned.

'Breathe through your nose and exhale from your mouth . . . feel your body relax and let go of all blockages. On the next inward breath hold for four seconds and release slowly for eight seconds . . . your thoughts are still and there is nothing but your breath and you. Feel the energy flowing through each muscle of your body . . . you are healing now . . . your chakras are relaxed . . . see yourself walking through a beautiful green garden . . . the breeze is flowing through the lush green trees . . . the warmth of the sun . . . feel it all, feel the ground and go deeper in the garden . . . it is never-ending, boundless . . . hear the birds chirping, the water from the spring . . . see the colourful flowers blossoming and keep going . . . here there are no tensions . . . no sadness . . . only peace and quiet . . . peace . . .peace . . . peace . . . just feel your breath . . . and nothing else . . . because there is nothing else but you . . . connect with the universe . . . merge with it . . . be the universe . . .'

As I listened to Guruji, I felt a cloud enveloping my body. And I felt the connection. With my breath at first and then with the guy who sang the bhajans. And suddenly I was in love. Suddenly the world was a more beautiful place. Suddenly this talk about energy healing and chakra balancing was interesting. Simply because Sandy was a part of the whole deal.

The 'hugging therapy round' at the end of the session nailed it for me. About him — I wasn't too sure what he thought of it as he seemed to be in a trance while approaching all people — girls or boys — with an equal and impartial warmth. As if it didn't matter.

But for me – it made a huge difference when I hugged Sandy compared to just another boy from the neighborhood. Maybe I wasn't spiritual enough. Maybe I still had to learn.

And I had found my teacher. Not guruji, stupid!

The next week, when Papa saw my excitement about going for the next session, he sensed trouble. I heard my parents having a huge fight over it in their bedroom.

'I am not going to let any daughter of mine get involved in this bullshit!' shouted Papa.

'Just because you don't understand it, doesn't mean nobody else will too. She is my daughter; she will do as I say. And she wants to go, can't you see that?' Mama shouted back.

'For God's sake, Seema, don't make her like yourself' he said softly and regretted it immediately when Mama started crying.

You know who won the argument, right? And I found myself attending another session. For some more bhajans, yoga asanas, breathing techniques and meditation. And the guy in orange who sang the bhajans with an accent.

And *rang de tu more gerua* became my favourite song for a long time. But no, I didn't get any of the promised peace . . . That night I couldn't sleep. I wondered if it was sitting still during meditation or the fact that Sandy completely ignored me – and which of these had been more grueling. So I did the best thing to ease off my restlessness.

I went online.

As I said before you just can't get over a guy whose profile picture looks like this:

The fact that he had that kind of swag, a medical-school dropout, a struggling actor, having a seductive voice and spiritual interests, curly hair and deep dimples, made him really, really sexy to a stuck-up girl completely bored with her life full of maths, science and swimming.

Who would believe that a person could be tired of winning all the time? But I was. And I was desperate for some excitement, which I thought Sandy would bring into my dull life. What I didn't realise is that even if you get tired of winning you still don't ever want to fail. And Sandy was already making me feel like a failure. By not paying any attention to me.

As I looked at his photos on Facebook, I started wondering if it would be a good idea to send him a friends request. But I did not want to come across as a cheapo like his sister Dolly who recently broke up with Karan, a guy that Tara was in love with too. I know that they got a bit too involved . . . you know, going beyond kissing and all before Mona Aunty made Dolly cut all ties with Karan. But Tara has a feeling they will get back together soon. Well, who cares? I had to do something about my own love life now and it was time I had one.

After all I was in Class X now and had Boards to take this year. And Mama was expecting me to be a state topper this year. Nothing less would do for her.

So that's what this 'could be state topper' did. I sent him a friends request. Imagine if Mama found out that I am on the road to failure. Her failure – as a *Momager*. OK, I will make it easier for you – a mom who is also your manager.

And I waited. For the next forty-eight hours I was online. I saw that his number of friends had grown from 1252 to 1270 but I didn't make the list. And when it got a bit too much, I decided to confront him. But I couldn't do this alone, I needed a trusted team. (Yes, I had learnt something from Mama's conference calls that ran in the background on weekends.) So I went over to Tara's house.

It was awkward. When you don't see your friends for weeks, it's kind of awkward to meet them face to face. All right, we exchanged videos and jokes on WhatsApp all the time but since the Prom Night, we had not seen each other. But this problem could not be solved over a chat application.

As we made ourselves comfortable on her bed, I spilled out the details, over chips and cola. Yeah, I needed some emotional support.

Tara: I know, yaar, I saw him looking at you at the party. And not just one time.

Me: He hasn't made any move, Tara. I met him twice during the meditation class but he doesn't give a damn. Can you believe it, he didn't even accept my friends request?

Tara: He will, yaar, just hang in there. How can he ignore someone like you? I mean, you have everything!

Me: That's what *you* think. And stop saying that. It's irritating.

Tara: Come on, Megha, you are a fighter. Don't give up so soon. He is not that great anyway, except that he is good looking.

Me: I don't know, Tara . . . all I know is that I love him. Don't know why . . .

As I burst out crying, I could see the shock on Tara's face. I knew that I was acting crazy but it was my first time and Mama had not prepared me for *this*.

What was I thinking? Tara herself had no experience whatsoever in matters of the heart except for her one-sided love for Karan. How could she help me?

Tara: Let's go to Dolly's house. Let's talk to her. He is her brother. She will know what to do. She might be kind of dumb but she is the only one we know who has been in a relationship. I am sure she will help us out, yaar.

So Tara and I went over to Dolly's house to help *us* out with *our* problem. Like I said. I needed a trusted team.

Dolly: Bad news, guys. Bhai already has a girlfriend in Mumbai.

Me: Oh thank God! That's why he was ignoring me. I thought he didn't find me good enough.

Now both Tara and Dolly were shocked. What was I saying? Was I relieved because my crush was already going around with someone else?

Me: Don't get me wrong, guys . . . I wasn't able to accept the fact that someone could ignore me. I mean, I am good, right? So what could be a reason except that Sandy is already taken.

As I burst out crying again, I surprised myself. What was happening to me? What was I really sad about? I guess I really did need the meditation sessions, and this time for some actual peace. And clarity of mind.

Or was I just fooling myself?

'Hare Krishna, Hare Krishna . . . Krishna, Krishna . . . Hare, hare . . .'

'Hey God, forgive me. I am not religious, but you know, I am a good person. I never hurt anyone. I listen to my parents. I respect my teachers. And I volunteer at the dog shelter. Help me, God, help me get over him. I know I don't exist for him, so why can't I stop thinking about him? Either help me move on or let him be mine. Yes, let him be mine, God, I promise to never take you for granted. I love him, God, can't you see that?' My prayers and Sandy's bhajans completed at the same time. We both opened our eyes simultaneously, and they met. I smiled. And it was all over for him this time.

So when we embraced each other during the 'hugging therapy', I knew that God listened.

As I packed my bag and collected my stuff to leave, he came over to talk. Yes. This was going to be my big moment.

Sandy: Hey Meghna . . . did you enjoy the session?

Me: It's Megha.

Sandy: Oops, here I go again . . . sorry. It seems you are becoming quite a regular here.

Me: Yes, it makes me feel good. (*Honestly, it didn't
                       but I didn't want to offend him again.*)

Sandy: Oh yes, when I come here, I forget about my past
                       . . . and my problems . . . and my struggles to
                       pursue my dreams . . . here it doesn't matter.

Me: I know what you mean. We become one with
                       the universe, right?

And he laughed. And he took my cell number. And that night, he accepted my friends request.

The best part was yet to come. In the next few days his relationship status turned from 'in a relationship' to 'it's complicated' to 'single'. Thank you, God. Really.

How and why he had a breakup was none of my concern but when he needed someone's shoulder to cry on, then who else but a swimmer could provide the support he so badly needed?

When Tara heard, she was as excited for me and we both went over to Dolly's house. But this time to talk to Sandy. Directly.

Since Mona Aunty was not home, Dolly and Tara actually made me go to Sandy's room to say 'hello'. You know what a guy and a girl do in a situation like this?

Sandy cried while I listened to his story.

'You know, Megha, I am going through hell . . . I have just had a breakup. I mean, I kind of knew it was coming. Since the last few months, she stopped listening to me. When I try discussing our relationship, she says I will never understand . . . I mean my career is not really looking up except for this teeny-weeny role in this damn *saas-bahu* show, which I had initially resolved to never be a part of . . . I am having my own issues . . . and now, she says she doesn't want to have anything to do with me as I am a selfish bastard. She has a great life, she is an only daughter of rich parents, she has no ambitions, no drive . . . all she wanted to do was spend time with me . . . but I have a life, I need to make it big – and she calls me selfish?'

It was too complex for me to understand. Did they break up because she stopped listening to his issues? But he said all she wanted to do was spend time with him. So what was the problem? I couldn't make sense of the contradictions.

And honestly I didn't care. I just wanted him to get over it so that he could start afresh. So I did a really stupid thing.

I proposed.

Now that's something which girls are not supposed to do but then I wasn't just any other girl. I was Ms All Rounder.

'Sandy, you might wonder what's got into me but I think I have fallen for you. And big time. I know you've just had a break-up but you will get over her. Trust me. You know, I have been such a busy girl, having more pressures than most kids. All these years all I have done is academics and swimming and have had absolutely no time to even think of anything else. But since I have seen you, I have only thought about you. Do you think we could have something going on between the two of us? As I really do. And I am usually never wrong.'

So when he gave me a hug this time, I knew I had won. As I wasn't good at failing.

When I gave the news to Tara and Dolly, they couldn't help hugging me either. Oh, to be loved by a guy who looked like Harry Styles. Unfortunately, this was his only positive point I could think of that time. But I hoped I would get to see a lot more.

Did I say I was usually never wrong?

Before I go on about Sandy and me, something more drastic was happening in my own house.

Something like a divorce.

When I came back home after the best evening of my life, I had no clue that my happiness was going to be this short-lived. As that same night they told me.

Papa: Megha, we need to talk, beta . . .

Mama: Come, sit down, my child (*Mom was kind of jittery – the first time I saw her like this and it was scaring the shit out of me.*)

Papa: You know, beta, things have not been good between Mama and me? We have tried to work it out, beta, but it seems we cannot go on being with each other anymore . . . in other words, we are getting a divorce.

Me: What? But you said you will give yourselves another chance! You have been into counselling, right? Tell me you are joking. (*I started to cry.*)

Papa: Yes, we have been seeing a relationship therapist but ours is beyond repair, Megha. But you know we both love you. We will never do anything to hurt you.

Me: Oh, yes? So if this is not hurting, what is? Give me a break, guys! (*I cried and cried.*)

Mama: Megha, it's all right, you will feel sad about it . . . feel it and let go.

Me: Spare me your spiritual crap, Mama. You guys

have let me down big time. I hate the both of you. I know you don't love me, so don't lie, OK? Just leave me alone! (*I ran off into my room, slamming the door behind me.*)

So this was what I had said was the best evening of my life.

The next morning, when Mama woke me up for swimming practice, I could not move. I felt completely drained. But when I told her that I felt sick she again gave me a lecture about dealing with obstacles and emerging as a winner. Oh, why can't she get over this 'winner' rubbish?

Because there was no point arguing with her, I got up to get ready. On most days it's our driver, Goldie Bhaiya, who takes me everywhere. From school to swimming to tennis to tuitions. But that day, when I saw Mama with the car keys, I knew she was trying just too hard. As she is careful to be never, ever, late for office.

More about mama . . .

Her work means everything to her and though she is called a superwoman in her social circle, she really hasn't given our home much time. I am sure she hasn't been a good wife either, as I have never seen her being nice to Papa. Usually she doesn't even let him finish a sentence. There is one thing she has given a lot of attention to, though – her daughter's achievements. She was always, always on my case. When I was younger, I liked the attention but slowly she got too overbearing. I was sick of her always trying to motivate and push me to do my best. But I did it anyway. Because what chance could a fifteen-year-old have against a ruthless career planner like her?

Maybe I am sounding mean, but before starting to write, I had promised myself that I would try to be as honest as possible.

But when we started talking in the car . . . she tried changing my mind.

Mama: So, how is your practice getting on?

Me: OK.

Mama: What does Coach Sir say? Are you improving your speed?

Me: Whatever.

Mama: You don't want to talk?

Me: I don't.

Mama: We have to, Megha . . . you know I only have your best interests in mind.

Me: Don't start, Mama.

Mama: I know you are disturbed. Believe me, we tried. We lost it a long time back, Megha; the only reason we are still together is you.

Me: So stay together, I am still here.

Mama: Megha, I don't like your Papa anymore. I cannot live with him anymore.

Me: You don't like him, yeah? A simple, straight, loving man like Papa, you don't like him? Have you ever thought what is there to like about you? (*I was crying.*)

Mama: Yes, there is nothing to like about me.

While I knew I had hurt Mama, I had to vent my frustration. This lady, who has always given her profession her top priority, she doesn't find Papa good enough for her now? Now that she is CEO of her company while Papa is still an Assistant VP or something . . . How arrogant is she? To even compete with her own husband! My poor father . . . I found myself hating her. And this time I didn't feel guilty about it.

She dropped me off at the pool where Coach Sir was waiting for me along with the other girls. We were all competing for the same thing – the State Level Championship due in July. The winner would go straight into the Nationals. Last year not one girl had even come close to defeating me but this year my coach had pointed out that I was losing my speed. He told me that though I had muscular, agile legs, I still had to work on my strokes. Some of the girls in my age group had grown taller over the last year and some had even lost weight. So they now had an advantage over me. My strength had been my speed but somehow it wasn't working anymore – at least not enough to have a shot at the Nationals.

As usual, I wasn't supposed to lose my sleep over it: just practise and practise. And improve. My breathing. My coordination. My focus. My stance. My dive. My drive. My everything. My last year's win was history already. The fact that I was a National champion last year did not matter anymore if I did not work on myself continuously. I still had to win the State Level to get selected for the Nationals.

The School Games National Championships would take place somewhere in November this year. All these years I could get away with some minor hiccups since I was still in the under-14s but now I would be competing in the under-17 category and surely this wasn't something I could take easy. Coach Sir was relentlessly on my case, as it was all about timing – and it wasn't my strong point anymore.

But I had another thing to work on, too. And I wasn't going to ignore it over a swimming competition . . . as I said, my timing was all wrong.

My new relationship was my new focus now. And my everything.

Sandy and I started meeting a lot more. I had to make the most of the time I had with him as in a month or so he would be back in Mumbai to start shooting for his show. Mona Aunty, who was almost never home, made it easy for us. And the fact that Dolly was my boyfriend's sister made it a lot easier too.

I don't think my parents could have guessed in their wildest dreams what their 'perfect' daughter was up to. And I am not talking about an affair. There was a lot more involved than being in love for the first time. Such as tensions. And nightmares.

What to do, I asked for it!

As when you fall in love with a Harry Styles lookalike, you tend to ignore the fact that he could well be a jerk. And that's what he was slowly turning out to be.

It wasn't that bad the first couple of weeks. Except the guy liked to talk a lot. About his dreams that changed a bit every time I met him. The only thing that remained constant was that he wanted to be a celebrity. Though his self-respect hurt when he thought about his part in this inane TV drama, he did not have the guts to let go of it. Sometimes he would talk about participating in Bigg Boss. Sometimes, of anchoring a talent show. And sometimes, of starting an acting school. Although he was still modelling in Mumbai, it was not enough to get him noticed. He felt frustrated at times and meditated for hours together to find his answers. But all he had was me. Or so he said. **My bad luck entirely . . .**

When he wasn't talking, he used his lips somewhere else. Like on mine. The first time it happened, I lost all my usual good sense and didn't even know how to respond. I just went with the flow and tried to enjoy it. After all, I had dreamt about this moment since the first time I saw him and now that it was happening, why wasn't I feeling great about it? I thought being in love was beautiful. Maybe it was in the movies. In reality I was in a relationship with a guy who had not said 'I love you' to me even once. Whenever I would confront him, he would start confusing me all over again about love not needing a proof and it was just a blissful emotion to be felt deep inside, without any expectations, blah, blah, blah.

I was going through a rough patch myself but he never let me talk about it. It was as if it didn't matter to him if I was disturbed because of my parents' likely divorce. Maybe it didn't. But I couldn't see it then.

When I told Tara about it, she said that he was just using me and did not really love me. But I rubbished it thinking that this immature kiddo was probably jealous that I had a boyfriend and she didn't. What to do, I was fifteen and could not understand a guy who was so much older. I was trying so hard but it seemed we were both in different zones.

But unlike Mama, I took my relationships seriously. I loved this guy and had to do everything it took to make it work. But now that I think about it, I was just very, very stupid.

For I was stupid enough to still carry on with him after he slapped me for the first time. What started off as some teasing about his Bollywood aspirations turned into a full-blown debate. And I was bloody good. As I said, I don't lose. But this time I did: when he couldn't shut me up with a powerful argument, he used his hand on me.

Yes, I got slapped by him.

I know what you are thinking, a confident super-achiever like me, in an abusive relationship with a failure? Is it even possible? Yes. If my parents' relationship could end up in a divorce, anything was possible.

But then there were good moments too. We watched *Pretty Little Liars* and *Arrow* on TV. We went on drives to Baskin-Robbins. We went for *Suicide Squad* and *Sultan* and shared the same honey-coated popcorn and Coke. I loved showing him off to the crowd, which always turned to look at him. I could sense girls giving me envious stares. But he was all mine.

Or so I thought.

One day he stopped taking my calls. He stopped answering my

messages on WhatsApp and never came online to chat with me on Facebook either.

He disappeared.

I called up Dolly to find out about him but I wasn't ever prepared for this.

'Hey, Megha, sorry, but didn't you know? Bhai left. Last night he took a flight for Mumbai . . . No, he just told Mama that something urgent came up, some audition or something . . . Oh? He didn't tell you? Well . . . wait for his call, Megha, I am sure he will call you soon . . . Bye, yaar, take care,' she said sympathetically. I guess she knew. That I meant shit to him.

My heart had shattered into a thousand pieces and I didn't know what to do. Except stalking him. So my next few days were spent ruining my eyes due to constantly staring at my phone. I sent him a million messages. I called him all the time. But he did not answer

And worst of all – he blocked me.

Now what could I really do? I had to give up. I had to forget him. If only it was that easy.

Mama tried talking to me as she thought it was the divorce that was affecting me so much. But I had now begun to give it back to her. I had had enough of her lectures about competing and winning. I wasn't interested in anything and cried all the time. My life was ruined. I didn't know what was more tragic, my own break-up or my parents'.

Papa, however, had never pushed me for anything. He didn't care if I lost or won. He loved me for who I was. I felt terrible for him to see his marriage break with a woman he loved. I didn't know the complexities of their relationship but I knew whose side I was on. Because I truly had started hating her now.

I wasn't just very, very stupid, I was also evil.

I learnt a lot of things in the next few weeks. One was that it was Mama who was the victim here. Yes, you heard it right.

Papa had to tell me. Because he could no longer bear the fact that I blamed her for the divorce. Yes – I used to think that Mama stopped liking Papa because she was super successful while he wasn't. Because she was extremely ambitious and he was happy to be where he was. Because he wasn't a go-getter like her. How wrong I was.

'I know, Megha, your Mama doesn't like me anymore . . . how can she – I have let her down. And it's not what you are thinking.

I am sure she would have still loved me if I decided to be a 'stay-at-home dad'. It's not that, beta . . . I am telling you this as I feel she does not deserve the treatment you are giving her. It is breaking her up from inside. So you have to know. I hope you will handle it with maturity.

'Megha, for the last three years or so, I have been involved with another woman . . . please listen . . . don't start crying. Just hear me out. She works in my company as an Admin manager. She is sweet and homely . . . Things were already strained between Mama and me, and no, it hasn't anything to do with her being too ambitious . . . actually I respect her for that . . . but still the fact is with her travelling and all, we have sort of drifted apart. Even when she was home, all her time was devoted to you. I know she loved me in her own way but she just wasn't there . . . honestly, I could have worked it out if I had really wanted to. But I had fallen in love outside. With a woman who is like me. It doesn't mean that I don't love your mother anymore . . . I still do, but differently now. But I don't see us having a future together. So this woman, her name is Anuradha . . . you can call her Anu Aunty . . . she is a very nice person, you know – very affectionate. Good-looking, too. I think you will like her . . .' Papa concluded.

'Like her? The woman who broke up my parents' marriage – I will like her, Papa? I hate that good-looking bitch of yours and I hate you too. You ruined it all. You ruined Mama's life. All you men are assholes!' I shouted.

Suddenly my cheeks turned red-hot and I realised I had got slapped.

And this time it was Mama.

'How dare you, Megha, how dare you ever talk to your father like this. You are too young to get into this. Apologise right now!' Mama said, very sharply.

'Oh no, Seema, she didn't mean it like that . . . I was just telling her about . . . you know who,' Papa justified.

'I don't care if she meant it or not. I didn't raise her to be this way. Come on now, Megha, apologise.' Mama was serious.

'Sorry,' I said, crying, but they both knew I didn't mean it.

'Now get out of here and think about what you have done,' said Mama.

'Oh Seema, let her be, you are stretching it too far,' said Papa.

'You stretched it too far, your affair with her, Ramesh. You started it . . .' Now Mama started crying.

And Papa gave up.

So nothing could save this marriage now.

And while I lay in my bed, thinking, I realised nothing could save my own relationship either. Except . . .

Sandy called.

And guess what? I did not disconnect. Despite what he did to me, I still thought he deserved to be heard. Maybe he really was in a big problem. I had to listen. Like always.

'Oh, Megha, I am so sorry, baby, you don't know what I have been through the last couple of weeks . . . I had to leave, yaar. I have been trying for the last two years for this production house, so when I was called for the audition, I didn't have a choice . . . No, no, it's not just you. I wasn't taking calls from anyone else, either . . . I was so damn busy. I had to focus . . . I knew you would understand . . . No, I am not coming back for at least two to three months. You know, right, my shoot is going to start . . . Oh, the audition? I didn't make it . . . I didn't know how to face anyone after that . . . Can you believe it, Megha, they called me "expressionless"? Yes, sweetheart, to hell with them. Thank you for believing in me . . . By the way, how have you been? OK, I need to go. Bye.'

And I felt nothing. Except that I didn't know if we were still going around. And there was an important issue facing me. School was going to open in the next two days.

So this was the most productive vacation I had had. I made a boyfriend who made me feel like shit. I tried spirituality, which made me feel like shit. Holy shit, to be precise. I did not finish even one unit in the Maths book and it made me feel like shit. I did not go to the dog shelter and it made me feel like shit. My mama had stopped forcing me to do the above and that too made me feel like shit.

Basically this is what I became over the summer – a piece of shit that nobody cared for anymore. Who had acquired one new hobby – self-pity.

I hoped things would change when school started.

As I said, Class X became a big deal right after the vacations. The year to get real. The year of the Boards. The year that can either make or break a future. Even though our school offered the option of internal exams, almost all of us opted for Boards, and honestly, it was driving us all crazy. It was even worse for me as I had not even started the project I had to submit when the school started. And neither had Tara and nor Dolly.

Tara didn't do it as she was working on her manuscript. A few months back she got an eating disorder called bulimia and it seems she handled it well. Can you believe it; she took it seriously when her mom suggested she pen down her experiences in the form of a book? What confidence, man! All she has done is those articles in our school newsletter and she really thinks she can pull it off? I am almost jealous of her because she is one lazy bum who is simply luckier than us all.

Dolly didn't do it either as she was working on something too. Like her affair with Karan. They broke up some time back but it seems they are back together now. To tell the truth, she would have not done the school project anyway, Karan or not. She is one of the few girls who are so damn clear about what they want from life: to be happy and look beautiful. That's all she cares about and the crazy thing is that I am feeling jealous of a loser like her too. I really must be going down the drain.

Who cares, as I still had Mama, though things have been kind of strained between us, especially after the *thappad.* But I needed her help to complete this damn homework.

As usual, she was there for me.

While we sat on the carpet in the drawing room discussing the plan of action, I realised that no matter how busy she was, she never, ever, refused to help me out with anything. Papa was there too – just watching from a distance and basically never getting his hands dirty.

OK, I was sent for tuitions and all, but she made it a point to always be on top of things when it came to my life – my school, my swimming, tennis, toastmasters, volunteer work – anything. And my diet – I don't even want to get started there. But if it wasn't for Mama, I would be eating chocolates through the day. But Mama made sure that I stuck to my diet and nutrition plan that looked like this on most days (as on special occasions the family liked to binge on pizzas, too):

BREAKFAST	Oats, a glass of almond milk, two boiled eggs, wholegrain toast
PRE-WORKOUT SNACK	Fruits, peanut butter sandwich, a handful of dry fruits
POST WORK-OUT OR LUNCH	Dal, chicken or fish curry with rice/chapattis, cup of yogurt
DINNER	Salad, sautéed vegetables, soup
NIGHT	Bournvita or protein shake

And about my project –

My school loves trying out new ideas. Some work and some don't. This year they decided to do something different. So no more electrical circuits or magnetic fields or potato batteries or even DNA models. This year we had a choice between interesting (and rather long) topics like 'Impressing classmates with a love story with the backdrop of India's struggle for Independence', 'Making a short horror clip for adults', 'Advantages of home-schooling over conventional education' and 'Auditioning for the role of a heroine in a Karan Johar film and getting the part'. So after a lot of arguments over which would be faster, smarter and more impressive, we decided on the love story. After we'd discussed what really we wanted to achieve, Mama had it all figured out.

Mama: Look, Megha, we divide the project into four parts – background, creating the story, synopsis, and final printing. I will work on the background, synopsis and printing . . . You get down to doing your part – writing the story. I think about five thousand words should suffice, no?

Me: Five *thousand* words, Mama, are you serious? I

can't do it: all we have is this night. Why don't *you* create the story and I do the rest?

Mama:	I can help you, Megha, but it's your battle.

Me: No, Mama, I can't do it – it's too much for me. You know school starts day after tomorrow. And it's not a damn battle, just a chunk of homework; surely you can help me?

Mama: I already am, but as I said, it's your baby. At least try. If you can't do it before morning, let me know and we will think of something.

Me: Baby, battle, war! Loosen up, Mama . . . can't you help me out just this time? You know I am not in the right frame of mind!

Mama: A man's gotta do what a man's gotta do – right frame of mind or not. In other words, you can't give up without even trying – whether it's your homework, your relationships, or life itself. You have to give your best shot.

Me: OK, fine, you win. I will show it to you tomorrow but don't blame me if you don't like it.

Mama: I will. Trust me.

As I started typing on my laptop, slowly the characters came alive and the story started taking shape. I realised that unless you actually get down to work, you will create nothing but doubts in your mind about your own abilities. I typed, I typed and I typed some more and before I knew it, it was morning.

When Mama came to my room, I looked at her for sympathy before collapsing in my bed.

When I woke up in the evening, she gave me my project work

along with my contribution of exactly five thousand words.

And along with it, my favourite London Dairy Mocha Almond Fudge ice cream. She announced that we were all going out to celebrate with a movie and then dinner at a new pizza joint where they actually make authentic wood oven pizzas, all of us – Mama, Papa and me – after a long time, we were family again. And the best part was that not once did she say that I could have done better. Because I already knew that I could have – if only I had started in time. But big deal: I can't change that, and I have my project ready for tomorrow – let me just have fun now and forget everything else – school, homework, the impending divorce and . . . Sandy.

Yes, it still wasn't over between us.

Last night of summer vacations . . . well, technically it was morning already . . .

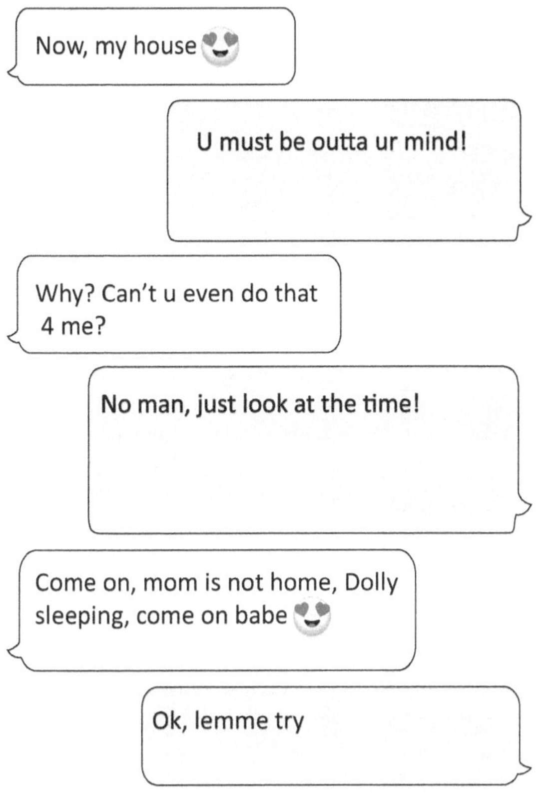

Guess what? No, better still, read on . . .

Now school was starting tomorrow and it was a really stupid idea to get out of my house at this hour and that too secretly. But as I said, Sandy brought into my life something which I totally lacked – some excitement. This was one adventure trip I just had to take.

As I changed into my new denim shorts and a pink tank top, I wondered if I was looking too desperate. Big deal, I thought as I applied some lip gloss and perfume. Nervous as hell, I prayed with quivering lips that nothing should go wrong. When I felt the same, familiar knot in my stomach, I ignored once again what my body was trying to tell me: *Turn back, Megha, or you will regret it.* I didn't. I didn't turn back and neither did I regret it. Because from this night on my feelings for Sandy were sealed. Feelings of sheer hatred.

Some time later . . . in Dolly's house:

'YOU DOG!! WHAT DID YOU JUST DO??' shouted Dolly.

As I ran towards Dolly, I felt his hands gripping my arm tightly from behind.

'Leave me, Sandy, let me go!' I shouted.

'Come on, Megha, I said I am sorry. Hey Dolly, tell her, I am sorry, guys. I didn't mean to . . . I don't know what happened to me!' Sandy blubbered.

'I should have known better than letting poor Megha near an animal like you! Can't you see what you have done – look at the bruises! That black eye! You beat my friend, Bhai, how could you? Oh God, you are drunk! Just you wait, I will call up Mama and tell her everything. You will be dead meat, Sandy; I will make sure of it.'

As I hid behind the so-called Dumbo Dolly, who shielded me like a wall, I loathed myself. How could I end up in a situation like this? Why the hell did I come here, what did I want from him? Why did he do this? But I knew – he did it because I did not stop him the first time. And continued meeting him, hoping that he would not do it again and believing him when he said that you only hurt those you love the most.

Tonight he beat me only because I tried being funny about his career. I thought I was going to cheer him up but I ended up offending him again. And when he couldn't take it anymore, he slapped me while the rage on his face said that it wasn't over – not yet. When I resisted, he pinned me to the floor and punched my face. Thank God, Dolly banged open the door just in time otherwise it was me who would have been dead meat. And now, his sister was standing up for me. She pushed him and he fell on the bed, crying profusely.

'Oh God, Megha, I am so sorry . . . look what he has done . . . wait, let me get some Dettol,' Dolly said softly.

As she applied the burning solution, I wondered what hurt more – my sore cheeks or my breaking heart? Or worse, my shattered ego? To be treated this way by a loser like Sandy! Suddenly I could see it all. I let him do this to me. Yes, I deserved to be beaten up. While all these thoughts were running in my mind, everyone entered.

Mona Aunty, Mama and Papa. And the police. Well, not, like, in uniform and all. But close enough to the real thing. So the drama unfolded.

Mona Aunty:	Oh God, what happened? Sandy, what did you do?!
Mama:	Megha, my poor baby . . . look Mona, look what this bastard has done!
Mona Aunty:	Why, Sandy . . . Dolly, can you tell me what's it all about?
Papa:	Megha, what the hell are you doing here in the first place and at this hour?
Mama:	Yes, Megha, I thought you were sleeping, what were you guys doing, some party or something?
Me:	Stop it guys!! Let me explain, will you? Sandy and I have been going around for a couple of months . . . it's been on and off . . . Yes, sorry, Mama and Papa. He

called me over tonight and as you know, like a fool I came here. When he told me the producers fired him from that show, I tried cheering him up by saying that he should not worry as he will get reincarnated as a fly or something . . . Well . . . it didn't seem important, it was jokes, and I didn't realise how he was reacting . . . he got so damn upset that he beat me for this! Mama, he beat me. (*Crying.*)

Papa: You were in a relationship? I mean, you were going around with this guy? So much older? But you are still a baby, Megha! (*Papa, with his bloodshot eyes looked at me contemptuously before turning towards Sandy to attack him.*)

Mama: Stop it, Ramesh, we need to control ourselves too. Oh sweetie . . . don't cry Mona, what do you have to say? And who is this man with you?

So 'this man' turned out to be Commissioner Uncle, the host of the party where Mona Aunty had gone. Their family friend. When Dolly called up Mona Aunty, sensing trouble he volunteered to come along too. Then she called up my parents.

Mona Aunty: Sandy, what do you have to say? Do you know it's a crime? I'd warned you to manage your anger but you didn't listen . . . and now . . . this?

Sandy: Sorry, Aunty, sorry, Mama, I don't know what happened . . . tomorrow I will go back to Mumbai; I promise I will never

	touch Megha again . . .
Mona Aunty:	You think we will ever let you come near this girl? And do you really think, you will be let off scot-free?
Commissioner Uncle:	Yes, Sandy, you are spending the night in jail. And if Megha's family file an FIR, it could be much longer.
Sandy:	What? Jail? FIR? Just for this? Mama, don't do this to me, I am sorry guys, I mean it. It won't happen again. (*He started trembling.*)
Commissioner Uncle:	You will be taught a lesson, son, what do you say, Mona?
Mona Aunty:	Of course, take him away, I don't want anything to do with him . . . Megha, did he force himself on you? I mean did he try to . . . touch you inappropriately . . . like kissing or something? You can tell us . . . (*She was perhaps the most embarrassed one in the room.*)
Me:	No, Aunty . . . we were just talking . . . before he beat me. (*I started howling.*)
Mama:	We are taking Megha home . . . Mona, you guys deal with it while I figure out how I should be dealing with this situation myself . . . Mona, I trust you to do the right thing.
Mona Aunty:	Don't worry, Seema, I am really sorry about Sandy, but don't worry, I will make sure he gets grounded for this. Take care .

I thought that was the worst night of my life but I didn't know the nightmare had just started. However, it did mark the end of the Sandy chapter for me. The next morning, I missed the first day of school and my parents didn't go to work either. All we did was watch television over some pizza and Pepsi. We didn't even talk about it as none of us were ready. But in the evening I learnt that Sandy spent the night in the lock-up and was let off after a stern warning. The grown-ups had a meeting and they decided not to file a police complaint as it would get complicated. Sandy left for Mumbai the following week and left a handwritten note for me. Maybe he really wanted to prove his sincerity by actually writing and not texting this . . .

Dearest Megha,

I know that chances are that you will not even read this but I will not be able to go on with my life until I spoke to you about my feelings. Yes, that's what I am...a self-centred jerk who gives a damn about how others felt. All these days, you accepted me with my imperfections, with my complexes and this crazy attitude. I know I don't deserve a girl like you – someone who always listened to me, who tried to make me laugh when things were tough, who even forgave me when I disappeared suddenly and who perhaps will never forgive me for doing what I did over and over again. I will not even ask for it as it doesn't matter. I have fucked up everything Megha – my career, my family and now my relationship with you . . . but all I can do is say sorry. Don't forgive me but believe me that I really, really am sorry. Not only for that night but for all the times that I didn't care about how you felt . . . for never listening to you. Hope one day I will stop being such a wimp. I guess even at twenty-two, I still have a lot of growing up to do . . .

Goodbye Megha, I have lost you but I will always love you . . .

Sandy

Yes, Sandy, now it doesn't matter. Because you have loved only one person. Yourself.

But life goes on and school does too . . . and it was July already

Hopefully and if you have read Tara's book, you already know that we all go to Patriotic Public School which mostly has ex-army officers in its management. The children too are mostly from an army background. Like Tara whose dad, Major Sharma, took voluntary retirement to get into the so-called corporate sector, thinking it would be so much more lucrative. But recently he has quit that too and has started his own academy that trains kids to get through the SSB (a wing of the armed forces that does the testing for potential candidates). Even though we are not really a typical army family, my nana gave up his life fighting for the country and my mother has studied in army schools throughout her life. Dolly perhaps is the only one who is a pure civilian. Honestly, even my own army connections are too remote to count. But there is something about the Indian Army that gives me goose-bumps – especially when I see men in uniform – the way they conduct themselves – it's amazing.

Coming back to my school, the reason I am sent there is partly because it is very supportive of Mama's, sorry, my swimming aspirations. Since I do ground practice (like gym, yoga, jogging – the works) most mornings, they allow me to miss assembly. If the dates of the competitions are clashing with school exams, they let me take the exams as per my convenience. And then it got better. We recently got a new principal – Colonel Shiv Kumar Tripathi – the name itself is so powerful so imagine how the man must be himself. And because he is new, he has brought with himself a lot of fresh ideas that he wants to implement.

Like overall development.

A grossly misused phrase. But here he meant it, as they say, in letter and spirit. So Sir introduced something which the lazy student dreads – he cut off five minutes from each period and created an extra forty-five minutes for physical exercise and called it **compulsory military training**. Yes, you heard it right.

MILITARY ACADEMY CAMP

Be ready to get mentally sharper, physically fitter and more confident then you have ever been!

An opportunity of a lifetime !!

SCHEDULE

PHASE	TIMELINE	Details
ONE: Foundations	August — Sept 45 minutes – school hours	Compulsory participation for all students from class VIII to XI.
TWO: Weekend Batch	October—November 2 hours every Saturday	Best 40 students would be selected
THREE: Winter Camp	4 hours for 10 days during Winter vacations	Best 20 students would be selected
FOUR: Summer Boot Camp	6 hours for 5 weeks during Summer vacations	Top 10 elite cadets will be trained for this gruelling and prestigious course

Under the guidance of qualified coaches, you will be working both as a leader and as a team to gain endurance and self-disciple through safe and tested outdoor activates.

GEAR UP, PARTICIPATE AND SUPPORT THIS EXCITING INITIATIVE !!

Student coordinators for this programme are: Vaibhavi Sharma and Megha Deshpande

This year I had got my promotion – I was now President of the Sports Club and since I was not really a lazy bum (like Tara and Dolly), I was right in the middle of the action! There was a big increase in my duties towards the school government. At another time and in another world, I would have welcomed such a move but this year I was not in the right frame of mind to take up anything extra. **I hated my name on that flyer!** Already my life was loaded with studies, swimming, homework, volunteer work, my parents' divorce, my own breakup. And what were the teachers thinking – didn't they know we had Boards?? That we were in Class X, for God's sake? I hated the responsibilities in the list that was handed over to me by Mrs Chopra, Teacher-in-Charge of the Student Council. So I decided to do something to save myself from the extra load of military training.

Like quitting

Chopra Ma'am:	You can't do that, child, you know it.
Me:	No, Ma'am, I have to. I don't think I can handle so many things and I am afraid I will let everyone down.
Chopra Ma'am:	What is it, Megha? Are you all right? (*She studied the marks on my face, which were almost fresh.*)
Me:	Oh this, I had a bad fall, Ma'am . . . but please let me resign from the post. I am not capable of it anymore.
Chopra Ma'am:	Well . . . let me think about it, child . . . but the new Principal Sir – he likes to get involved in everything – I don't think he will take it well.

Me:	Please do something, Ma'am, you know we have Boards, how is it expected for a student to do that much? Sorry for being rude, but it's a bad idea – this extra period for this so-called military training! Do you know the kind of work that is? Participating in and coordinating this thing?
Chopra Maa'm:	Megha, I did not expect this from you. Making it to the summer camp itself would be an achievement and most appropriate for students seeking a career in the army. Even if you are not, the experience will be an advantage wherever you go. Think ahead. You have a bright future. Don't mess with it. Do you know that next year you are our best bet to be the Head Girl in Class XII?
Me:	Somehow, Ma'am, being the Head Girl does not motivate me that much now . . .
Chopra Ma'am:	I guess your mind is made up. Write a formal resignation and let me get it approved from Principal Sir. Till then you need to do what you need to do.

So the next two weeks were spent doing something that I hated the most – 'Admin' work.

Yes, I was human too. There *was* something I wasn't good at.

Like the prospect of getting involved in any kind of paperwork that called for making lists, compiling data and drafting reports – it used to make me nervous as hell. I was good academically and in sports but that didn't mean I was good at working on these kinds of projects as well. One look at this form and I knew. This new Principal Sir was just bad news and nothing else.

- **Name of the student:**
- **Date of birth:**
- **Class   Sec**
- **Height, weight**
- **Games you participate in school:**
- **No of hours spent on physical activity at home per week:**
- **Favourite sport:**
- **Fitness Level: Very Fit, Moderately fit, Unfit**
- **How much do you know about Military Training?**
- **If recommended, would you be willing to spend Saturdays as well as Winter and Summer vacations in the Military Camp?**
- **Any suggestions**
- **Signature:**

So here I was, the chosen one to make sure that in the next two weeks every student class VIIIth and above fills up the form, then compile the data into this:

- **Class**
- **No of Students**
- **Average height**
- **Average Weight**
- **Average fitness level**

I am not sure how this data would have really helped as there are the overactive nuts like me and then there are kids like Tara who refuse to move a finger, so I am not sure what an 'average' would really imply. But since I did not have a better idea, I had no choice but to do the job. And it happened to be more irritating and time-consuming than any exam for which I had studied. But as Mama said, I couldn't give up without trying; I had no choice here either.

Sometimes I really wonder if it's at all worth it – like following these damn principles about trying, determination, success and failure!

I mean, for example, if I didn't like singing and wasn't even good at it, why should I be pushed to try it and not give up soon enough? Giving up would save so many people from failing at stuff they were not meant for in the first place. But then, what chance does a confused fifteen-year-old Indian student have against the system?

Yes, I was confused and for the first time in my life I had started questioning authority. I didn't like the fact that we had to blindly follow what our elders said. A lot of stuff around me didn't make any sense but I did not have the guts to rebel, rather I did not have the time to even think about it for long. You know, I read somewhere: it is such a great responsibility to really want something. Because the day you know what you really want, you must put in your all to work towards it. It's so much safer not to have passion because then you have nothing really to lose if you fail – because in your heart you know it wasn't meant for you anyway. And it doesn't hurt that much in the end.

Yes, for the first time I didn't know what I wanted. And if I really wanted anything at all. There was a time I enjoyed swimming but I wasn't even sure if I wanted to compete first for the States and then for the Nationals again this year. I was great in studies but clearly it was not my forte – I had absolutely no passion to learn those subjects. It was sheer hard work that got me through. I was brought up to be competitive but now I was losing it all. **I wasn't interested in anything –** swimming, studies, this damn military training, my friends, my parents, my life . . . nothing mattered anymore.

But I carried on . . . rather, Mama made me . . .

Mama: It's a phase, Megha. You will get over it; you know you are a fighter.

Me: Mama, I am doing everything I should be, I am still going to school, studying, tuitions, even birthday parties . . . but it's so damn . . . boring.

Mama: You have your hands full, Megha, how can you be bored?

Me: I am, Mama, and I am kind of sad . . . you know since the Sandy incident, we haven't even discussed it . . . I feel really angry, Mama, I want to kill that guy!

Mama: Oh Megha, channelise this anger, this frustration – use it to your advantage in swimming . . . you know you have to work on your speed . . . and we don't have a lot of time – just three weeks, to be exact. The other day I had a talk with Coach Sir, who –

Me: Stop it, Mama, you won't understand . . . just leave me alone.

Mama: OK, but promise you will be a good girl and never have these negative thoughts in your mind again, promise, my little baby? Or Mama will be really upset.

Me: I promise, Mama. (*Now go to hell.*)

As I said, when you are in Class X, you can't afford to lose focus – in my case, on anything.

Regarding the Military Camp Project, now that my two weeks were over, I handed in the compiled data, along with my resignation. All I knew was that I had had enough of proving myself to the world. I did not want to succeed at the cost of my peace of mind. And I was still having these nervous attacks, which got stronger and more frequent over time. It was such a shitty feeling that I thought taking the extra pressure off myself would solve the problem.

To
The Principal
Patriotic Public School
Sec 25, Gurgaon

Subject: Resignation from School council

Dear Sir,

With due respect, I would like to seek your approval for my resignation from the post of President of Sports club. The reasons are personal and I hope you will absolve me of all duties pertaining to the school council.
Yours sincerely
Megha Deshpande
Class Xth B

Cc: Mrs KK Chopra

There was no point actually . . .

When I got the summons to Principal Sir's office during Biology class, my hands grew ice-cold and my heart started pounding with an overwhelming fear. I couldn't face him. What would I say if he asked me why I resigned? I just couldn't think straight. My head started spinning and I fainted in the classroom. Embarrassing as hell, as while we did have such moments of fainting – especially kids who couldn't tolerate the heat during the long morning assembly in school – for a strong, agile sports captain like me, it was a shame. What my classmates didn't know was that my reasons were different and I had no clue what they were.

So after a trip to the nurse's office, who gave me some glucose, thankfully I was sent home. But I knew I still had to face him the next day and had to have my list of excuses ready. I just prayed that my resignation got accepted without a fuss, because if they called Mama for a meeting, there would be no looking back for me as she would make sure that I didn't quit. She had made my life really difficult. Unfortunately, there was no use talking to her – yes, we could *discuss* it – but we couldn't talk.

But the next day, I did have my talk

Me:	Good morning, Sir, may I come in?
Principal Sir:	Yes, Megha, come in, child. How do you feel now? I heard you collapsed? Was it the heat, or is there anything else?
Me:	Nothing, Sir, I didn't have breakfast, so maybe that's why. I am all right, Sir, thank you.
Principal Sir:	I am glad. Sit down, my child, and tell me everything. Why did you resign? Are you not excited about the programme?
Me:	No, Sir, it's very exciting but I am afraid I am not the right candidate to push the project through. You have seen the data. Most kids don't even want to come on weekends. I am sorry for being so frank, but I am not sure how you will convince them to commit their winter and summer vacations for this training.
Principal Sir:	Interesting . . . Is that all?
Me:	Yes Sir, I just feel that it will not work for our school. (*My cheeks were red-hot and my legs shaking.*)
Principal Sir:	Sit down, Megha . . . If I assure you that this will be a big success, will you promise to be a part of it?
Me:	Sir, do I have a choice? I mean, I really don't think . . . *(I gulped)* I have the State Levels due in about ten days . . .
Principal Sir:	Don't worry, Megha, just concentrate on

your swimming for the time being. As it is, this course starts in August. So you have time to feel prepared. Participate in the Foundations course wholeheartedly – it's during school hours so you have nothing to lose. Give yourself two months and then decide. Do it just because I say so. Don't resign now. I am saying this as I trust you will be fantastic. Come on, soldier – think positive and I will see you in the field. (*He patted my back.*)

Me: Yes Sir, thank you Sir . . .

As I closed the door softly behind myself, I wondered if it is any use to even talk to grown-ups – they haven't learnt to listen at all. So he was another version of Mama! Of course, he too would not understand. That I wasn't interested in his brownie points at all. That I was changing. As my life was changing.

That I was sick of this positive thinking shit!

I had to be; when your parents are getting divorced, only a psycho would think positive! As if the developments in school weren't taxing enough, I had to deal with my parents' relationship, which was going down the drain by the day. While I could distract myself outside with school and sports, at home there was no way I could help being a part of the melodrama.

Mama, who had always maintained dignity, was now having these angry outbursts and had no hang-ups about attacking Papa over 'this extramarital affair with that slut': she abused them with the choicest of Punjabi cuss words while Papa had no choice but to bear it all. After all, he was the guilty party here. She stopped giving a damn if I was around or listening. Slowly this spiritual conduct business stopped working for her anymore and she let go of all inhibitions when it came to fighting with Papa.

Not only that, she tried poisoning my mind too (in Papa's words) but she really didn't have to as I had already started hating Papa. Family counselling, mediation, therapy were all useless now, as they had made up their minds.

According to the law of the land, they had to get separated for at least six months, while the courts would still intervene when it came to parental rights. So in a few weeks from now, Papa was moving out while I would stay with Mama. I soon found out what the big fight was about – neither would let go of their claim over me. And because both wanted me, both could afford me and provide me with equal material comforts as well as a solid, loving environment, it was up to me to decide whom I would like to live with.

But this time too, I really did not have a choice. Seriously, although I was confused as hell. Even though I knew Papa had been very wrong, he still was more caring and less pushy than Mama. He let me breathe.

But it wasn't a good enough reason.

Everything I was, was because of the way Mama had brought me up. Papa didn't do anything – if left to him, I would have been an average, silly teenager having a crush on Justin Bieber, struggling with her Maths homework and freaking out with her equally silly friends.

But here I was – an All Rounder, under extreme pressure, who recently had a breakup with her abusive boyfriend, struggling at everything and dealing with these episodes of nervousness and anxiety.

Yes, I was confused, but I did know that Papa did not deserve me as no matter what, you don't betray anyone's trust – specially of a woman like my mother. I didn't care if she was always on my back, the fact is she really did want me to be the best. And I had to be the best. For her. I could no longer bear to see a strong woman like her breaking down and I knew that her only chance to any happiness in our present situation was my winning the State Levels.

So I geared up.

I had wasted enough time on things that didn't count. Swimming was my life. Or so I desperately wanted to believe. I had to consistently better my endurance, muscle tone, flexibility, breathing rhythm, technique, sprinting, kicks – everything. I started getting up at 5 am for my ground practice, which was two hours in the gym – cardio, weights, yoga – the works, followed by school and then another three hours in the pool in the evening. Yes, you heard right. Kids who are serious about swimming do at least that much. Some even more. On weekends and during holidays it could be as much as six to eight hours of practice. Kids who are serious. Like me. At least for now.

And before I knew it the School Games State Level Swimming Championship had arrived.

'I am the fastest animal in the water. I have the strongest legs possible. I love swimming and I love winning the most.' I brainwashed my mind into repeating and believing these affirmations as I visualised myself in the pool. With my eyes closed I saw myself in my costume and heard the crowd roaring.

I perform the pre-race routine and get on with it – I go faster and faster and hit the wall within my goal time. Yes, I did it – I am strong and no one can touch me. And then he comes and mocks me to my face. Sandy slaps me – in front of everyone – and I don't do anything about it.

Oh God, it's not working today . . . I quickly opened my eyes and ended my meditation abruptly.

'Megha, come on, hurry up. We need to move now.' I heard Mama call for me.

'Please, God, let me do it this time. It's really important that I win. I promise you I will never take swimming for granted and will practise even more but please don't betray me. I am counting on you.' I prayed continuously during my drive to the club. There was an eerie silence in the car and I hoped Mama would not start again about having a *killer attitude* – her favourite phrase these days.

Anyway, we reached our destination where Coach Sir was waiting for us. Very impressive, I thought to myself as my eyes roved over this new facility. They recently had got a new fast pool constructed – a nine-foot consistent depth and spinning lane dividers. I could also see my competition. Perfect bodies, perfect shoulders and perfect expressions on their faces. They were here to win as well in this eight-lane, 50-metre perfect pool.

'Don't get intimidated, Megha, you know you have the potential to beat them all,' Mama whispered in my ears.

'Yes, I do. Now is not the time to get nervous.'- I commanded my body and thankfully it did not let me down.

Somehow my mind and my body aligned to do it for me. And I took the plunge.

I stopped thinking of Mama and anyone else. When the whistle blew — I just flew. For the first time I did not distract myself with another girl who was pulling fast. I was in a trance, and that moment I realised that I truly did love swimming.One stroke at a time. Megha — it's no big deal. I stayed calm, positive, in my own lane, focused, and trusted my training and my body that it would make it happen. But most of all I had fun.

And guess what – I won!

Under those circumstances, I did my best and mama agreed with me too. I was extremely proud of myself and happier than I had ever been.

And Mama-Papa too started looking closer. That night I caught them cozying up on the sofa and watching that classic *DDLJ*. Maybe the romance of Shahrukh Khan and Kajol would bring them together again, just the way they were in college, bunking classes to watch this blockbuster – first day first show. But then I thought of their comeback *Dilwaale* and sighed . . . some things are not really meant to be, specially when I saw Mama looking bored at the train scene which she had patiently endured probably twenty times before. Yes, my parents had moved on, so this nostalgia or even a State Level Championship could not fix things for them. Or me.

Invariably, when the excitement died down over the next few days, I started having a nagging feeling- is it that I just got lucky? Because God listened to me when I prayed so hard? I didn't even practice that much during summer vacations and had lost my will. So what happened?

Did I really deserve to win? What was happening to me? Why these doubts?

Win or lose, life goes on . . . since it was August already and there was no way of escaping the compulsory Foundations Military Training course that each one had to participate in – thin or fat, tall or short, active or lethargic!

In my school, most kids, except the few of us who were pushed into sports by overzealous parents – were big slobs, it didn't matter if they were thin, tall, short or whatever. Most of them hardly played any sport and always had their noses dug deep in their text books.

Obviously the first day was nothing but a big flop.

Because we were asked to do what we had never done before and that was:

Self-introspection!

'Good afternoon, cadets ! My name is Major Rajput and on behalf of the Camp Selection Board, I welcome you to the Foundations batch of the Military Training. Today, you will have it easy. So no running or obstacles or physical tasks – all you have to do is write. So students, start writing and don't stop till you hear the whistle – write **about yourself,** your ambitions, your likes, dislikes, achievements, failures – everything. There is no prize for creativity or perfect grammar so just be honest. But there is only one rule be yourself. You have half an hour and your time starts now.'

Writing was no big deal but being ourselves? Was he serious?

As I stared at the blank page with my pen dangling from my fingers, I had no idea where to start. I mean, there was so much going on in my life that these thirty minutes were not enough; but then I didn't have to write everything. *Just keep it school-type – don't go deep –* I said to myself as I started scrawling.

I had barely finished when the whistle blew and we knew it was over. As I looked around, I was amazed that some of the kids were actually revising their write-ups. Come on, guys, this is not an exam, I thought to myself, fingers crossed.

'Thank you, students. Now take your paper home and read it when you have ten minutes at home. Oh yes, I promised Principal Sir that you would not get any homework – so do it in the toilet so your parents don't complain. Just read what you have written and ask yourself: "Was I really honest?" That's all for the day.'

'Sir, sir, will we get another topic tomorrow? Can we prepare something?' A hand went up – Kawish Chaddha, my classmate, trying to impress our new coach with his ever-smiling face and boundless enthusiasm. But he forgot, this was an ex-army officer and not some usual teacher who loves getting his butt licked by swotters like him.

'Please leave it to me, son,' was all Sir said as he concluded the class.

Back home

As I sat reading my paper, I realised that the facts were right but it did not sound like me for real. I had a gut feeling about what was going to happen tomorrow. We would be asked again to do the same thing all over again. And this time I'd better go prepared. I had to sound truthful but at the same time, this was my one chance to lead this course. I liked the fact that I was still motivated, and got down to serious work and wrote a nice little inspirational-type essay on 'myself'.

Did I once say that this course wasn't for me?

Tonight was also the first night my papa wasn't going to be home and this time it wasn't a seminar or an official trip. He was moving out of the house for a few months – a legal separation during which my parents still had a chance to reconcile, as it's not like in the movies – divorce is a long battle and even if it is mutual, can get complicated if there is an extramarital affair or a child involved.

By now I knew reconciliation was impossible.

I went to Papa's room while he was packing his stuff. I needed to talk to him so badly but the problem was – we were not used to it.

Me: Papa, so you are moving out, right? You won't be coming back, I guess?

Papa: Hey, Megha, don't feel sad, baby, we will always be together. You can always come and meet me. I am just leaving this house, not your life.

Me: Papa, we used to be so happy . . . what happened, did I do something? Don't leave, Mama loves you . . . I – you know I love you too . . .

Papa: Don't worry, champ, everything will be alright. Tell me, how was school? How is swimming?

And he packed up his stuff and left. Just like that. Without looking twice at Mama, who was sitting in the drawing room, staring at the TV with moist eyes. I went to her and hugged her. There was nothing to say. As I said, this family was not used to talking about anything except school and swimming. So we both cried. Because we couldn't help noticing that he seemed almost relieved on his way out.

Next day at school

During Interval, as I sat down with Tara I felt an extreme pang of jealousy for this loser. She didn't do so badly in Class IX, was now working on her book and getting popular in school. Worst of all, she got appointed President of the Literary Club. No, the worst was that her parents were still together. OK, she was still fat and all, but she always seemed so damn happy. As I looked at other groups of girls around, chirping about boys and movies, I felt my heart pounding again. I had an intense feeling of hatred for the world. Doomsday struck and I actually started trembling. Tara looked at me helplessly before I fell down to the ground.

As I opened my eyes in the nurse's office, I saw Tara sitting next to me on the bed, rubbing my hands.

Tara: Megha, don't worry, yaar, your mom is coming.
               Go home and rest, yaar.

Megha: Tara, you don't know what is happening in my
               life. It's over.

Tara: Oh God, Megha, what are you saying, yaar, what
               happened?

Megha: Remember I told you that my parents could be
               getting a divorce? It's becoming a reality. Papa
               left the house last night. They are separated
               now. And in a few months a divorce will follow.
               I hate them, Tara, I hate my parents. How could
               they do this to me?

And finally I talked. I told her everything. About my father's girlfriend and the story behind my own breakup with Sandy. About my studies and my swimming and my duties in the School Council that I could no longer cope with. About my life, which was nothing but a disaster. I cried and cried and Tara did the best thing possible.

She listened.

Yes, this loser whom I had grown jealous of – this immature kiddo who happened to be fortunate enough to be getting those prizes in school – this happy-go-lucky friend of mine – she did the best thing possible by not opening her mouth. She had no advice to give, no motivational speech about staying positive. I realised that she really was my best friend. Hopefully I also understood what true friendship meant. Which was just being there.

I called up Mama from the reception and asked her not to come. That I hadn't had lunch and hence the fainting. I was feeling much better and could not go home as I had something really important to take care of in school.

Like the second day of the Foundations course.

It wasn't just me who felt like this, it seemed everyone here was discussing the same thing. All of us had prepared a better-written and more honest-sounding write up. We were all taken by surprise as Sir had something else in mind:

'Students, today again is your lucky day. No physical tasks. I am going to show some words on the screen and you have to write the **first random thought** that comes in your mind. There is no right or wrong answer and no points for the best-written thoughts. Again, it is NOT a test of your proficiency in the English language. That's what you have to practise every day – being honest to yourself,' announced Sir.

Oh God, I wasn't ready for this! But a man's gotta do what a man's gotta do! And as it is, they were not going to read the shit so I could actually be myself!

Word Association Test (WAT)

Love: *Can only happen in movies*

Friend: *Tara and…Dolly*

Life: *Life stinks*

Sky: *Want to fly in the sky*

Water: *I love swimming*

Mother:…………………………

Pen: *How do I write faster?*

God: *I need help*

Dark: *We should not be afraid of dark*

Anger: *Sandy, I haven't forgotten.*

And guess what? This time they did the unthinkable!

We were asked to deposit our papers with Sir. Oh God, I am finished. I am sure my score would be the lowest, I thought, trembling all over again.

The next half hour was spent in discussing the answers; thankfully no names were taken and thankfully there wasn't enough time to discuss all the papers so I got spared here.

The word-association tests were meant to test our basic perception and could give a picture of our psychology. Though the fundamentals cannot be changed, no matter how many lectures you go through, we were taught that we could train our mind to be reasonable and positive. We were told that over the next few months and especially for the students at higher levels going into the weekend and vacation camps, there would be a noticeable shift in the attitudes and frame of mind.

I had started enjoying it as it was so damn different from the usual sin, cos, tan phooey!

Surprisingly, there was an air of excitement in the school. All we could discuss was these last 45 minutes that gave us the freedom to be ourselves and yet strive to be the best we could be. The psychology tests were just the beginning. We worked on teambuilding exercises, leadership skills and some serious coordination. A lot of challenging physical stuff too. We had a whole list of tasks ahead and it was getting really interesting.

Such as situation reaction tests, group discussions, military planning exercises, individual tasks, group obstacles, story writing. Yes – we were shown pictures about which we had to write **short stories** of about 70-100 words. We were also asked to avoid too many 'I's, or use quotations, refer to celebrities or be too self-righteous or preachy when writing. And though the instructors claimed that they were not judgmental, I knew I was in trouble when Mama got called in by Principal Sir.

I am not sure what they talked about but Mama told me he discussed this story:

Thematic Apperception test (TAT)

Radha, a fifteen year old girl is really sad as her father has died. She misses him a lot and keeps looking out of the window, thinking that he will come back. She is not able to share her grief with her mother who is also going through this terrible loss. Radha knows that she has to be brave and support her mother but also worries that if her mother died, she would be left alone in this world. But one day she wakes up in the morning to sounds of laughter coming from the kitchen. She is shocked to see that her mother and father are baking a cake for her birthday. So it was a nightmare. Her father had not died and everything was fine. Radha thanks God and hugs her parents and they all live happily ever after.

I knew it wasn't a good performance but it was a nice little story of a girl with the most common textbook name and a happy ending too. So what was the fuss about?

Apparently, Principal Sir felt that I had to see the school counsellor and discuss my issues. So, one more item in my 'to-do' list. But my mama was on my side and told him that her daughter was a fighter and she knew how to take care of her. For once I agreed with her as I was in no mood to discuss these home truths with a school staff member. Also this military training was helping me take my mind off my troubles. Or so I thought.

Over the next two months I got busy as a beaver – whatever it meant!

Which meant waking up at 5 am for gym, then school, then one to two hours of tuitions and then two hours of swimming practice. I would be back home by 8 pm, have my dinner and collapse in my bed around eleven after finishing off my homework. On weekends it would be more tuitions before six to eight hours in the pool. It was the year of the Boards, and the Nationals too were round the corner, and I could not afford to take a minute's rest. This was my one big opportunity. I wasn't going to let it go. No matter what.

It was the end of September and the Foundations course had come to an end. I am sure all of us had become stronger, fitter, more disciplined with a lot more integrity and character than before. OK, I might be stretching it too far, but we did feel that something had changed within us and I couldn't point out exactly what. Maybe it was just that we were on our way to becoming better people.

I was even more excited as they recommended just a handful of us for the weekend camp. The shocking part was that of all people Tara made it to the list too!

Principal Sir was right: not only were the students excited about it, the parents loved the programme too. The tables had turned.

His initiative was a huge success.

Almost everyone wanted to go to the next level. Almost. But not me.

Despite being recommended. Actually, my mama wouldn't let me.

Mama:	Don't even think about it, Megha
Me:	But why, Mama, I love it, and it's really going to help – imagine if I went all the way to the Final Boot Camp! Everyone wants to go there, Mama, but not all can.
Mama:	Everyone else is not aiming for the Nationals. And everyone is not a topper as well. I don't see the necessity, Megha, especially if you have to dedicate two hours every Saturday. You know you don't have the time.
Me:	I have, Mama; we could cancel the Maths tutorials. I don't need them, anyway.
Mama:	Oh yes, you do. I am not going to let you compromise on your studies. You know your academics score is as important as your swimming. Actually, more. And this new hobby of yours – this military training and all – there is no place for it in your life. I didn't say anything first as it was during school hours but I am not going to sacrifice academics over a fad.

Me: But Mama, I love it, isn't that a reason
                        enough? Even Tara is going.

Mama: No more discussions, Megha. One day
                        you will thank me for this.

I cursed her in my mind and knew it was no use arguing with
her. All I could do was cry. But there wasn't even time for
that. Principal Sir tried fighting my case with Mama but she
wouldn't budge. Actually I heard they had a big argument when
she accused him of diverting students' minds in these useless
activities. I felt really let down as I thought a martyr's daughter
would understand. But as usual, she didn't.

Now I was really, really angry.

But I carried on like a robot. The one thing I had started feeling
passionate about – she took it away from me. If only Papa was
around, he would have stood by me. But that would have been
useless too, as no one, no one, can change Mama's mind.

Not even her mother.

I guess it is time to tell you some more about my grandma,
whom I was missing like crazy. She lives in Ambala in her big
colonial bungalow, with her four dogs, three cats, her driver and
a maid who has been around since . . . probably before I was
born. Nani used to be really involved with the cause of finding
a better future for disabled children but since her heart attack
five years back, she is taking it easy – which is a couple of hours
of yoga and meditation in the mornings, free cooking classes to
the ladies in the neighbourhood in the afternoons and *satsangs*
in the evenings. Not to forget the old age home she visits
regularly – as if she is all that young herself! I guess for seventy-
plus it's a lot that she is doing but Mama says she is wasting her
life as with her kind of capabilities she could have been running
a successful business in the education sector. Well, what should

I say – we all are like this only. High-strung, high-potential, high-achievers – forever on the move but never satisfied.

Mama told me that she had been asking her to come and live with us, which she politely declined every time – she couldn't trust her dogs and cats to her so-called worthless servants. I guessed she was being way too selfish as now we really did need her, with the divorce and all.

Anyway, one thing was leading to another and I was caught up in my usual problem – which was becoming more real and bigger than before.

Like Panic Attacks. Yes I said it. And so did the doctor.

It happened in school during a surprise Maths test. Suddenly I realised that I wasn't able to solve this problem.

I struggled with the damn thing for what seemed like ages and before I knew it the bell rang and we had to hand over our papers. What was even more sickening was that I could not complete the exam because of that one whopper!

It was probably the most embarrassing moment of my life when I fell down on the floor and started howling uncontrollably, clutching my answer sheets tightly against my chest: 'Let me do this question, I know I can do it, give me ten minutes . . . no, five. Please, Ma'am,' I pleaded in front of my shocked teacher and classmates, who couldn't believe this was a real situation.

Getting something like this to handle was extremely rare for our school counsellor so Mama was called, who had to accept how serious it had all become.

Yes, I was a psychic case.

'Well, from what I see, it seems that Megha has been having panic attacks, and if left untreated, it could lead to a case of full-blown panic disorder. I would suggest you schedule some therapy sessions and once I understand the case better, I could decide what medication she should be put on, if any,' explained Dr Devi to my mother. Dr Devi was a sought-after child psychologist in her sixties or something, recommended by my school counsellor.

'Oh no, no, no, Doctor, Megha is a strong girl; you know children throw tantrums for attention. Probably it's my divorce that's stressing her out. But anyway, thanks for your time, let me think about it,' Mama said curtly and rose from her chair, ready to leave, pulling me along.

Back in the car . . .

Mama: That old witch, what does she know about my daughter. I don't trust these doctors – all they want is your money.

Me: What if she is right, Mama, maybe I am getting a panic disorder.

Mama: I won't let you, Megha, I will seek a second opinion before deciding the course of action, don't worry child. Just concentrate on the Nationals. Once that is over – no more swimming till the Boards. Except for recreation, so that you don't lose your form. But I promise – no more competitions. You can take it easy then, but for now don't think about anything else, and don't panic, OK? I am with you.

As usual that was the end of the discussion.

Of course, therapy could wait as all I had was one month till the School Games Championship and I seriously didn't want to waste it on bullshitting with a shrink. Especially when Mama told me that she spoke to a friend of hers who was a practising psychiatrist in USA. It seems they decided over a Skype call that Dr Devi was a big crook and there was no urgency to get into anything for now. How very convenient. For Mama and me.

And because I was a bit too overconfident, I did a really stupid thing – I went on Google.

So for the next week or so, whatever free time I had, I was researching panic attacks. I read, I read and I read – everything from signs to causes to medications to some extra links on conditions ranging from depression to anxiety to bipolar disorder to insomnia to insanity to every damn mental disease in this world. And guess what – I started believing that I WAS going mad! I saw my symptoms everywhere – there was no hiding now – I was on my way to being crazy for life!

Oh God, I did need help.

I was living in intense fear. For the first time ever, I started having these terrible dreams and hardly slept. I could not concentrate on my studies, either. I was even zoning out in class, especially if it was Trigonometry. My friends were busy with their own stuff. Tara's manuscript was in full swing and Dolly . . . well, even though she had stood up for me that night, things had changed between us over the days. Maybe she didn't feel right siding with me instead of her brother. Or perhaps Mona Aunty had told her to keep her distance from me. Meanwhile my own Mama got even more charged up about her career since Papa moved out. But as I said, we just didn't have the time. So help came from nowhere. I didn't ask for it, either.

Basically, I was living my worst nightmare!!

The only thing that kept me going was the Nationals, due in November. They were going to be held in Kolkata. I had to divert my mind and stop thinking about my psychic issues. Oh God, let me win this time and then I will take care of the rest of my life.

But before I continue:

Guys, don't diagnose yourselves, especially with any kind of mental condition – you are not a doctor, even if you want to be one eventually! The more things you read about on the Internet, the more you will feel certain you have something. Don't get me wrong – Google is an amazing, most wonderful tool to get our answers but sometimes we don't have the right questions. If you still feel kind of weird – talk to your parents and seek medical advice immediately. But stay out of it yourselves. Trust me.

Anyway, this roller coaster wasn't going to stop anytime soon – now that it was November.

Why the hell did I read up so much stuff about mental toughness, I thought to myself while packing my bag. I was desperately looking forward to this trip – anything to break the dreary monotony that home and school had become, even if it happened to be a swimming competition.

But it wasn't some ordinary competition: it was THE NATIONALS! A shot at international events, a shot at making Mama proud, a shot at my own happiness. But the fact was that so much useless research on Google had led me to doubt my own mental toughness and it was making me panic – a feeling that I was trying hard to suppress. I had no idea when the lid would blow off again; I just prayed that it doesn't happen in Kolkata.

The Big Day – finally!

'You can do it, Megha – remember the States – you are the fastest fish in the water – no one can beat you . . . except . . . that *son of a bitch* Sandy . . . Oh forget it, let's do it again. You know you are tough, physically and mentally . . . do it – just like last time – one stroke at a time,' I thought to myself as I tried to shut down the voices inside me and diverted my mind to the autos, hand-pulled rickshaws, taxis and slow-moving trams on the crowded roads of this city. In normal circumstances, I would be clicking pictures all along my way to the stadium but today, I didn't bother. All that could wait.

First I need to win this damn race, I reminded myself. *Try to* **enjoy yourself in water**, I instructed my mind . . . and thought of the times when swimming used to be fun . . .

'Ladies and gentlemen, welcome to the 61st National School Games Under-17 Girls' 50-Metre Freestyle. The race is going to begin any minute and the girls are champions from their own states – all record holders and recipients of various prestigious awards. But this is the Nationals and anything could happen. It is a race of nerves, more than anything. Now you see the girls taking their stance and eyeing the pool. Just a few seconds and all will be over. One-two-three-GO and what a sight – there is no difference in the speed – seems so well coordinated as if rehearsed, but Megha has raced past them . . . Somehow she can't keep up – look – Sana has caught up and so have Manjeet and Sreelatha – it could be anyone's race now – the four of them neck and neck . . . who will be the best among equals? . . . Yesss! Sana from UP hits it. Then Sreelatha from Andhra and Manjeet from Punjab! We have our winners. What a beauty – a fight to the finish!'

Too dazed to understand the reality for the moment, I felt hot tears streaming down my cheeks. I pulled myself from the pool but the world spun around me. My mouth went dry, face felt flushed and this body was on fire as I tried to make sense of my pounding heart. Before I could ask for help, my so-called strong legs gave way and I fell down unconscious – into the pool, where I had come from. Oh Mama, sorry, I failed.

I woke up in the hospital. Now it was becoming a habit!

'So what is it – dehydration?' Mama asked the doctor attending to me.

'You tell me, Mrs Deshpande. Is this the first time?'

'Well, not really . . . maybe a couple of times before in school ...' Mama replied, avoiding the doctor's eyes.

'If it has happened before, then you know what it is – panic attacks. I cannot fully diagnose it just now but you might want to show her to a psychiatrist when you are back in Gurgaon ...' the doctor replied, as if it wasn't a big deal, and walked off.

'Mama, I am sorry, I couldn't control myself . . . I lost, Mama, I lost the Nationals! I let you down . . . I hate myself for this! How could I let it happen?' I cried helplessly.

'Don't worry, Megha, it's over now . . . stop brooding about it and get over it,' Mama, said without a hint of emotion in her voice.

Back to Gurgaon.

Now that my dream was over, I had mixed feelings about it – there was an uncanny relief, which made me feel really amused about the whole situation. And bizarre moments when I felt almost happy that I lost. While at other times, I wouldn't be able to sleep all night, thinking about my humiliating defeat. My timings were always better then all the girls in the competition, so how could I not even manage a bronze? I had no injuries, had been practising with utmost dedication, was in great form, especially after the States . . . then why? I bought some self-help books and indulged myself in those words of wisdom – that shouted at me to stop worrying and start living, talked about the secrets of leading a happy, productive, successful life, and about the power of positive thinking and, of course, about the cheese that got moved! But I still had no idea why I lost, but then . . . I remembered Mama had asked me to stop brooding about it, so . . .

To hell with that stupid competition – or so I thought . . .

'You know, Megha, I didn't want to make you feel sad about it, so I stopped myself from commenting but you know, you haven't really done a good job . . . I mean, I wouldn't have felt so bad if you had tried but you gave up even before the race started . . . and you let them swim past you so easily – why? Where is my fighter? The one who never lost a race before? And then you collapsed right after the event! You are a sportsperson, Megha, you can't do *that*. Do you remember the famous lines – it's not the dog in the fight that matters but the fight in the dog?

'You know there are kids in your school who look up to you . . . and your younger cousins – you have a responsibility towards them . . . Now I have to be blunt – you *have* disappointed me. You were bloody slow out there, if the three winners had beaten you with their own timings it would have been still OK, but kid, where was your speed? I wish I could say that it was just a race but let me clarify, those were the Nationals, do you even know what you have done?'

As Mama vented her frustrations I wondered if she had called me a bitch or a dog or whatever. I looked unbelievingly at her before realising that perhaps I had got what I really deserved! How can it be expected for this bloody slow girl to win such a big event? I was nothing but a loser. I had fallen in my duty as a daughter to this wonderful, great woman 😵 whose one chance of any happiness was my gold medal and I blew it. Big time!

To make matters worse, my parents got legally divorced. Once and for all.

Today was the last hearing of my parents' case in the court and as expected, the judge coolly granted them the privilege to keep out of each other's way. Mama got appointed as my primary caretaker. Papa got weekly visiting rights. No accusations. No fuss. No drama. A piece of paper releasing them of the vows they took on their wedding. To love and to cherish. In sickness and in health. Till death do us part. Sorry, I got mixed up with the English way. In our community usually the onlookers are either drunk or caught up in the 'shoe-hiding game' during these ceremonies so these vows are neither understood nor taken seriously by the already anxious couples, who want to get over with the rituals as early as possible. Yes, I am sounding too 'off-track' but I had no idea what was I supposed to feel. And it's not important, anyway.

All I knew was that this strong woman that I had as a mother wasn't going to be of any help to me whatsoever. She carried on with life as if nothing happened. She had meetings to attend, a growing team to manage and was vying for an international assignment in the emerging markets of the Middle East.

That's the way we dealt with it . . .

Over a Chicken Margarita at Pizza Hut with the news that we could be moving to Dubai in a few months. To begin a new life. New school. New friends. If only I could get excited about it. Clearly I wasn't. I didn't want any more changes in my life and I was courageous enough to tell my mom that running away would not solve our problems for us. As usual — she didn't listen.

Meanwhile for me – it was the usual life . . .

Because I could no longer think clearly, I decided to go with the flow. As I said, I was slowly becoming indifferent to everything around me. I did what an ideal Indian student is supposed to – attend school and tuitions daily. I also did what an ideal swimmer is supposed to do – practise in the pool daily. And I did what an ideal daughter is supposed to do – never ask questions. Perhaps I already had the answers – that this is life and it is supposed to suck.

I missed my younger days with Tara and Dolly. But that was before I discovered swimming and Mama discovered that I had it in me. If only I was an average girl without any special gifts or talents – life would have so much easier. But then even as I was becoming indifferent, a part of me had got used to living like this. At least it was familiar territory. So what if it was damn lonely here?

I remember when I used to crib about not having enough, my mom used to show me pictures of malnourished kids starving in extreme poverty. Somehow it never did make me feel better or grateful about my own life. Obviously even now, it wasn't working for me so I gave up trying.

I know I am rambling but the point of it all was that I was very sad through it all. But I did not realise that it was becoming a real situation because I was too busy with stuff that really mattered.

Such as winter vacations, then Pre-Boards, Farewell Night and God help us all – Boards.

Usually winter was my favourite time as we always spent New Year's Eve at an exotic location outside the country. I still remember the fun we had on our trip to a small tropical island called Bora Bora (!) – with its dormant volcanoes, luxurious resorts and sunny skies, this was paradise on earth. And nothing could have spoiled it for us except that Mama and Papa again had a fight. About nothing in particular, except that Papa refused to try adventure sports and Mama made a big fuss about it, calling him a sissy. And I couldn't do anything but watch and pray that we would get on to the next activity before they both decided to sulk and call everything off.

Well, that was last year and despite these little fights here and there, we were together and happy. But now that Papa wasn't on the scene anymore, I wondered what Mama was planning.

But now guess which place it was going to be?

Ambala!

Me: Oh no, Mama, I don't want to go there!

Mama: How can you been so selfish? Nani has been calling us for a long time, it's just five hours' drive on the road and I haven't seen my mother for so many months!

Me: Is it my fault, Mama? Why can't she come here or why don't you visit her on a weekend? Why are you spoiling my winter vacations?

Mama: Oh no, you guys used to be so close, Megha, don't lose it. She is getting older; God knows how much time she has. And I don't have to give you explanations. You are going to Ambala and that's the end of it.

Me: What do you mean? You are coming, right?

Mama: Yes, almost . . . but I have a seminar to attend around the same time. Don't worry, I'll drop you there and then come over for a day or two to pick you up.

Me: I have nothing to do there except *samosas* and *kulfi*! And I hate her dogs, too!

Mama: Learn to cooperate, Megha, and no more arguments.

Obviously, I didn't have a choice. Actually I had been wanting to visit Nani for quite some time, I mean I would have insisted during the summer vacations if Sandy had not happened. But now I was not only single but friendless. I don't know how it happened. Or maybe I do. Now that Tara's book was getting published, she was getting more popular by the day and making new friends. Yes, this wacko did not need me anymore. The signs were there. Especially when it took her a day or two to reply to my WhatsApp messages. Even in school, we weren't meeting a lot as we were in different sections this year. Even though we were still officially 'best friends', it seemed to be the beginning of the end between us. No real reason – except that times change and people simply grow out of each other.

Imagine – an all-rounder, super-achiever, good-looking girl –

having no family and no friends!

Except an old Nani who had a better social life than me! Yeah, she had her hands full with yoga, meditation, cooking classes and lots of visitors from the neighbourhood who came for advice on crazy stuff like *saas-bahu* squabbles, making pickles and organising *mundans*.

My trip to Nani's house too was going to be a learning experience for me but not this one.

This trip was super boring! I am not supposed to be writing the irrelevant stuff in the book so all I will say is that those seven days were the most uneventful moments of my life.

I did nothing except watch TV and gorge on the world-famous Ambala *chaat papdi* on New Year's Eve.

And two, I learnt that my mama was a big liar.

Yes, you heard right. When I confronted Nani about never making an attempt to give us support during the divorce, she told me that it was Mama who stopped her from visiting us. Mama felt that she was capable of handling everything herself and did not want to depend on anyone to fix her life.

Unbelievable! Are these adults for real?

Well, more on this later as I got busy again. Schools reopened and the Pre-Boards were round the corner. Though they were not the real deal, I had to brush up my act. Over the last few weeks, I had started losing my place in the class. Two times in a row, I didn't even make it to the first three positions. Worst of all, Tara was getting better by the day. For the first time in her life, she scored an average of 90 in the unit tests! I wondered if things could get any worse.

But they did.

I don't know exactly what happened but I wasn't able to concentrate anymore. Maybe I thought that the results didn't count but I just wasn't able to work hard. Yeah, if a Class-X student is not able to work hard – that's a disaster waiting to happen.

In short I didn't do well in the Pre-Boards.

In fact, for my standards, it was the worst performance till date. So with a 76 per cent score on my report card, I joined the ranks of *'have potential to do better'* of my class – the likes of Dolly who are absent half the time and can't tell the difference between blue and green! On the other hand, Tara rose in her ranking and got branded as a *'high achiever'*! Good for her as I had stopped caring a long time back. I guess the miserable Pre-Boards result failed to give me a wakeup call! I still had a long time to prepare for the Boards. Or maybe it felt good to be in denial.

So what if Mama had been disappointed again; I didn't care about her feelings either. She got called in for a meeting with the Principal and the class teacher to analyse what was happening to an 'intelligent student' like me. It seems they attributed my Pre-Boards results to my loss at the Nationals and the divorce too (!). Finally, the grown-ups concluded that all Megha needed was some more motivation to do better.

Meanwhile, I still had to attend counselling in school as I got a couple of fainting spells again. Mama had started to look worried but so far did not consider therapy. It could wait. Plus, she tried fixing the problem with vitamin supplements and some more protein in my diet. She also became a bit too overbearing as many a time, I caught her checking out my cupboards and going through my Instagram and Snapchat for some clues. What can you find, Mama? I don't smoke and neither do I have a boyfriend, for heaven's sake! Actually mine is the dullest life possible on this planet!

Claustrophobic as hell by constantly being under the scanner, I diverted my mind with the Farewell Night. After all, I was still a winner and a top contender for the Ms All Rounder! Hey there, losers of Class X – you can't touch me here, as title belongs to me!

Now we had to gear up for the Farewell!

Unlike last year, the Farewell Night was a month before the exams and trust me, this was a very wise decision. Last year, the school tried experimenting and scheduled these events after the exams and had to face flak from angry parents who blamed the administration for the school's debacle in the Boards – yeah, because not even one student could go beyond 95 per cent while the competing school had ten students scoring more and one nerd actually making it to a perfect score! With these kinds of statistics, the school had to play very safe but I really wondered if this year things would be better. With this military training and all initiated by our new Principal, who anyway wasn't very academically inclined **– God help us!**

PATRIOTIC PUBLIC SCHOOL

FAREWELL TO CLASS X

Students of Class X are invited to the party of the year!
The Farewell Night!

Have fun while aiming for exciting titles like:

- Miss and Master class X
- Miss and Master All Rounders
- Miss and Master "Most Likely to succeed"

Please prepare a short introduction about yourself

Dress code:
Smart and decent formals
Date:
25th February,
7 pm onwards in the Auditorium

Anyway, this year the Farewell wasn't going to be an extravagant affair, the credit for which again goes to Principal Sir. So no more cat walks, cultural items or couples' dances. Even if it was going to be as simple as it gets, I was actually looking forward to this night as it was time to claim what was rightfully mine – the **All-Rounder title**. But as things were kind of sour between Dolly and me, I thought this year we would not be getting Mona Aunty's help in getting dressed up. Last year Aunty, a fashion expert, had made sure we looked like beauty queens and all of us had won our own prizes.

But now, we had no professional help at all! My mom has a personality and all – but she is not the saree and makeup sort and as for Tara's mom – I don't want to be rude but she is kind of quirky – you know – wears these short kurtas over Patiala salwars and freakish metallic jewellery! Basically it meant both Tara and I were on our own.

Thank God Tara WhatsApped me to discuss the event otherwise I had practically zero excitement in my life. But I was surely in for a surprise. Tara told me that **Mona Aunty had offered help to the three of us.** The best thing was that we would be getting ready in Tara's house instead of Dolly's as . . . well . . . I don't have to explain again, do I? Pay attention, guys!

Without getting into the details of lipsticks, mascara, hair and accessories . . .

...this is how we looked like on the big night:

(*As they say – **no matter how you feel – get up, dress up, show up and never give up!**)*

School Auditorium same evening:

Since it was truly a simple affair – we got it over with before we even knew it (at least I did). All we had to do was go up on stage one by one and introduce ourselves. For the first time in my life, I was not prepared at all and for the first time a stupid self-introduction took me by surprise, especially when I realised that almost all girls from my class were well-rehearsed, but not me. Can you believe it, both Tara and Dolly had an idea that this was going to happen while I had completely missed it by not paying attention to the Farewell flyer?

Dolly: Hello, friends, someone once said that people will stare, so make it worth their while. And I believe that someone. So here I am – your own Dolly, from X B. Gorgeous is my middle name and I am proud to be a student of this reputed school and a citizen of this great country. All for women empowerment and global peace, I hope you will support me as your Ms Class X!

Tara: My name is Tara and well . . . . I hate public speaking but I have to do this. I believe that beauty is not about having a pretty face – it is what is inside you. So don't wait to get loved by others – start by accepting yourself a little more. An endearing smile is cuter than a red pout. So friends, remember – happy girls are the most beautiful.

To hell with this rhetoric about the meaning of beauty and global peace. When my turn came, I took the easy way out. I collapsed!

After a while I found myself yet again in the nurse's office.

Mama, Tara, Dolly were all around me. I learnt that I panicked on the stage before even opening my mouth. How embarrassing! They told me that after getting me here, they carried on with the function as if nothing happened. I guess these episodes of fainting had become a bit too regular to warrant any special attention.

But guess what they did to me?

They gave the title of Ms All Rounder to Tara!

Tara! How could you? You betrayed me – my so-called best friend – you joined the grown-ups and plotted against me? You think you deserve to win, you fat slob?

I screamed inside while congratulating this frenemy of mine, avoiding my Mama's piercing eyes. I had lost once again. Even Dolly had done it by winning the Ms Class X title but that was OK. It wasn't mine, anyway . . .

I had nothing more to feel except that my life was over.

Hey Megha, u there ?

Well, hello?

?

Hey M, r u not gonna talk to me yaar?

What is my fault?

Can I come over, let's talk.. 

Hi Tara, sorry was in the bathroom, kind of busy

I will c u in the school tomorrow, ok?

What?? It's Saturday

What's wrong with u yaar? 

As I rested my head on the pillow, I stared blankly at the screen of my cell phone . . . but tonight, I wasn't just going to go on some random sites. I had something more important to think about.

Such as dying.

Google

10 ways to d	
10 ways to die	
10 ways to die in the west	
10 ways to deal with stress	

As I read about dying of carbon monoxide inhalation, lethal injection, drowning and hanging, I dozed off before settling for sleeping pills as the quickest and easiest way to kill myself. I had seen a bottle in Mama's medicine cabinet so all I needed was an overdose and that would be the end of this useless life.

The next morning, I got up with a nasty feeling in the pit of my stomach. I don't know what hurt more – my losing the All-Rounder's title or Tara winning it. Seriously, it wouldn't have hurt that much if it wasn't Tara.

I mean here is the girl who followed me around like a dog when we were little, took my advice over petty issues like clothes and boys, felt complexed about being overweight and got a 90 per cent only once in her life! And the school already thinks her worthy of being an All Rounder? OK, she had written a book but what was the big deal? I am a State champion and have brought laurels to the school countless times. Just one bad year and they stripped me of my title? It's a very selfish world out there.

Yes, maybe it was better that I died . . . because I could run but could not hide . . .

So this was when this creepy thought had first entered my mind. I was a lost, lonely loser, beaten by everybody whom I was used to beating. Those sleeping pills in Mama's cabinet looked good. As I lay in bed, remembering the past year, flashes of the military-training Foundations, course lit up my mind. It had not mattered who came tops there; I had accepted who I was. I realised I was being a melting blob of self pity.

'Pull yourself together, Megha!' I scolded myself. 'Everything will be all right – just work through it.' The old, sensible, down-to-earth (OK that's an exaggeration) Megha was struggling to get past the person I had become – bogged down by failures and disasters. It was not easy – it was so much easier to be angry and resentful and sorry for myself. I decided to push aside those thoughts.

I did get back to my senses soon enough and gave myself the weekend to recover. I was a sportsperson – a winner. I wasn't going to let a damn farewell party ruin my life.

And I had to get serious about studies too. I opened my Maths book and started from scratch. I solved one question after another and did not move from my study table for two whole days.

Monday morning things were kind of different in school...

I am not sure if it was my imagination but I felt the whole class staring at me. They were whispering behind my back. I heard voices in my head: look at Megha – that loser, what did she think of herself – good she didn't win – serves her right . . .

When Tara approached me I gave her the cold shoulder. Call me unreasonable but I wasn't ever going to talk to this back-stabber. For the next one week, she tried and tried but I wasn't going to give her any more chances. She had betrayed me and it was over between us. Once and for all. And the other girls of the class – *I give a damn for them, they don't deserve any attention from me anyway.*

I got summoned by Chopra Ma'am as probably she thought she owed me an explanation. Oh yes, she did – the whole school did.

Chopra Ma'am: So what is it, child? I heard that you have been acting strange in class. Why were you rude to Aggarwal Sir during the Maths period?

Me: Oh that? No Ma'am, I was just trying to show him my way of solving a question.

Chopra Ma'am: Really? But you do realise that you could have done it politely, no?

Me: Sorry, Ma'am, if he felt offended but I didn't mean it.

Chopra Ma'am: What is bothering you, Megha? Are you still upset about the farewell night?

Me: No, Ma'am, it was just a damn party.

Chopra Ma'am: There you go again, Megha. Do you know why Tara won?

Me: I am not interested, Ma'am, but I realise that the school perhaps took pity on her . . .

Chopra Ma'am: Tara won because she made a comeback. Yes, she suffered from a food disorder, but she didn't let it pull her down, she put up a fight and got her life back. And

	she is in fact helping others by talking about it.

Me: Ma'am, in all modesty, I am a state champion. Surely writing some articles here and there doesn't even come close.

Chopra Ma'am: She has also written a book, is President of the Literary Club and has been consistently improving her academic performance. And don't forget the Military Base Camp that she has been an active member of – something you refused. If that's not being an all-rounder, what is? And her soft skills, I don't even want to go there but she is the friendliest girl around who has always been nice to everyone. OK, she might not be into sports like you but at this moment she is definitely the most deserving of the title. You could have won, Megha, but you are losing your advantage. Get a grip on things – your grades are falling and you have developed an attitude too.

Me: I understand, Ma'am. Now if you will excuse me, I have a class to attend.

I stalked off from the meeting room. I felt a deep, seething anger in me at this school, to which I had given my blood, sweat and now tears. They all had let me down big time. Mama, Papa, Tara, Sandy, this school, every one of them. How I hated them. How I hated this system! This whole goddam world!

But there wasn't much time for more brooding . . .

For the next month we all forgot about everything else except studies. Well, not exactly, as I also started having these crying spells. There were no real triggers – sometimes it would be an irritating Chemistry equation, a lost pen or even if my cell phone battery died. The only saving grace was that it never happened publicly or I would have the laughing stock around.

All this while, I had no contact with Papa, who had moved in with his girlfriend. I know I am being blunt but I had lost respect for the man who was coolly starting a new life, leaving Mama and me to struggle with our set of problems.

Yet again, I was wrong . . .

Actually, I learnt, rather Papa told me over a rare phone call, that Mama had forbidden him from seeing me until the Boards were over. She did not want me to get more upset than I already was with my swimming, academics and the farewell fiasco. She did what she thought was best for me, or so she said. As usual Papa couldn't stand up for himself. If only they had asked *me* what *I* wanted. On second thoughts, it was better that they didn't as I myself was confused as hell. I knew there were a million things going wrong with my life but now was not the time to resolve it.

It was the time to face the big beast – every student's nightmare – the colossus – the one and only – the Boards!

The month before the Boards was an emotional roller-coaster ride that wasn't going to end anytime soon. This so-called 'most important phase of life' has its own set of strategies that students need to follow apart from the constant nagging from parents and teachers: aim for a 10 CGPA, make a time table and stick to it, don't study at the last minute, don't watch TV, forget Facebook, forget Twitter-*shwitter*, develop a conceptual understanding, do numericals thoroughly, mug up your formulae, make mind maps, practise last year's papers, munch on almonds, have *chyawanprash,* drink Bournvita . . . the list is endless.

As if this were not enough – Tara did her bit to irritate me even more.

This month's newsletter included an article from Ms Know-it-all, Holier-than-thou – that ex-best friend of mine – Tara Kapoor! Can you believe that now the kids have to take advice from an average student like her?!

What is the world coming to?

Patriotic Public School

Newsletter for the Month of March

Dealing with Exam Stress
— by Tara Kapoor

It's that time of the year which we all dread whether we are 'poor' students or are in the 'bright' category. A time when we actually don't have a choice but to face it and no matter what — no one but no one can do it for us. It is our own personal battle. And though I am sounding a bit nervous myself, I still have some rules my topper sister follows and guess what—they work for me too !

1. Plan your day and stick to it
2. Take baby steps but keep an eye on the big picture
3. Don't overload your body with heavy food, eat healthy, light food
4. Keep hydrated, drink a lot of water too
5. Don't compromise on sleep or else performance suffers

Stand Tall —
whatever your height

निकलो घरों से।
— by Pradumn R Chourey

Tv को तकते हो,
घरों में तुम अपने
बाहर तो निकलो, बहारें आई है।
Mobile निहारते हो, घरों में तुम अपने
खिड़कियां तो खोलो, फ़िज़ाएँ आई है।।

राह तकती तुम्हारी, सड़कें सुबह को,
वो बल्ला, वो बॉलें निराश पड़े है।
मन ही मन उड़ते हो,
घरों में तुम अपने
पंख तो फैलाओ, आसमान खुला है।।

पत्ते भी ताली बजाते है, सुनो तो।
परिंदे भी सुर में गाते है, सुनो तो।।
सुनते हो खट-पट।
घरों में तुम अपने,
मीत भी गीत सुनाते है, सुनो तो।।

Sixer's अब लगते है **Mobiles** में सारे।

Goal-post तुम्हारा,
I-Pad में बना है।
बाहर निकल अब दौड़-भाग मचा दो,
तुम्हारे कदमो का मैदानों को इंतज़ार
बड़ा है।।

Daniel, an eighth grader had always been referred to as a 'small fry' and all these years of having 'eight almonds with a glass of milk' for breakfast wasn't helping either. Teased by his classmates and advised by well-meaning aunts and uncles, there were times when he wanted to just disappear from this cruel world where all the grown-ups cared about was how much height he gained over the summers! Well, it wasn't so bad actually as he was loved dearly by her parents. Still, every night Daniel would measure his height with a tape and sleep dejected. On one particular bad day, when he got teased by his friends in a basketball match at school, he came home crying into his mama's arms.

"Why me, mama, why did God make me the shortest kid in class?" His mama said, "Danny, don't focus on what you don't have. Focus on what you can do. And whatever your height, you can do everything. Go to school, excel in your studies, play sports, act normal and forget about your height. If you are meant to be tall, you will be. If not, accept it and move on. If you still feel sad sometimes — think about Mahatma Gandhi, Beethoven, Picasso...all of them were short, but they were great as they stood tall" His mama's words gave him the boost his needed and he decided to follow the footsteps of these famous people who ruled the world by their talents and achievements. So children, the next time you get teased over your height, say — "I am not short — I am just compact and ridiculously cute".

The thing that worried me sick even more than the exams was the fear of panic attacks – that was the last thing I needed in my life.

'God, I know I haven't been a good girl but I have no one but you to discuss my problems with. Please, God, no matter what happens, please spare me these panic attacks or fainting episodes. Not only are they extremely embarrassing, they will ruin my performance too. You know the Boards are extremely important – they could make or break a career . . . please do something. I don't want to panic. Just this time. Once my exams are over, you can do anything to me but please let me take my exams in peace. Please, God, I beg of you. If you do that for me, I promise to stop eating non-veg for at least a year. I swear. But don't let me down.'

Yes, God is kind and he always listens period.

I was able to give my exams in peace. No nervousness, no anxiety and no fainting. Just like old times. If only I had studied like the old times too, as every time I looked at the question paper, I got down to work knowing that the days of being a topper were over. Despite the tuitions, despite the sample papers, despite

the countless hours on Quadratic Equations- something was missing. There were too many questions that I could not solve. It seemed that the whole world schemed against me to put me in a spot. Yes — my papers didn't go well. Why? Really, I had no answers why but I knew that my days were numbered.

And I felt exactly like that dumbo in my class who hardly passes any exam!

March-end, the exams were over and so was any chance of happiness.

Tara's book was released and she became a celebrity overnight. Nobody knew if it was going to be a hit or not but the fact that an average girl in her teens could write a book was enough for the world to fuss over this so-called debutante author. By now, it was practically over between us but for old times' sake I took the initiative of messaging her. But I wasn't going to forget everything else and start afresh if that's what she was thinking. Unfortunately, it got ugly as I should have known before trying to be nice to Ms Hoity-toity!

Just then Mama came to my room.

Mama:	Megha, what happened, darling? Why are you crying?
Me:	Oh nothing, Mama . . . I probably stared at my phone too long.
Mama:	Look, I have something to cheer you up! Ta-ta-da – **Tara's book**!
Me:	What? Why did you get me this?
Mama:	Come on, Megha, it's your best friend's first novel. You should be so happy for her.
Me:	I hate her, Mama; don't you know what she did to me?
Mama:	What did she do?
Me:	You know – the All-Rounder's title, it was mine! And she took it away! Why did they give the title to her, Mama, what's the big fuss about her?
Mama:	Do you really mean that, Megha? One, I hate to see that in your envy, you have become blind to her achievements, and two, she couldn't have refused, could she?
Me:	If it was me in her place and if that title belonged to my best friend, I would have.
Mama:	The title doesn't belong to anyone, Megha, you have to earn it. You had a bad year, that's all. And she did pretty

	well for herself, I must say. Her parents must be so proud of her and look at you . . . well . . . I don't even want to go there.
Me:	Don't, Mama, I am already very upset.
Mama:	But trust me, this book will cheer you up . . . Here, go through the 'Acknowledgements' part.

> *I begin my expressing my gratitude to my mother as she is the one who encouraged me to pen down my feelings since I was very little. I am grateful to my dad, my sister and even my grandmother who have been very supportive of my work. My teachers, who have been so motivating. I also want to thank my best friend Megha, for she taught me that it's not enough to be talented – if you want to achieve something, be prepared to work hard. Thank you, Megha, for being a constant source of inspiration in my life.*

As I read this, I felt tears rolling down my cheeks. What was I supposed say except that I was so damn ashamed of myself.

Me:	Oh Mama, what have I done? Tara thanked me in her book! I don't deserve this!
Mama:	Yes, you do, Megha; don't undermine yourself so much.
Me:	It's all because of you, Mama. If only you had not made me feel like a loser!
Mama:	Are you serious, Megha? The only purpose of my life has been to see my daughter happy and this is what I get in return?

Me:	The only purpose of your life has been to see me win, Mama. Even if it came at the cost of my happiness; but now, I don't want to go there.
Mama:	Yes, you shouldn't, either. Thank you very much for opening my eyes, Megha, how proud I am of you today!

As my Mama stormed out of the room, crying, I felt guilty as hell. I had messed up the two most important relationships of my life: with my best friend and now my mother. How would I ever, ever fix this?

Thereafter began this cold war between my Mama and me. Papa started visiting again but things were not the same with him. I still hadn't called up Tara to apologise. And the weird part was that I didn't have the energy for it either. With everything screwed up in my life, I thought that probably time would heal these wounds. And I felt too drained, anyway. All I could do was hope that things would get better.

But they didn't as Class XI started and Tara and Dolly left the school. Can you believe it??!!!

Yes, my best friend did not continue as she opted for Arts, which our school did not offer. Despite the 90 per cent in the Pre-Boards, she still wanted to study Arts. I mean, come on, Tara – there is a limit to being rebellious. And Dolly – it wasn't really a surprise as she wasn't the academic sort anyway. Tara was lucky enough to join a prestigious institution for Arts in Delhi and Dolly decided on private education! However, my heart was broken. I was extremely lonely and longed for the good old times with my pals.

What happened afterwards . . . read on.

Mama's career was skyrocketing and she was asked to move to Dubai for her new role as head of the MENA (that's Middle East and North Africa) region. The plan was to leave around July. Like I said, it was going to be a new school in a new country. Maybe it was God's way of helping us, too, start our lives afresh.

As it was, I didn't have anything much to do in my school either. I didn't try to make my place in the new class. Literally, as for the first time, I opted to go to the back row, far, far away from the teacher's desk. We had a lot of new kids joining from other schools and everyone else was also trying to settle down and get adjusted to the new faces.

We, as in Mama and I, opted for Non-Medical as my career was already chalked out – I had to walk in my parents' footsteps or even further, as Mama always made it clear that I would be studying engineering and later an MBA at one of the Ivy League colleges.

About the extra-curricular activities – I was swimming regularly and was in the school's football team, but somehow, things were not moving. Last year I was President of the Sports Club and this year I was supposed to become the Vice Head Girl but due to my poor performance, they restricted my powers and my movement to the sports arena. So I had to be content with the title of Sports Vice Captain. Actually I was made to feel that it was a favour to me. I guess that was the price I was paying for taking my duties in the School Council for granted. Or the price for not being oh-so-politically-right and teacher's pet like other kids in the school government!

Eventually the summer holidays started. For a long time, I waited for Mama to bring up our holiday plans but it wasn't going to happen, it seemed, so that it became even more difficult to face those holidays which most regular kids from regular families look forward to. Unlike me whose days of taking those exotic vacations were over. And there was something else too that both Mama and me did not have the courage to face:

That it was 28 May – time for the Class X results.

So this was the day I had been dreading all along. I knew that my chances of a perfect CGPA were close to nil but I was still hoping for the best; like they say – hope for the best but be prepared for the worst. But I trusted that God would do it for me even when my exams didn't go so well; God wouldn't play around with the Board results, would He?

As I entered my roll number and date of birth on the Secondary Examination portal, I thought I could hear Mama's heart beating even louder than mine. Just a few seconds more and all will be out in the open. Open and out!

Now that it was the perfect moment for me to pass out and escape Mama's baffled look, my body refused to cooperate. I just sat there and stared unbelievingly at the computer screen. Was this some kind of a joke?

English:	82
Hindi	66
Maths	64
Social Studies	63
Science	72
Total=	347/500

Oh no! So God did play around with my results – 69.4 per cent??!!! I didn't even make it to a 70!! This was as good as failing! Tell me, Mama, that it's not true . . . Come, let's check again.

As we helplessly logged in three times more – we got the same result. God had played a cruel joke on me.

Megha Deshpande – topper from the bottom!

'Don't worry, Megha, this is not the end of life,' I heard Mama call out as I locked myself in my room.

Disheartened, dejected, defeated . . . I don't have words to describe how I felt. The game was over. I had failed. Yet again. But I made a promise to myself that this was going to be the last time.

And yes, mama, this is the end of life

As I went through descriptions of some fascinating near-death experiences on the Internet, I felt at peace. Yes, my time was up. Need to move on. Because . . .

CAN'T

TAKE IT

ANYMORE!!!

Part 2
Some lessons to learn . . .

Don't judge me by my success, judge me by how many times I fell down and got back up again period.

– Nelson Mandela,

late inspirational world leader

The woods are lovely
dark and deep
But I have promises to keep
And miles to go before I sleep
and miles to go before I sleep
-Robert Frost

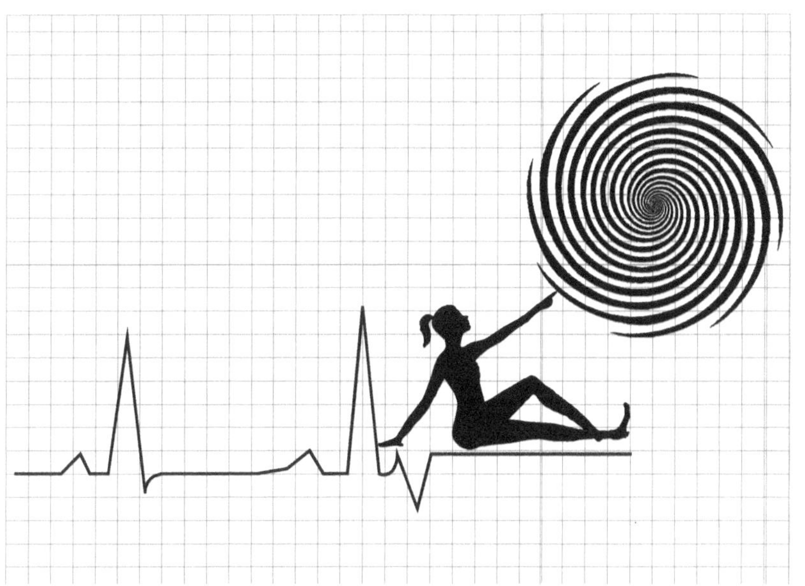

10:30 pm, end of May, St. Teresa Medical care

Gurgaon, India

This *can't be happening . . . it seems I have failed yet again.*

I am able to think, so it means I am not dead yet. But I am not able to open my eyes, I am not able to speak, so does it mean I am dead? Oh wow, now it is time to go through the tunnel I have heard so much about, and merge in that white light at the end of it. Now it is time to be one with the universe, to feel a magnificent energy, to feel that bliss, that infinite love . . .

But all I am able to feel is this damn headache. And a lot of drowsiness. I guess this must be the end. Goodbye, cruel world. And sorry, Mama and Papa.

I drifted into a deep sleep. I started to feel lighter and floated in the clouds above. Finally, I was in the 'other realm' I had been fantasising about – the place with no school, no exams and no swimming competitions. And no Sandy. Here I would get my answers. Here I would find peace. Here I would be happy. And be left alone.

'Oh Megha, why did you do this to us? Why, Megha, why?' I heard Mama cry. And Papa was talking to someone – probably a doctor. Which meant I was still awake. And alive. Only, my body felt so heavy that I could not move. I tried to make sense of the situation but did not have the strength to concentrate. Give it up, Megha, just give it up.

It's time to go, Mama, I thought as I looked down at my body lying on the hospital bed, with tubes and an oxygen mask attached, and Mama's helpless and sobbing face down on my chest. I felt warm rays of light surrounding me and taking me upwards. Just then Mama got hysterical: 'Come back, baby, don't give up!'

Who would believe me that I could not dare defy Mama's orders, even when I was dead?

I let out a deep breath as I opened my eyes slowly to look at the shock and relief on my parents' faces. 'Yes guys, it's not the time to give up,' I whispered and went back to sleep.

It must have been an hour or two later when I heard my parents talking softly.

Papa:	How could you be so irresponsible, keeping sleeping pills so easily accessible to her?
Mama:	What do you mean? Did I know that she was going to commit suicide?
Papa:	How could you miss it, Seema, surely there would have been signs?
Mama:	Oh God, you are so right. . . . I did miss it. Even when it was right in front of me. Megha was screaming for help all these days but I completely ignored her. You know, she had been seeing her school counsellor. They did warn me . . . I was supposed to get her therapy started but I thought with the Nationals and Boards, it could wait . . . you know my experience, I don't trust these doctors . . . but it's my fault. Completely. I just wasn't there for my daughter. (*She started sobbing softly.*)
Papa:	Don't cry, Seema, I wasn't there either. I failed Megha. I failed both of you. Badly.

I opened my eyes and saw Mama in Papa's arms. They were

both crying and looked closer than I had ever seen them. *Does that mean this relationship still stands a chance? And about me, once the sympathy dies down, my life will be over. Mama is not going to spare me. Megha, be ready for the thrashings and the never-ending lectures!*

How could I be so stupid, to think that killing myself would be the answer? If only it was that easy. Because now that I was alive, I felt enormous exhaustion and a sinking feeling of extreme guilt and shame. What did I do? And why did I make my parents go through with this drama?

I should have died before thinking of taking my own life!!

After a couple of days, we came back home. Mama made me promise that I would not talk about it to anyone. *But Mama, I have to talk about it,* I thought to myself. *I know the last time you spanked me was when I was six, but I am actually waiting for it. Why are you not saying that you are disappointed in me, like always? Can't you see how ashamed and embarrassed I am? Don't be so nice to me, Mama, I don't deserve it.* This time, Mama heard my inner voices.

Mama:	Relax this week, Megha, and then you are going to Nani's house in Ambala.
Me:	What about swimming?
Mama:	Swimming? I'm surprised you are still thinking about it. There is a big Olympic-size pool nearby, which you can join. Nani is very influential – she will find you an instructor too. But that is not the important thing.
Me:	So what is it, Mama, are you sending me away because you are angry with me?
Mama:	No, Megha, I am not angry with you, child. But

I have my limitations. I cannot deal with this situation as well as my own mother can. I trust her as the only one who can help you. And I hope you know that you need help.

Me: I know, Mama, but how will she help me? You know I am not the spirituality and yoga sort.

Mama: Be open-minded, Megha, and believe me when I say this: you will be healed.

My suicide attempt had shifted something in my mama. She looked calmer and at peace with herself and her life. She even started updating Papa about my condition. Can you imagine, she took a week off from work as well, to be with me! We talked, we cried, we played Scrabble, went shopping, polished off countless pizzas, watched TV all day and slept together. She read out stories for me and never did bring up my studies or career or swimming. All this love and attention was kind of awkward but I started getting used to it. Maybe the suicide wasn't such a bad idea, after all, I thought to myself, smiling.

But then, it was time to go.

Ambala

City of Mangoes (*Amba-wala*), city of scientific instruments and home-town to Bollywood's Parineeti Chopra, this so-called small town in Haryana also has the world-famous *Pooran Singh ka Dhaba*, which is frequented by thousands of visitors every day. Well, the only reason I am telling you this is because Ambala is technically my place of birth and it is here I would be getting reborn again. I mean, nothing miraculous would happen, really, but for the next two months, Ambala would be my transit towards being a more . . . sought-out girl.

If you are interested to know more – Nathuram Godse, Mahatma Gandhi's assassin was hanged at Ambala's Central Jail! Ambala is also mentioned in *Kim,* a novel by Rudyard Kipling. If you are still intrigued, please go on Wikipedia and spare me.

It wasn't the first time I was visiting this place but this was the first time I went with an open mind. Or at least I tried to, as Mama had asked me to trust her this time, and though I still had a million confusing thoughts in my mind, I had decided to go with the flow.

Mama spent the weekend with us before going back to her office in Gurgaon. Yes, like always, she had critical things to take care of at work. Such as looking good to her bosses and being nasty to her juniors. Well, what was I expecting? No matter how much I tried reasoning with the situation, I was pissed off at her for not spending more time with me. I guess those Scrabble games had spoilt me rotten, to actually start believing that she cared.

For now, it was only my Nani and I.

As we sat on her lawn, sipping our morning coffee, I felt her looking at me as I played with her dogs. *Probably she is cursing Mama for having left me here for this course of 'healing' when the last thing she wants is distractions from being a celebrated Mataji (an old female spiritual guru) of her neighbourhood.* Maybe I was being very hard on her but the fact was that I had become very negative; even though I thought this suicide experience would have taught me something, in my heart I knew that I had a long way to go. And that this was the time to really open my eyes and my ears, and start learning.

Nani:	Do you know, Megha, why are you here?
Me:	Mama says I need help and that you will do it for me. Frankly, I am not sure how you can . . . you know nothing about my life.
Nani:	I know a lot more than you think I do, but

why don't you tell me yourself. Start from the beginning. Like you are writing your autobiography. Remember, tell me everything and be as honest as possible. I am not going to judge you, no matter what you say. But talk. As it's time now.

And I did.

I went on and on about this wretched life. About Mama-Papa's divorce. About the other woman in Papa's life. About Mama's ruthlessness. Her attitude towards Papa. And me. About her career that became more important than her family. About my so-called affair with Sandy. And how he treated me like shit. And how it came to a point where he hit me badly. And that no matter what, I couldn't get over that humiliation. About the one thing I badly wanted – to be a part of the Army Boot Camp- and how Mama took it away from me. About my swimming debacle and my loss at the Nationals. About losing the Ms All-Rounder title at school. About my regular anxiety attacks. About my poor performance in the Boards. About my broken friendship with Tara. And my broken spirit. My bitterness about my own parents. And the school that let me down big time.

Finally, I talked about my suicide attempt. And how my hands trembled and my lips quivered when I gulped down half a bottle of the sleeping pills lying in Mama's medicine cabinet. And how I collapsed in the bathroom – out of sheer panic or due to the effects of those pills, I still didn't know and perhaps never will.

And that even when I thought it was better that I died, deep within I never did want to die. And I was never the one to give up.

At last I ran out of words and sat staring at the coffee mug in my hands for long minutes. Finally, she spoke.

Nani: That's all for today, Megha. Come let's go to the kitchen and bake a cake. Do you remember when you were little – that was your favourite hobby? Mixing the batter till the lumps are gone?

As I beat the mixture of eggs, butter and sugar till it became light, fluffy and creamy, and carefully folded in the flour and chocolate powder, I realised that I was already feeling better. And then Nani added a pinch of salt. When I looked at her questioningly she said, 'the salt enhances the flavour and balances the sweetness. That's what problems do in our lives, Megha. So that it doesn't become so sweet that it's bitter.'

Well, perhaps my life had just too much salt in it, Nani, I thought to myself. But I didn't argue as I also knew that in the coming days, I would find my own balance.

The next morning Nani and I went to Jain Soda Water Factory, a decades-old restaurant that I used to frequent as a child. Here, sipping their famous Milk *Badaam*, I marvelled at life's little pleasures this simple drink could provide.

Me: So what do you think, Nani, does this also have salt in it?

Nani: If only I knew their secret recipe, Megha, but yes, it seems like it. Enjoy it without worrying about the ingredients.

Me: So, Nani, what else are we doing today?

Nani: Today we go home and do nothing. I just want you realise what it's like to do nothing. But before you get used to it, we will start our journey. Perhaps day after tomorrow.

Me: Journey? Where are we going, Nani?

Nani: We go within, Megha.

Me;   Nani, I already told Mama, I am not into this spirituality nonsense!

Nani: Don't worry; all I am going to do is share with you some truths of life that I have realised over a period of time. I don't claim originality; you will not hear anything out-of-the-box or revolutionary. But I hope listening to me will give you a different perspective. You can call them rules or truths or lessons or even quotations – doesn't matter.

Me: Oh, you mean, I will find my answers.

Nani: You might find some answers, but not all. Experience and life will teach you much more than I could in the next two months or so. All I can ask of you is, be a good student. In other words, follow these three rules:

One – listen carefully;

Two – think about it; and

Three – ask questions.

Me: Oh, sounds so exciting . . . I can't wait to start.

Nani: Me too. We start day after tomorrow. Tomorrow, we will practise silence. If you can, please don't talk to me or anyone else. Detox yourself of your cell phone so no Internet, WhatsApp and Snapchat, promise?

Me: Promise, Nani, let's do it.

So over the next few days, I learnt what I would call '**Grandma's Truths of Life'**. I am not asking you, the reader, to follow everything blindly but it will give you a perspective. And who knows, you might even end up being a happier person. Like me. So here we go – Grandma's Truths of Life:

1. Shit Happens

Nani: In other words, bad things happen. Sometimes to good people like you, too. Actually to **everyone**. What can we do about it? We accept it. We have to accept that there will be problems and miseries and bitterness and everything that comes with the whole wonderful package called life. Yes, your parents got divorced; yes, your own relationship failed; yes, you flunked an exam and you had a breakdown. Who knows why it happened, so don't ask. Just accept it. **Stuff happens – get used to it.** And now here is the next one:

2. Now get out of the bathroom

Nani: Yes, bad stuff happened. And it wasn't your fault. You accepted it, you cried over it, you became resentful and you ended up staying that way longer than necessary. **Get out before you start enjoying the torture chamber**. That's what the human mind does – it seeks sadistic pleasure even in pathetic situations. Sometimes, it helps you to zone out, it might even get you some attention. But get out. Before it's too late. Obviously, the third would be:

3. Seek help

Nani: All right, you are strong and perfect, but seeking help is actually a survival skill. Doesn't matter what you think yourself to be, there will be times when you will feel that you need help – it could be an emotional trauma, a tough Maths problem, a disease or any other shitty thing. It's OK to ask for help and you should not feel inadequate in doing so. Seeking help doesn't make you weak but admitting that you need it is a sure sign of strength.

Me: Oh yes, Nani, that's what I did. I kept asking why 'shit' was happening to me as I didn't deserve it. But about the seeking help part, I think you need to explain it to Mama more. She was advised by my school to get therapy for me right away but she kept procrastinating; firstly, saying that her daughter was a fighter and did not need any help from outsiders. Secondly, she always had the excuse of these upcoming swimming competitions or exams. If only she had thought about me and been a little less selfish and arrogant!

Nani: That brings us to our fourth truth, Megha.

4. People have their reasons

Nani: Remember, it's not about you. People have their own reasons. Why your mom did what she did has nothing to do with you. She had a really bad experience herself and that is why she has major trust issues with psychologists. I remember it was a few years back.

You were just born and your Papa was never around – always travelling. She thought she did the 'right' thing by quitting her job and was a stay-at-home mom for a while. It didn't work and eventually, she fell into a deep depression. Yes, you are right, she did not seek help from me as probably she wanted to avoid the usual lectures. Yes, Megha, all mothers are guilty of it. But she went from one doctor to another who gave her a different diagnosis each time and confused her further. Fed up and helpless, she finally spoke to me and took my advice of getting into meditation and alternative healing. I am not going to claim any credit for it, but it helped her tremendously.

That is the reason she did not seek professional help for you, Megha, and please remember that I am not implying that one shouldn't either. But before that, talk to the people you trust, seek help from your inner circle, pray, meditate and take it easy. That is also the reason she sent you here.

Megha, she is your mother – she has her issues and some mental blocks, but she loves you the most in the world. Never forget that and never ever doubt her intentions. As she has her reasons and will always have. So will everyone else. Even the mean ones, even the jerks. Even those who hurt you. **It's not about you.**

As I listened to the truth about Mama from Nani, I felt warm tears rolling down my cheeks. Oh, I had misunderstood my own mother. How could I ever doubt her love for me, she is my mom! I felt guilty as hell and cried for a long time.

Nani: It's OK, child . . . let it out. When you are ready, I will tell you the next one.

Me: I am ready, Nani, please go on . .

5. Only the good feel guilty, but know when to stop

Nani: If you feel remorse that you have done something wrong, let anyone down or messed up somewhere – it's actually a good sign. It means that you are a good person and have a conscience. But don't carry on with this feeling forever – either make things right or stop feeling guilty about it. In your case you don't really have to feel guilty as you had no idea why your mother wasn't taking you for therapy and you judged her wrongly. But now you know so don't waste any more time over it.

Me: Oh Nani, it's not just her, it's my best friend Tara. You know, I wasn't able to accept the fact that she was getting more popular than me. Instead of feeling proud of my friend for her achievements, I got jealous! I ridiculed Tara, saying that she hadn't done anything great by writing a book for children, although I damn well knew that it's a very big deal! I was really nasty to her, Nani, and I don't have the guts to face her anymore. I wish I could tell her how sorry I am!

Nani: Now that you are sorry about it, listen on:

6. What is done is done

Nani: All right, in your words – you screwed up with your mother, you screwed up with Tara, and you haven't been exactly nice to a lot of people. Accept it. It's over now. What is done is done and now move on. You have all the time in the world to make up for it. In simple words – stop being rude. And apologise to Tara when you get back. You guys need to really talk and it can't be done over WhatsApp.

               Now let's talk about something else that you are not exactly proud of. Something more serious. Your suicide attempt. In this case you shouldn't be let off so easily. You should feel remorse for it and you should regret it for a long time, actually, because this was the most foolish and selfish stunt you ever tried pulling off. So here, you can't say what's done is done and move on. I won't let you. Do you know why?

7. No matter what – you can never ever take your life because it is not yours to take

Nani:

You know, Megha, suicide does not take away the pain – it just gives it to someone else. I am not going to say that it is a cowardly thing to do; actually it takes guts. But it is definitely the most selfish thing you can do. When that bottle of sleeping pills was whispering your name, did you not hear your Mama shouting at the top of her voice, through her lungs, inside your heart and your mind, TO STOP as she loves you? You know, every few minutes, someone in the world dies by suicide. And the next minute, someone in the world is left to clean up after it.

And you wanted to kill yourself because of a few failures here and there? Did you not see the opportunities life has given you? A loving family, a great school, wonderful friends and a shot to be whatever you wanted to be. I understand that it wasn't a perfect life and that you were in pain but there is no excuse for what you have done. Even if I tried hard reasoning or rationalising it, Megha – **Suicide is not the answer.**

You were lucky that you survived, but you were luckier that you didn't end up with permanent brain damage that those sleeping pills could have caused! Yes – you could have spent the rest of your long life tied to an incubator, like a vegetable, in a hospital bed. Did you ever think of that?

> Remember child – death is still not the greatest loss, the greatest loss is what dies within you when you are still alive. The real loss is when you let yourself give up, lose that spark which makes you get up and go on after every fall. You still have the spark. You still have the will to fix your life. To get on with it. That's why you are listening to this. Don't lose it. Ever.

As I cried, listening to Nani, I felt my heart breaking in a thousand pieces when I realised the enormity of this blunder. Of what it could have done to Mama and Papa. But yes, I also understood that Nani wanted me to feel this as deeply as possible. And I needed it. To be able to get over it.

Nani: Megha, my baby, even when I so want to hug you badly and say it's OK and it's over, I won't. You need to feel it and then let it out. Cry as much as you can – and about anything – there is no agenda. It's OK if you cry over Sandy, Tara, the Nationals, your marks or your suicide. If it's important to you, it's not silly. Let it out, baby. But this is your moment and I will leave you alone. We will talk again, but not today. Till then, vent it all out. But before you sleep – repeat to yourself — **Tomorrow is another day.**

As I lay in my bed, staring at the fan above me in the hot summer night, I played back in mind everything bad that happened to me in the last year or so. I relived those moments of panic, of being punched by Sandy, of the Nationals I had so badly wanted to win and how empty the house feels when Papa doesn't live there anymore. I hugged my pillow and cried myself to sleep. Perhaps my tears washed my eyes so that I could see life more clearly. But I wondered what would be the next pearl of wisdom . . .

I guess Nani changed her mind about giving me another dose next morning and I was actually feeling thankful that she did. I needed time to process it. She knew that and decided to give me something that I truly needed – like **some swimming practice.**

Me:	Do you mean it, Nani, are we going for swimming today?
Nani:	Oh yes, your mama told me that this was your first concern – that you wouldn't be able to swim in Ambala. Of course you can. There is an Olympic-size pool in the cantonment area. And I am not done as yet.
Me:	Oh, is there more?
Nani:	Yes, over the next few weeks you will get trained by a very special person.
Me:	Trained, as in? And who is this special person?
Nani:	You have the State Levels in July. Have you forgotten that? And this special person – his name is Lieutenant Colonel Paramjeet Singh.
Me:	Are you kidding me, Nani? How did you manage this? He is in the International league !!
Nani:	Oh, he is the son of a very dear friend. He's here on his annual leave. When I talked about you to him, he volunteered to help out. Don't worry – he will give his best. He is an army officer, after all. But you have to promise – you will not take it casually either. You still have time to think about it. Tell me, do you still love swimming?
Me:	Nani, at this point honestly, that's all I really know: that I love swimming.

As we hugged excitedly, I couldn't help feeling thankful for this wonderful second chance that life had given me! But I was feeling out of form and wondered if I even had a chance . . . in fact I was even thinking of dropping out from the selections. It would be enough if I just started enjoying it again. A win would actually be a big bonus and could wait for the time being. As I wasn't over my last defeat and perhaps would never be.

As we stood eyeing the pool, those dreaded feelings came back. I felt my legs trembling but I diverted my mind to the figure preparing to dive. He took three steps before leaping to land on the edge of the diving board with arms over his head. He dived off the board, his hips raised above the shoulder level. His hands reached his toes, his body bent from the waist to become a beautiful angle, before he straightened it, to complete a perfect *jackknife* – an advanced form of dive.

Woooo! Who is he, I thought to myself before realising that the figure was walking towards us.

'Good evening aunty and hello young lady, you must be Megha,' he said.

'Good evening beta, yes, met my granddaughter Megha. Your Protegee' Nani responded.

As I shook hands with Col. Singh, a warm feeling enveloped me. I always had this thing about Army officers. What manners, what height, what shoulders, what personality and what a dive of course! Surely Singh is King, I thought.

'So Megha, ready? Let's see what you have got. Please can you do a 200 metres' freestyle, just to warm up?' he turned towards me.

'yes Coach Uncle,' was all I said before I dived into the pool awkwardly. But thank you God, for creating water!

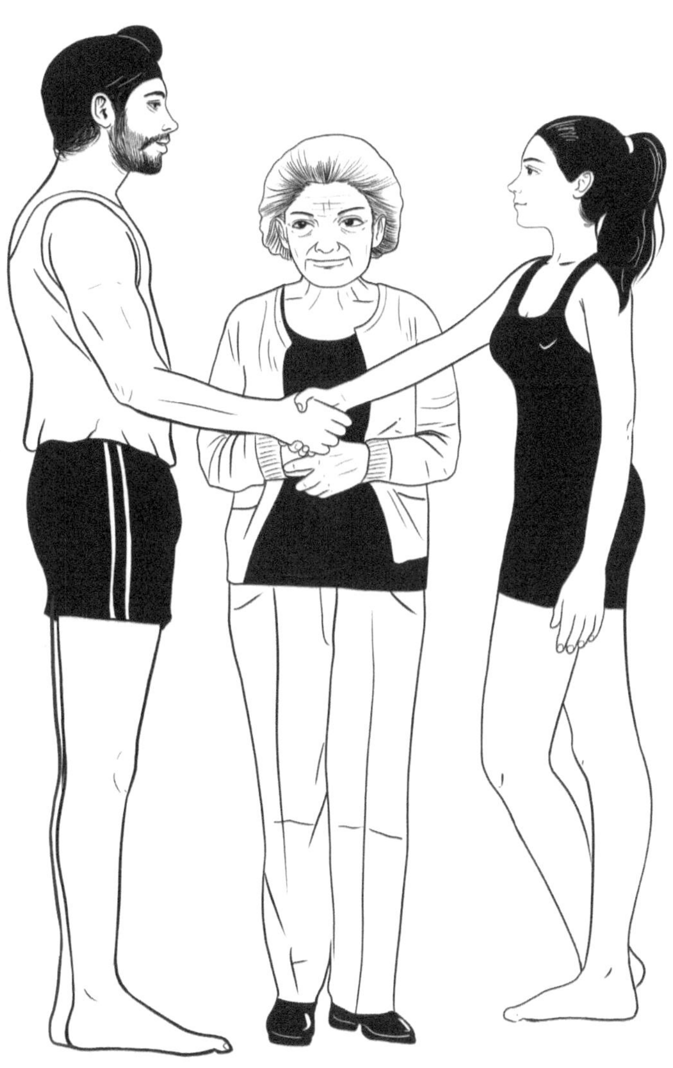

The next few days, I was in that water almost six hours a day. Even then, I felt things were not happening. There was something holding me back, and I wasn't happy with the way I was practising. Uncle did not look too impressed either. And Nani knew that it was time for the next principle, which was:

8. If you get too used to winning, failure is the best thing that can happen to you

Nani: You may not realise it now, but take it from someone who has been through a lot more than you. Yes, you failed and failed again. But it gave you an opportunity to bounce back with more enthusiasm. You have known defeat. And frustration. And a whole lot of sorrow that comes with it. It has made you humble; rather, it has made you more human. You know exactly what you have to work on. Now you have a great chance to show the world what you are really made of. Get up and walk out of those failures. Because it is the only way to succeed.

Me: Wow, Nani, it sounds great in theory. In reality, it was the worst and the most humiliating thing that ever happened to me. Look at me – I am not able to focus during the practice sessions, either. Perhaps I am not able to get over those failures; actually that's what I have probably become.

Nani: Oh girl, I told you – you will not realise it now – the only time you fail is when you say 'I give up'. And I know for sure, Megha, you are not the one to ever, ever give up. That's why you are here. That's why you still practise swimming, even when you say that you are not able to focus. That's why you are alive. Remember, child, failure is an event, not a person. OK, it happened to you but that's not what you have become. As long as you don't stop trying, you have no right to call yourself a failure – even when you want to get dramatic and indulge in self-pity. And anyway,

9. Failure is a bruise, not a tattoo

Nani:

This so-called failure that has thrown you off the cliff, it's neither fatal nor final. It's temporary, and an important part of growing up. Of getting smarter. And wiser. And better. You are going to do really well in life, Megha, I know that – you have the talents, the brain, the personality and a whole lot of opportunities. Plus, a mother who will make sure of it. It will not be easy to fail, Megha, but when you do, thank God for this gift as it will stop you from becoming arrogant. And the best part being – this setback will make you appreciate success so much more. **That is why it is so necessary to fail.**

Me:

I get it, Nani, but your own daughter had made my life miserable by always commenting on how I could have done better – even when I won. Imagine how she made me feel when I actually failed? With a mom like that, how can you expect me to stay motivated?

10. Forgive your parents

Nani:

I understand where you are coming from, Megha. Even if it is my own daughter, I am not going to defend her actions. I know that she wasn't exactly soft with you and sometimes she got too overbearing, but forgive her because whatever she did, it was out of love. All mothers, rather, all parents want this, Megha – to see their children happy. And most think that success is the ultimate happiness. They push you to work harder towards doing well in life. They make it difficult for you now so that you can have it easy in life later. They do it for you and for that reason alone, even if you have to suffer in the bargain, be magnanimous and forgive them.

Me: Oh Nani, who am I to forgive my parents, I am just a child . . .

Nani: Yes, but you will grow up, too. Secondly, a lot of children's lives get messed up because of the wrong choices their parents make. But parents do whatever they think is right at that point of time. Some people are not so great at this job of parenting, just like there are lousy teachers or lousy doctors. But take my word for it, that's the only way they know how to do it. So make peace with them. So that you can be at peace with yourself. And also you need to preserve the most beautiful and important relationship you will ever have in your life – with your mother. Even if you think she hasn't exactly been good. But trust me, don't grow up with any grudges. Ever. At least with this person. Your mother.

Me: I promise, Nani, I will try . . .

Nani: You know, Megha, your mom wasn't an easy child. She was aggressive, stubborn and mostly in her own bubble. She gave me a really hard time, growing up, with her tantrums and arguments. But I made peace with the fact that there is a limit to which I could influence her and started paying attention to the positives in her. It might seem absurd but it's not easy to love unconditionally, even if it's your own children, so I had to really work on it. And over a period of time, she mellowed down, got busy with academics and developed a personality. You have been a good daughter but like me, it will be you who will have to learn to love unconditionally. She is an amazing woman, Megha, and she deserves your love and respect. Just like all mothers.

Me: Nani, you said that parents think that success is the ultimate happiness. Isn't that right?

Nani: No, Megha, it's the other way round – happiness is the ultimate success. But we will talk about it later. For now, you need to tell me what you have learnt so far.

Me: I learnt that problems are a part of life and we need to first accept them and then get over them. Also don't judge, as people have their own reasons. That you don't become a smaller person if you seek help. And yes, failure is the best teacher. And ultimately whatever parents do, it is out of love.

Nani: Wonderful, Megha, I am so proud of you. Tomorrow, after your swimming session, we will start something new. For now, take a break. Which means read a book, or sit in the lawn, listen to the birds and smell the flowers. No cell phone or iPad, OK?

> *If you can meet with Triumph and Disaster*
> *And treat those two impostors just the same;*
> *Yours is the Earth and everything that's in it,*
> *And—which is more—you'll be a Man, my son.*

With Rudyard Kipling's book in my hands I went over these beautiful lines before shutting my eyes and listened to the sounds of nature — the birds chirping, the dogs barking, the water sprinkling . . . Everything is perfect. What have I been afraid of? The world is mine and everything in it.

And I dozed off dreaming before waking up to the slurpy tongue of Caesar all over my face. Yuck — get out of here, you dog, I shouted at him while he continued licking away.

That moment, **I experienced unconditional love.**

The next day, I woke up more energised and upbeat than I had felt in the longest time and when I heard myself singing in the shower, I knew I was on the right track. I also realised why I was feeling so happy. **Because I was alive**. Alive to sing, to learn, to love and to swim. Oh thank you, God.

'You need to swim faster, not harder, girl!' Uncle shouted when I finished my length. 'Don't lift your head that much to breathe as you lose balance, and you don't need to kick harder. Don't waste energy. OK? Now, another length. Come on – go!'

Oh God, this guy will kill me, I thought to myself as I went for another length, my fiftieth of the day.

'Great, Megha, you did well today. But before you go home, repeat those rules to me again,' Uncle commanded.

'Yes, Uncle. First, stay as horizontal in water as possible. Second, swim taller, use your recovery arm more efficiently, and lastly, don't break the water with your kick,' I sighed.

'Good girl. Tomorrow we concentrate on two areas – high elbow catch and developing your core muscles. Good night, pay my regards to Aunty,' said Uncle.

When I reached home, my Nani had a surprise waiting for me!

'Mama!' I cried, as I went running into her arms! As we hugged, I couldn't help feeling how much I had been missing her.

'Oh, I am so happy you came, Mama! You know I am having so much fun here. Nani treats me with *chaat-papdi* every day. And the Milk Badaam – you must try it, Mama, it's yummy!' I spoke excitedly.

'Oh, Megha, I have had my share of *chaats* and Milk Badaams and I am not a swimmer like you to be able to burn it all! How is it going, my child – I mean, your swimming?' Mama asked.

'Oh, I am doing well, Mama, Coach Uncle is so proud of me!' I exclaimed happily.

'What a relief, Megha . . . so, do you agree with me that sending you to your Nani was a good idea?' Mama asked.

'Of course, Mama, mothers are never wrong.' I kissed her bewildered face before we both burst out laughing. Just like old times.

But just like old times, Mama had to leave the next day. I felt cheated that she didn't even stay for the whole weekend, but she was travelling out of the country, had important meetings to attend. As usual. But I tried not to harbour any negativity about my own mom. I tried but couldn't help feeling it.

I guess I had a long way to go before becoming a saint like my Nani.

'Yes, darling, you know I do . . . Really? Oh, that would be a pity if you can't make it next month. But do not forget the date, OK? It's my birthday . . . I can't believe you forgot, sweetheart . . . bye . . . love you too.'

Nani was coochie-cooing on the phone with God knows who! I couldn't believe that at her age, this lady who gave me lectures on morals and principles, had a boyfriend! What hurt more was that I didn't.

'Oh, hi, Megha, I didn't know you were standing here . . . what happened? Why do you look so irritated?' Nani asked.

'Nothing, Nani. I heard your conversation with your . . . sweetheart,' I replied and felt my cheeks burning red.

'Oh that!' she giggled. 'Yes, he is an old friend – actually more, much more.'

I couldn't believe Nani was behaving like a silly school girl but I felt extremely let down. So I just went into my room and did what an actual school girl does in these kinds of situations. Net Surfing. After a while, she entered.

Nani: What happened, beta?

Me: You know, Nani, I cannot believe that you have a boyfriend.

Nani: Why, I am single and ready to mingle, why not?

Me: You are old, Nani, isn't that reason enough?

Nani: Ouch, that hurt! But seriously, I am perhaps younger than you are, Megha – remember you are as old as you think. And what is it that is troubling you? That I seem happy in my relationship?

Megha: No, Nani, I am sorry . . . It just seems weird! I mean I had an image of you – the pure, wise Nani who does yoga, meditation and social work and all . . .

Nani: Oh the burden of expectations! Megha, I guess it's time for the next rule – which is:

11. Everyone deserves a second chance

Nani: Honestly, I don't need to give any explanations to you but I still want to say one thing. Everyone deserves a second chance to happiness. Just like a failure — you deserve to get back into the game, the same way I have a right to fall in love, doesn't matter how old I am. I don't want to elaborate as it's very personal but I am telling you this as you might have to face it yet another time in your life. With your mother. She is single now Megha, your dad is not in her life anymore. Sooner or later, she might seek happiness in another relationship. Accept it, rather, encourage her to move on, if that makes her happy.

Me: Nani, I can't even imagine Mama with anyone else than Papa but I will remember what you said to me even though it hurts like crazy. You know I can never get over their divorce. It's the worst thing that ever happened to me. Why couldn't they live happily ever after nani?

Nani: Which brings to our next rule –

12. Happily-ever-after does not mean together

Nani: Megha, I understand that you think that you will never get over their divorce. You have gone through tremendous amounts of anxiety, anger, shock and disbelief. But trust me, these reactions will ease off on their own and completely disappear. I am saying that after a lot of research and my own experience. People are meant to be resilient, especially children – we don't give them enough credit. So much so that often parents remain in extremely unhappy and emotionally traumatic marriages, just to protect their kids from being scarred for life. But it doesn't happen. Most kids cope well in the long term. You will too. Your parents tried for the longest time possible to make it work but what could they do, they had lost it.

Me::   What did they lose, Nani? Love, respect, admiration?

Nani :   A bit of all those but they also lost the most important thing that keeps the marriage going. They stopped being friends. In other words, they started judging each other, they stopped laughing together and they stopped being interested in what the other was doing. I don't know the details, but from what I can see, that's what happened between them. They lost that friendship.

Me :   Yes, Nani, I agree with you. But I still pray every day that they get back together. At least for my sake . . . just see how much I have been hurt.

Nani: Megha, accept it that it will never happen. They don't have to be together to live happily ever after. If you really want to pray for your parents, pray that they find their lost happiness – without each other. And about how much you have been hurt, it leads to our next rule. Take note:

13. Scarred tissue is stronger than regular tissue

Nani: You go to the gym, right, Megha? Do you know what bodybuilders do? They damage their tissue. So that it repairs and rebuilds itself. And in the process becomes stronger to bear even more weight. Philosophically speaking – what wounds you can also wake you up. That's what happens when we get vaccinated. Our immune system gets activated to fight the virus more efficiently and protect you in the next attack. I know it would be absurd to even ask you to welcome the pain, but trust this wise old lady's words when I say this, child: Christ gives you a cross you can carry. You can deal with this pain because you are strong enough.

Me: Oh no, Nani, it was awful. So much happened to me . . . how can you expect me to be strong?

Nani: Oh, my poor baby, but now is the perfect time to bring up our next rule:

14. Stop playing the victim

Nani: A famous writer once said, 'there has been much tragedy in my life; at least half of it actually happened.' All right, you are a victim. People did horrible things to you and you fell into terrible circumstances. It won't help you to keep whining and narrating your sad story. Stop blaming others, Megha, and take responsibility of your own happiness. Sorry to be blunt, but you need to stop getting addictive to your past, don't build your present around it.

On the way to the pool, I thought about it. Yes, I had made this pain, my identity. It made me feel sick about myself. And I made a promise in my heart.

Meanwhile, mercury was soaring in Ambala After few days of temporary relief, heat wave was back as maximum temperature was sizzling at 46 degrees and there were no signs of the rains. All the more reason to be in the pool, I said to myself.

Yes, I was becoming positive again.

Like Dory said in *Finding Nemo*, my favourite film as a child — *When life gets you down, wanna know what you gotta do —*

keep swimming!

So here we are again, at the swimming pool:

'Hello, young lady, so today we talk about the "Hourglass Pull" – you know about it, right?' Uncle said.

'Yes, I know – it means when pulling both arms together

simultaneously, the path should look like an hourglass,' I replied; maybe he forgot that I went up to the Nationals.

'OK, but you have to work on it. Even the most experienced swimmers don't do it perfectly. Since the shortest distance between two points is a straight line, don't pull your arm through the water in a straight line as you want to maximise the amount of water pulled. Practise an S shape because that's the longer way to complete a stroke. Don't shorten your stroke, you lose efficiency as you will end up taking more strokes per lap. All right, young lady? See how I do it.'

As I watched his body gliding through the water seamlessly, I couldn't help feeling a pang of nervousness. It was almost June-end and the State Levels were due in a month. Was I ready for that fight? Was I even ready to face school? With Tara and Dolly not there, it would never be the same again. I was missing my friends a bit too much but things were really strained between us. And Nani had advised me to not sort it out on WhatsApp. Just a couple of weeks and I would be back in Gurgaon again. Same old school. Same old boring exams . . . *Oh, how could I forget – what about Dubai? Mama hadn't mentioned it either* Anyway, all that could wait as I still had a few more laps before calling it a day. *And how do I stop my mind from running in all directions? Why can't I just concentrate?*

Back home, as usual Nani had the solution.

Nani: It calms you down, Megha.

Me: I knew you were going to start this, Nani – but I've tried all this. Honestly, it didn't work for me. And you know I met Sandy during these stupid meditation classes.

Nani: What didn't work once does not mean will not work ever. Everything worth its while comes with practice. And meditation is no different. Remember, you promised to keep an open mind about it. And for the time being, can you forget about Sandy?

Me: No Nani, I can't. If it was a regular relationship, I, would have. How can you forget that I got beaten by him?

Nani: OK, let's forget about meditation. Tell me more about Sandy. How did you get attracted to him? How did you really feel? Do you still like him?

Me: What are you saying, Nani?!! That jerk, he beat me up! I hate him! Actually, I want to kill him. But you know what hurt me more?

Nani: Go on, beta . . .

Me: What hurt me more is that the grown-ups didn't do anything about it. All he got was a few hours in jail and that too unofficially. And Mama asked me to never talk about this to anyone. Can you believe it, my own so-called new-age parents? We never discussed this! Mama advised me to vent this anger out in the pool. And look what it did – I lost the competition.

Nani: OK, let's go over it again. There are two issues. One – he beat you but did not get the punishment he deserved. And two – your family never talked to you about it. Right?

Me: Yes, Nani. What kind of an example is Mama setting for me? Then you tell me to forgive her and I am sure you are even going to tell me to forgive that son of a bitch!

Nani: Yes, I will ask you to forgive him. Only because it will give you peace. Along with that, you will make a promise to yourself to never get into an abusive relationship again. Stop it the very first time anyone raises his hand on you. About your mama, I am sorry about it. I admit that it wasn't a good idea – not talking about it. You guys should have . . . but why didn't you call me?

Me: Nani, Mama told me that you cannot be with us – you have this house and your dogs and cats and a pretty active social life!

Nani: Really? I told you last time too, Tara, your mama didn't want me to come even when I offered several times. She said she could handle it.

Me: Yes, you told me, Nani, but still, why did you listen to her? You are her mother – **you should have taken a stand there**. You know about your daughter's ego much better than I do! Couldn't you have known we needed you? How selfish could you be!

Nani: I need time, Megha . . . leave me alone . . . I need to sort it out in my head first before I can explain it to you.

'To hell with everyone!' I called out as I went to my cell phone. And why should I have to listen to them – no Facebook, no Instagram, no Snapchat, no YouTube, no life! Why can't these grown-ups just leave us alone?

The next day, Nani didn't speak to me much. Maybe she was guilty. But I knew her just too well to think that she would admit making a mistake. After all she was my mother's mother, no less! But I was wrong as

15. Nobody can be right and wise all the time, even the oldies.

Nani: You know, child, even though I am decades older, I have learnt a very important lesson from you and that is being older does not mean being wiser – atleast not about everything. Especially about relationships. Because as we get older, we get more rigid and stop learning from our mistakes. Only because we think we are beyond making mistakes. But no one is. We all do keep making them. I am sorry, Megha my dear, that I did not provide the much-needed support to your family when it was breaking up. I actually gave more credit to my daughter than I should have, Megha, as no matter how strong a person portrays himself to be, **deep down we all need love and care**. Especially the wise, old guys – they are the most vulnerable. Even I do. Just like your mother. Just like you. Just like everyone else. And that is why, Megha:

16. Be brave enough to start a difficult conversation

Nani: Divorce, break up, failures, weaknesses, low self-esteem, fears – these are all touchy topics that most of us don't want to touch. I know nothing is more awkward than talking about this stuff with your parents . . . Perhaps the fault lies with our generation that we did not teach our own children to argue, to question, to doubt and to reason out. Even though times are changing, most families stick to the safer topics like academics, schools, sports, etc. Megha, I really want you to work on it. And I will discuss this with your mother too. You guys need to start talking. Especially about the tough issues. That's how you both will help and heal each other. And the same goes for Tara and Dolly too. They are your best friends – a very important part of your life. Talk to them. Unless you don't mind letting go of them. Open up, child. Open up.

Happiness is having a conversation that matters

Me:	You have hit it, Nani, I guess I really need to open up. Do you think my anxiety attacks had something to do with not talking about my fears?
Nani:	I am so proud of you, my child – you said it. I strongly feel in my heart that when we keep

things bottled up inside us, it creates a volcano waiting to erupt. Our bodies are very smart – they explode in the form of these panic attacks so that this negative energy doesn't turn inwards and harm our organs. You will perhaps laugh when I say that tantrums or panic attacks could be a good thing as they protect us from diseases that manifest from fear. Of course, it would be impractical to welcome these episodes. But don't be ashamed of them, my child – go deep within and discover what's bothering you. Of course, as I said before, talk about it with someone you trust. Take advice. And now that you seem more open about it – let's go to the dreaded topic:

17. Practise going within – meditate, have a belief system, trust, feel and let go

Nani: We are not human beings having a spiritual experience, we are spiritual beings having a human experience. If it's too much for you, Megha, then remember – each one of us has a spiritual side, a consciousness, a power. A vital energy that tells us that we are alive. To experience this life, this love, our successes, our failures, our broken relationships – everything. And that's all it is – just an experience. It will not be so hard if you learnt to detach yourself from it. And it will happen if you learnt to connect with yourself.

Me: Oh no, Nani, don't go there – isn't it self-contradictory? What do you want me to do? Connect or detach?

Nani: You need to do both. Connect with yourself first and you will realise that you are becoming more detached with what is happening around you. It doesn't mean you stop caring anymore; it just means that it will stop bothering you so much. Like your failures, your parents' divorce – witness it, feel the sorrow, learn from it but stay objective. Because you are not in charge. **Some things are not in your control**. You should know when to let go. It can happen with practice. I will teach you, my child, but for that you need to learn to trust. Me. And the universe.

Me: OK, Nani, I trust you. But I can't promise that I will start with daily meditation and all. You know I don't have the time.

Nani: That's funny; actually, Megha, your daily twenty minutes of meditation will help you do hours of work more efficiently. But I don't want to force you. Do it and you will realise it yourself. But as I said before, the key word is trust. Keep the faith. And have a belief system.

Me: What do you mean, Nani? What is a belief system?

Nani: It is what you think about yourself, about God, about the ultimate power. About having the consciousness to take the right decisions, to do the right thing, to have the generosity to pray for others, to help them. In other words – believing that being a good human being is our ultimate tribute to the God who created us. Practise gratitude, be thankful for everything – and you will see how abundant and fulfilling your life will become.

Me: So is it not about religion?

Nani: Far from it, my child, but it is about God – that
           sacred power you turn to when things are not
           going right . . . that someone who watches over
           you – and the trust that everything will be all
           right. The courage to hang in there.

Me: But sometimes I feel so sad, Nani, so frustrated,
           ashamed and sick of everything around me . . .

Nani: Megha, it's OK to feel intense emotions. As I said,
           it's your body's defence mechanism. Vent it out.
           But be careful about one thing – don't do it for
           attention. Be very protective about expressing
           those big emotions – they are very precious.
           Don't waste your feelings at the wrong time, on
           the wrong people. But if by any chance you do,
           don't fret too much. It's still OK.

Me: So it's OK to cry, Nani? Won't it make me look
           like a loser?

Nani: Nothing will ever make you look like a loser. That's
           what I taught you earlier. Cry if it comforts you.
           Don't be hard on yourself by judging your each
           and every action. Remember – you are a human.
           And you will feel. That is why it is so important
           to meditate – to get in touch with your feelings.
           We start tomorrow, Megha, but before we call it
           a day, promise me that you will let go of all your
           inhibitions and open up yourself to the beautiful
           surprise morning will bring you.

Me: Ok, let me go over this once more:

- *Each one of us has a spiritual side*
- *You are not in charge*
- *Trust*
- *Keep the faith*
- *Gratitude*
- *Everything will be alright*
- *It's OK to feel big stuff*

As I lay down, running in my mind again the lessons Nani had been teaching me, I felt a sense of peace. Yes, everything will be alright. And I wondered what surprise morning would bring for me?

The next morning, I woke up to the sound of laughter coming from the drawing room. So the surprise was Mama, who seemed to be actually cracking a joke. Where was the other familiar sound coming from?

Coach Uncle!

Me: Mama, you didn't tell me last night that you were coming!

Mama: I wanted to surprise you, darling. And how is your coach teaching you, Megha? I hope he is not bothering you as much he bothered me in school!

Me: Oh, you guys know each other?

Coach Uncle: Oh yes, we do . . . we were in school together . . . when my dad was posted in Ambala. Remember, Seema? Army school? Batch of '90?

Mama: Can I ever, Param? You were such a brat . . . I hated you, man, actually all girls did.

Coach Uncle: All, except one . . . but she broke up with me; did you have anything to do with it?

Mama: Oh shut up! I couldn't care less.

Coach Uncle: Oh yes, you did . . . the whole school knew you liked me, that's why you plotted and poisoned her mind till she dumped me. Don't worry, I will take revenge one day, you crazy girl!

As they continued pulling each other's leg, I wondered what the hell was going on. Mama was actually enjoying the teasing and was blushing like a red tomato while I went green from extreme jealousy. How could she sound so happy with another man? Had she forgotten Papa already?

Nani looked at me and smiled, perhaps to remind me of that lesson about everyone deserving a second chance. But no, Nani, I am sorry but I am not ready for this. Unlike Mama, I still love Papa. All right, I had started to like Coach Uncle too; the time that I spent in the pool with him challenged me, pushed me to do my best and made me realise my strength and regain my lost speed. Apart from the usual swimming techniques, I learnt about grit and determination and well . . . generosity. Who would give these many valuable hours to a stranger? But he gave his time, his experience to me. Yes, I admired his personality and was in awe of his army background . . . Yes, he was everything I wanted to be. But as I said, he wasn't Papa.

That afternoon, Coach Uncle stayed back to have lunch. Nani and I looked on, she amusedly and I resentfully, at these old school friends reminiscing about the good old days of bunking classes and playing tricks on their teachers. Why didn't Nani tell me about this? When we were alone, I confronted her.

Nani: Oh, I told you he was a family friend's son. It must have skipped my mind that your mom and he went to the same school. But why are you looking so paranoid? You should be happy, actually; he told me you are ready for the big competition and he feels really proud of the progress you have made over these few weeks.

Me: It's not about me, Nani, did you really miss it? I am sorry but it looked like some serious flirting was going on between them.

Nani: Megha, he is an unmarried man so he has a right to seek friendship with a single woman. And if it leads to something, you should actually be happy about it.

Me: Nani, don't you think they are moving too fast?

Nani: Megha, be kind and do the right thing.

Me: Which is?

Nani: Keep out of it. At least for the time being. Don't ruin an old friendship that has the potential to become a beautiful relationship.

Me: I will try Nani, but I am not happy about it

Nani: Megha, you were right – **it's not about you**. Not as yet. Give it time.

Mama spent that weekend with Nani and me. The three of us bonded over nostalgia pasted in albums, which had mostly black-and-white memories of Mama's first day at school, of a six-year-old Mama on a pony in Shimla, of Nani's countless relatives enjoying picnics and weddings and holidays together . . . faded group photographs in front of the Golden Temple in Amritsar, the Taj Mahal in Agra and crumbling monuments of old Delhi . . . how simple life used to be and how happy they all looked back then. And now, it's getting just too complicated. When people look for fun and thrills in exotic destinations like Bali, Switzerland and Dubai but are still unhappy.

That reminded me, mama had not mentioned her transfer to Dubai in a long time.

Was there a change of plan?

Mama: Oh that? No, Megha we are not going . . . remember, you said that running away will not solve our problems for us?

Me: Really, Mama? Oh, I am so happy. You did it for me?

Mama: I did it for myself, Megha. Your suicide attempt was a wake-up call for me. I didn't want us both to go into unfamiliar territories with an unstable frame of mind. Now that you brought it up, child, can I say sorry to you?

Me: Mama, I am sorry. I was so stupid, so selfish! You know I love you and never wanted to leave you. Still I hurt you so much. I am too ashamed to even own up to it and say sorry. But believe me, Mama, I am. I really am sorry for doing that to you.

Mama: No, Megha, it wasn't your fault entirely. I was in denial about your situation for a long time. If only I had listened to you. If only I had not pressurised you into winning all the time. If only I had taken your panic attacks seriously. I was a horrible mother, Megha, I know. But I promise you, child, I will make up for it. I will prove it you soon.

Me: No, Mama, you don't have to prove anything. Whatever you did was out of love. I have nothing against you. I love you.

As we hugged, cried and let go, it seemed that we both were near our final steps. Towards complete healing.

The next morning, Mama left. And it was time to face the music.

Nani: It's all very simple, Megha, there are two things that you need to remember right now. One, you are just a beginner so you have to be receptive. And two, you are doing it because you trust me. I am not going to make any tall claims that you will achieve some mental or spiritual breakthrough. Nor will it lead to some intuitive understanding of the subconscious or help in hitting the next big idea. All it will do is help you relax and focus. A lot can happen and it does, but with time. Be patient and practise. That's all I can ask for, as of now.

Me: OK, Nani, go on. I am open.

Nani: Sit on the mat cross-legged and adjust your body in a comfortable position. Now close your eyes and be aware of how you are feeling. Are you anxious, restless or eager? Whatever it is, just acknowledge it. Now turn your attention to your breath. Just focus on your breath as it comes in, and release it through your nose. Just feel your breath – in . . . out . . . in . . . out. And that's all. In–out–in–out. Your mind will wander, let it, acknowledge it and bring it gently to your breath. If you start feeling something like anger, frustration, anguish – don't fight it. Stay with the feelings for a while and return to your breath. Don't resist anything. Just be. Gently come back to your breath. In–out–in–out. Now slowly open your eyes.

As I did, I felt cheated. Is that all there is to it? What about chanting, or imagining beautiful scenery or floating in the clouds and that blissful *samadhi*?

Nani: I know what you are thinking, Megha. But that's basically all for today. Just five minutes. In about a week we will increase it to ten minutes and then twenty. That's our aim. To be able to sit still for twenty minutes, shutting out the world outside and focusing on the vital energy – our flow of breath. Now is not the time to take up something challenging or to expect miracles. But with practice you will get there. Don't rush it. Till you want to do it for yourself. And not because I asked you to do it.

I laughed. So that's what I had been resisting all along? It's all very simple. Just keep breathing. Just keep living. In the end all will be OK. If it's not OK, it's not the end. Not original – but so apt. So my trip to Nani's house was working. I was feeling so much better and lighter. I knew that I wasn't there yet, but it didn't matter as long as I was on the right track. School would be starting soon and I had just about a week left in Ambala. But my lessons were not over.

Nani: Yes, Megha, you keep learning as long as you live. But sometimes you need someone to spell it out for you, to structure it, to put it into words. That's all that I am doing. I hope you know that I am not trying to be preachy.

Me: Even if you are, Nani, it's OK . . . I don't mind. I enjoy our discussions. I have the State Levels due in July. But it doesn't make me so nervous now, Nani. Even if I fail, it's fine.

Nani: You don't say that before you start to race, Megha. Before you misunderstand, I believe it's time for a few more rules:

18. Take it easy, but take it

Nani: Basically, these words by the famous singer and song writer Woody Guthrie mean that you don't get stressed out or nervous or worked up about what life throws at you. It's great to take it easy and relax before a big event but you still have to face it. So, if you have to take it, take it with your full enthusiasm, your full strength, knowing that you have worked hard for it, believing that you can. Loosen up your arms, spread them wide and take it head-on.

19. Be your best version but be yourself

Nani:

It is the concept of **Swadharma.** If you don't know it, Megha, then please look it up. In the Indian tradition, *dharma* means an essential way of being, which is individual and personal. It is not destiny but a set of capabilities that allows us to take our place in the world. Our ultimate, sacred duty is to realise and fully develop those unique capabilities that each one of us is born with. **That is *Swadharma.***

However, fully developing those capabilities or achieving the best that one can be is really hard. Because human potential has boundless possibilities. There is no end to it – you don't know what really to strive for. So set your own standards, be your own judge, scale your own heights and keep raising the bar. Don't get stressed out about competition. You don't have to defeat others to be a winner. You don't have to be better than others. You have to be better than what you were yesterday. There is only one you – celebrate that uniqueness and never aim to be someone else. Pursue personal excellence and create your own best version.

20. Thoughts have life

Nani:

You can never create your best version if you constantly pull yourself down. Don't fret or underestimate yourself. Recognise when you find you are getting into a pattern of negative thinking and remind yourself constantly not to go there. Thoughts are living, they have physical energy; they can even change the world. And your thoughts belong to no one but you, so only you are responsible for what goes on in your mind. Be protective about your mind, guard it ferociously and don't let any negative thought enter it. **Be positive**.

While being positive means that you are positive and hopeful that all *will be* all right, Megha, it also means you still feel positive about your *present* circumstances. If they are good – it's great. If they are hard – even better. You will learn from those hardships, child, and get stronger. Being positive means being positive always – see the good in everything – in people, in situations – everywhere you go. It means not being cynical and having a fault-finding attitude – you are no one to judge others. Even then if a negative or pessimistic thought enters your mind – it will be unrealistic to say that it won't – don't let it stay longer than necessary. Remember, Megha, it's your mind – only you have the control so it better listen to you!

21. Unfulfilled passion turns to pain

Nani: Being passionate, being ambitious is great! You already have it in you – all you need to do is realise that potential. Don't let the fire die, child. Keep it burning and keep going. Remember, when you grow older, if for some reason you did not fuel that fire or you wasted that passion – it will turn into pain. You don't want that, do you? So give a good fight for the sake of your passion, if you have to. So don't let the universe down by not justifying that gift or talent or capability or skill – whatever you want to call it. Or it will be very sad indeed.

22. Keep the balance

Nani: There will be days when you do fifty laps and there will be days when you refuse to get out of the bed. There will be days when you tidy up the whole damn house and there will be days when your room will be the messiest in the world. There will be days when you will want to hang out with your friends and there will be days you will want to be left alone. There will be days when you would want to rule the world and there will be days when you couldn't care less.

Now, you will know how far you can go in being an achiever or get away being a slob. It will be your responsibility to keep the balance. Know yourself and keep yourself sane. Don't be extreme in anything but remember, it's not fifty-fifty. You CANNOT swim and laze around in equal measure. You cannot have proteins and fats in equal measure. That's not balance – that's stupidity. Balancing is all about prioritising. Those little sins of watching a useless soap or having junk food – it's all good so long as you don't go overboard. For each one of us – we have to know when and where to stop. In your case, Megha, since you want to win the Nationals, you have to be even more careful about striking that balance. For kids who are aiming for academic excellence – they need to know exactly when their little breaks end. In other words, whatever you do, don't lose focus on what you really want to achieve.

Me: I understand Nani . . . that is why you have stopped taking me out for Milk *Badaams* these days . . .

Nani: Yes, darling, this is a very small price you pay for what you want to achieve. You know these wonder girls of India who won medals in the Rio Olympics recently. Read about them and you will realise the sacrifices they made, the hardships they went through to make it to their goals. Or just watch *Dangal*. Life is not easy, Megha, and really wanting something – it's a great responsibility. You know that already, don't you?

Me: Yes Nani, about wanting something . . .

Nani: What is it, Megha?

Me: Last year, my school introduced Army Camps. Kind of like military training in order to get the kids to be more physically active and mentally alert. This was something I had major hang ups about initially but over a period of time, I really wanted to participate wholeheartedly. You know my fascination for the army, its values, its practices . . . the uniform . . . but Mama didn't let me . . . I don't blame her as I really did not have the time.

Nani: That's a shame, Megha. You should have. Don't worry, if the school is still doing it this year, go for it.

Me: Mama won't agree, Nani, I did really badly in the Boards too. The only reason that I am still in school studying science is because of my sports record; otherwise I would have been chucked out a long time back. Now I need to do well in studies, Nani, I have really let everyone down. Army training and all can wait.

Nani: You don't have to be a topper in everything, child. That's what striking a balance is all about. Now let's do an exercise. Close your eyes and think about what are the times when you felt amazing, energetic, alive.

Me: I don't need to, Nani – I feel alive when I swim. And I felt alive during those military exercises – specially the physical tasks.

Nani: I am so excited, Megha, we might have hit upon something important!

Me: I don't get it, Nani . . .

Nani: Tell me, Megha, what do you want to do in life? Let me rephrase, what do you want to do professionally?

Me: Mama has it all chalked out for me. I will be studying engineering and then MBA. Just like them all!

Nani: And swimming?

Me: Oh, Mama is very particular about it as she wants a powerful CV when I apply at international business schools. A National win will surely help. That's why I am in the school football team also, have learnt a bit of karate, can speak French, play the piano – you know, she wants to create credentials for me. But she is not going to let me do the army camp as surely my studies will suffer; you know – academic score carries huge weightage too.

Nani From where I see it – I see you joining the Indian Army, or maybe IPS – a physically and mentally demanding job, that will not only bring you status and respect in society, but which will actually help you in achieving the greatest heights in professional swimming too. Google it – Lt. Col. Rajyavardhan Singh Rathore, a veteran shooter who rose to fame after winning the Silver Medal in the Olympics at Athens. Think about it, Megha, the army could be your best bet. I will speak to your mom. And I am with you on this.

Me: Oh Nani, what are you saying? Is it even possible? Can I join the army? Look, I am getting goosebumps . . . but wait – what if it doesn't work?

Nani: If at any point, in your career, your personal life, you feel it's not working, remember the next rule:

23. You have a right to change your mind

Nani: It means that even if you think right now that you have found your calling, you can still change your mind later. It doesn't mean you are fickle-minded or indecisive. All it means is that you have to be open to the opportunities life brings you. There are many such great people who changed their careers in their forties and even later. Keep seeking, without being a rolling stone either, Megha..

Me: I get it, Nani, it's all about finding the balance. And staying dedicated to your goals, while being flexible.

Nani: Yes, child, that's something a lot of us don't realise. Your profession is not set in concrete. Be sincere to it but it is not you. Give your best and hope for the best. If it still doesn't work for you – look for something else.

Me: What if I don't know what I want, Nani?

Nani: That's also OK. At fifteen or sixteen it's absolutely OK to not know. You will figure it out eventually. But you should at least know what you don't want to do, right?

Me: Yes, Nani, I am not an engineer-MBA type of a person. I am not Mama. I am a sports girl; I like to move and sweat it out in the field. Attending seminars in air-conditioned offices is just not my scene.

Nani: I get it, child . . . but don't disparage her, she works hard too. Anyway, I will discuss this with your mom. Remember – trust that everything will be all right.

Me: I hope so, Nani. In a couple of days, I will be back in Gurgaon. And school will start. Mama and I will get back to our same old routine. But . . .

Nani: Yes, child?

Me: Tara and Dolly will not be there. Oh, how can it still hurt so much? I really miss my friends. They both joined other schools as they did not want to study Science or Commerce and my so-called elitist school did not offer Humanities.

Nani: But they still live in your society, right?

Me: Yes, thank god for that, Nani. But we are all drifting apart. I want to start all over again with them but things have got too complicated.

Nani: That brings us to our next rule:

24. Some friendships are so worth it – don't let go of them

Nani: It's easy to be a friend but it's not easy being a true friend. No blood relation, no legal contract – just an understanding, an unsaid promise to be there for each other. If you find such a person who is loyal, straight, honest and loving – never let go of them. Our childhood friends are perhaps our best friends and now you have to do everything in your power to protect these friendships. Work on it. Get back to them. Start having fun again. Tell them you love them and say sorry if you have to. If they feel the same, they will come back. If they don't – try again and again until they do, as having true friends is the most wonderful gift. And so, so rare.

I am not talking about the social media friends – you can be lonely even with a thousand of those friends. I read somewhere: being popular on Facebook is like being rich in a game of Monopoly – it's not real. For the young generation like you, recognising the blurred lines can be tough as you haven't really seen what true friendship was before the Internet and all came in. I am not asking you to dump it altogether – you can still find friends there – but know who will really stay true to you. Tara and Dolly will. So get them back into your life. Before it's too late, child. And remind yourself – what Dolly's brother did, does not make Dolly a bad person. And if Tara is getting popular – it doesn't make you a smaller person either.

Oh God, why didn't I think of it before?

I didn't know how the next few days whizzed past as suddenly it was my last night at Nani's house. Lying in bed, I hoped and prayed to achieve the following goals:

- *Settling down in school*
- *Getting reunited with my best friends*
- *Joining the Army Camp*
- *My marks improving, and most important,*
- *Winning States and then of course – the Nationals!*

I guess I was ambitious like Mama, but in my own way. The next morning, when she came to pick me up, I knew that I was reaching the culmination of my stay with Nani – of the most important rules I learnt about in the last few weeks. I felt an enormous sense of gratitude to Mama, who had sent me here, and for once I knew that she had done the right thing. I had learnt so much about life, about my inner feelings and had accepted my history while walking out of it into my present. I had met my swimming teacher, who had filled a void that I didn't know I had, but I was still not courageous enough to accept it as it wasn't easy admitting that Papa too had not given me enough of his time. I had started liking him a lot and would not mind if Mama and he got together. But I felt guilty to even dream of such a possibility as I didn't want to be unfair to Papa either. Yes, Papa was gone but I guarded the time spent with him possessively. Because in my heart I knew, that even when he had promised that he would be a very regular and integral part of my life, things would never be the same again. I needed to move on. We all did.

But now, it was time to go . . .

As we stood at the gate to Nani's house, I felt warm tears streaming down my cheeks, which was kind of embarrassing. I didn't know I was so damn emotional. And I didn't know that I loved my grandma so much. Oh, thank God for family. As we bid tearful goodbyes, I looked at Nani for my final rule. I knew it was not over. Smiling, she looked at Mama to complete it for her.

Mama: So, Megha, are you ready for it?

Mama smiled and gave me the final rule:

25. The only golden rule is that there are no golden rules

Mama: I know what you are thinking, but hear me out. Basically, it means that the rules are not engraved in stone. Take what works for you and leave the rest. They are guiding principles to make your life simpler, more fulfilling and productive. Trust these rules, do them, they work. And with practice, everything will come instinctively and you will become a natural rule-follower. But if at any point of time you feel it's not practical to follow a certain rule – don't. Let only your conscience guide you at all times and that's the secret of attaining a happier kind of life. A life that you deserve to live. A life that each one of us deserves to live.

She smiled again and hugged me.

Me: Oh Mama, you summed it all for me. Thank you, Nani, for giving us both this clarity of thought. I hope I can live up to your expectations.

Nani: Don't be so formal, Megha, and loosen up. You don't have to prove anything to me. Be yourself. And take care of my daughter. Bye-bye, darling.

Me: One more thing, Nani, can you thank Coach Uncle on my behalf – he was amazing with me and I learnt so much . . . I wish I had told him how grateful I always will be for his time . . .

Nani: This is not the end of it. Megha. Call him – he will be delighted to hear from you . . . So long, girls . . . stay happy!

But before we begin Part 3, let's do the quickest recap possible:

Part 3
The comeback . . .

Screw it, let's do it.

– Sir Richard Branson,
founder of the virgin group of business

If this was an enchanting tale of self-discovery through the roads of India, I would have given you at least a paragraph or two about the gratifying and scrumptious chicken curry that spiced up our souls, which we had at a highway *dhaba,* of the sentimental old film songs we listened to, which took us down memory lane, of the intimacy Mama and I were slowly developing through unsaid words . . . but I will skip all that as first, I don't have what it takes to be fake and second, I want to get back to the real story, which is:

Back to school

The vacations were over and all of us geared up for the big day. As I packed my bag the night before, the familiar nervous feeling returned. What was going to happen? Would I be able to make new friends? I had not touched my books at all during the last few weeks, would I be able to get back to studies easily? Does my school know about my suicide attempt? Is it supposed to be a secret just like the Sandy episode? What should I do if anyone asked?

Just then Mama came over to check if everything was all right and looking at me she knew that it wasn't.

Mama:	What happened, Megha, you look worried?
Me:	Oh no, Mama, I was just packing my stuff . . . I was wondering if you told the school about the suicide . . . Did you?
Mama:	I didn't, Megha, but I have a feeling that people would know, it's a small world after all.
Me:	Oh God, it's so embarrassing . . . what if someone asks, Mama?
Mama:	I don't think anyone will, Megha, but even if

someone does – you have to own up to it. It's not a stigma. Just acknowledge it and politely say it's behind you and you have moved on. Don't be ashamed of it, child; at the same time you don't have to give any explanations, either. If you want to talk about it, find a trusted friend. Like Tara or Dolly.

Me: Yes, I guess I might want to talk about it with a friend. But not now. First I need to get started with the school stuff, then it's the States and tuitions, homework. I have my hands full, Mama and I really have to make up for lost time.

Mama: I agree – there is a time for everything. Talk when you are ready. Remember, I will be listening whenever you need it, too.

Yes, things were changing between Mama and me. Even though she was busier than ever before with her office, she was more present when I was around. At first it seemed kind of awkward, as I wasn't used to the attention. Like she would quickly put her cell phone down if I came over to talk. I wasn't able to figure out what was really going on in her mind. But she was so attentive to me that it almost seemed artificial. I wondered if I'd asked for it.

My first week at school went . . . well. The usual. Same old morning assemblies, Maths, Physics, Chemistry, Sports, Intervals, a bit of politics in the School Council – nothing extraordinary happened. Actually, something did, so I need to put it down too.

I made friends with two of the weirdest girls in my school.

Now that I had become more down-to-earth, rather now that I wasn't the star student anymore, I was approached by these girls:

Gayatri and Ragini

They are both in Tara's book but most people wouldn't remember – two crazy, rebellious, misfit *chuddy-buddies* who had not grown since Class VI! These petite girls talked different, walked different and looked different. Gayatri is an aspiring poet who uses words from a dictionary printed in another world. Nobody understands what she is trying to say or where her thoughts come from. And Ragini – don't even ask – is a feminist, NGO, social worker type who wants to start a revolution one day. But both seemed extremely confused about their causes and were often the subject of mindless gossiping by the other so-called 'normal' girls, including me. I didn't ever want to be seen with them but now that my options were limited, I had to . . . open up, as Nani would say.

And it turned out to be a wise move. As I was really, really lonely. You know the feeling, right? When you don't have company during lunch breaks and you have to eat your tiffin all by yourself? I didn't want to be that pathetic person who sits in a corner all alone during free periods. I wanted friends, like before, and all right, I had lowered my standards but who knows, they could fill in the gap until someone better came along . . . be positive, Megha, be positive – about your present, people – see the good in others, don't judge, I reminded myself.

And guess what? I actually started enjoying those weirdos

Honestly, the fact they let me in their little group made me relax about school. I don't know what triggered it but the three of us started hanging out together during lunch breaks, though often I used to wonder what were they still doing in this school, studying science. It seems those rebellious, abnormal girls had very 'normal' parents who did not let them decide. I think that it was a good thing, in these particular cases – they both had no idea what they wanted from life.

Anyway, the fact is that they were so different that they were cool. They always got into trouble over discipline and loved giving lectures about social issues to anyone who cared to listen. Kids listened so that they could have their share of fun later on. I thought maybe having me in their group would get them some respect from other girls but I guess I was wrong. I probably lost mine too. But it was still a small price to pay for the experience I was getting, as just being with them – discussing matters of national importance, about education, development, demonetisation and all – was really new but fascinating. It was too soon to say if they were just a 'time pass' or if it would lead to something special, but for now – I was relieved. Actually, happy. With girls who didn't care about marks or competition, fashion or boys. Yes, I liked them. A lot.

Settling down in school – done !

Now that school was settled – it was time to move to my next point in my list of goals to achieve

Yes, some friendships are so worth it and I had realised it. And some things need to be faced head on – I wasn't going to use a chat application to solve this. I needed to talk to her directly, to tell her about the hell I went through without her by my side and to apologise for misunderstanding her, for being jealous of her success, for being such a lousy friend. Tara, ready or not – here I come.

Her mama welcomed me with open arms and sounded so excited to see me after so many days. Tara seemed as if she was expecting me and I felt kind of disappointed by her usual poker face. *Come on, girl – it's me, Megha, your best friend*. But anyway, we settled down on her bed, we both looked at each other and we started laughing. We laughed and laughed till we hugged each other and cried. How can some people be so nice, so good, so . . . pure, for the lack of better words?

Me: Oh, Tara, you don't know how much I have missed you, yaar . . . do you know about it?

Tara: I know, but I still want to know – why, Megha? You have everything. You are good-looking, a sports champion, popular, your parents love you, your friends love you . . . so why did you attempt suicide? It's crazy !!

Me: It's a long story, Tara, do you really want to know? It's kind of complicated . . . sad, too . . .

Tara: Yes, Megha, I will always want to know – whatever you do, whatever you think, whatever that goes on in your life – good or bad. I want to know and I have every right to know. I am your best friend forever, remember . . . I came over to your house when I heard about the suicide attempt but your mama told me you were visiting your nani. Aunty also said that you will come yourself to meet me and settle all our differences. That I shouldn't contact you on the phone as we needed to talk it out personally. I have been waiting for you all this while, Megha, and I am so happy you finally came. And I'm so excited!

Me: Excited as hell! You liar, I am sure you have made many 'arty' type of friends in your new school!

As we continued joking and pulling each other's leg, I wondered how I could have taken this friendship for granted for so long. Even now I had not said sorry properly to this crazy girl who was always there for me. And always will be. Is that why? Because she seemed a bit too available? Tough question and I didn't have the answer. Do you?

***My best friend** – she is fat, I am thin*

She is funny, I am, well . . . not really

She is complicated and I am even more

She is weird and I am getting there too

But I know I will get through anything that may be

Because no matter what, she will stand by me

When I came home there was another surprise waiting for me . . . but no so pleasant actually

It was Papa! I hadn't seen him for the last two months or so. Mama told me that his office had sent him for a project to

London and there was a big possibility of him moving out of the country permanently. I had been in denial as I had so many other things to deal with, myself. But now, I really wanted to know. *Come on Papa, come out with the truth, I can handle it.*

Papa: So, how have you been, baby? Come sit with me child, I have missed you so much.

Me: Oh, I have missed you, Papa, you haven't really been around, have you?

Papa: Oh, I am sorry, Megha, I was travelling and all . . . but now I am back. I promise to see you every weekend, just as we decided.

Me: You don't have to, Papa, if you don't want to . . .

Mama: Megha, please control your self.

Papa: No, it's OK, child . . . I am guilty as charged. But I have some news for you . . . have you told her, Seema?

Mama: No, but please go ahead.

Me: I know you are leaving, Papa. What's the big deal; actually, you have already left.

Papa: Oh no, Megha, I am not going anywhere. I am just getting married.

Was he for real?

Now this was something that I had never dreamed of – my own father telling me that he is becoming a goddamn groom in his middle age! Even though I knew about that Anuradha woman, it never crossed my mind that he could think of starting another family. I spaced out for a long time before I caught Papa looking at me expectantly. Almost excitedly.

Me: What do you want me to say? Well . . . congratulations – may you have the most rotten life ever!

Papa: I didn't expect this from you, Megha . . . Seema, I thought she had gone to your mother's house to learn something . . . and this is what she has turned out to be? How can you be so rude, Megha? I am your father! And I always will be!

Me: Prove it to me, Dad. And about what I have learnt – Nani taught me to forgive my parents. But I don't think I can. After what you have done to us. Couldn't you have waited?

Papa: I will have no more of this from you. Excuse me, but I am leaving right now.

Me: Finish it off, Papa, don't run away. Explain yourself. Why couldn't you have waited?

Papa: End of conversation, Megha. Here is the invitation card. I will be happy if you ladies came. Good night.

As he banged the door behind him, I looked, flabbergasted, at the invitation card. Oh God, couldn't he have chosen a better day? It was the exact date of my State swimming competition! I couldn't believe it, how could he be so desperate to get married, it hadn't even been a year since the divorce! How could he have become so indifferent to how we felt? I looked at Mama for answers but she had none. And honestly, she was the one who seemed indifferent to the whole situation. As if it stopped mattering to her what her ex-husband was up to. Or she seriously couldn't care less. Then who was I, to be getting so pissed off about it? To hell with them all! These unfeeling grown-ups. As I had my own worries – my big event – the States was due in less than two weeks . . .

. . . and I wasn't going to let a stupid wedding ruin it for me!

Now I had had enough practice in Ambala to know that there was nothing stopping me this time. In my mind, I was a winner already. What was amazing was that I actually tried feeling nervous by thinking about the Nationals defeat, but still wasn't able to feel anything. All I felt was so, so damn ready.

The big day arrived and I woke up with the sound of a message on my phone . . . from Uncle

> *Hey champ, the hard work is already done-now is just a formality. Give me the good news when it's over.*

And another one from Nani

> *All the best Megha, I am praying for your victory. Go for gold, my DHAAKAD Girl !!*

And another one from Tara

> *You will do it, but don't forget to celebrate with me !*

And another one from Dolly

> *M, I wanna let u know that I am thinking about you. Good luck, I love you.*

And another one from Papa

> *It's a big day for both of us. I can't be with you but hope that you will be with me. All the best my darling daughter, God bless u*

With a load of good wishes, I had an amazing clarity. Though I hoped to win and wanted to win so badly, I also knew it won't hurt as much if I didn't. Yes, the meditation sessions were working. Thank you nani. And Megha – take it easy, but take it.

As Mama and I drove to the stadium, we did the same usual talk about speed and stuff. But it was different this time. For the first time ever, Mama did not threaten me to win! Like it was OK if I lost and honestly it was a big burden off my shoulders.

As I said, I was so, so ready

'Good morning everyone and welcome to the State Level Under-17 Girls' 50-metre Freestyle championship. We have the best swimmers from all over the state but all eyes are on Megha, who has been everyone's favourite since last year with her remarkable victory in the State level. But it's a new day and all the other girls look equally prepared and ready to go. One, two, three! (*Whistle.*) Wonderful start by all and it's too soon to say who is leading . . . but here is Megha, catching up and speeding past the rest . . . she might even break a record or two here – and yes – a final stroke and she hits the wall. A big lead over the runners up. Brilliant timings – a one-woman show, so to say. Megha Deshpande it is. Our winner!'

Oh yes, I did it – the invincible Megha!! The fastest girl in water! I am the best!! Watch it, Megha – stay humble . . . Triumph and disaster – treat them the same . . . These were my thoughts before I saw Mama running towards me to give me the tightest hug possible.

Mama: Megha, I am so proud of you. You did it my child, beautiful race! After the prize distribution ceremony, let's go shopping, then pizza for lunch, then movie and finally a celebration dinner! Even Tara and Dolly want to join in.

Megha: All that can wait, Mama; I have a wedding to attend. Are you coming?

Yes, that's what we did that evening! We went home and got dressed to attend the big show. When Mama looked at me, mystified, I reminded her of Michelle Obama's recent speech (so what if it didn't really work):

'When they go low, we go high.'

Mama: Yes, Megha, you are doing the right thing by rising to the occasion. I am going because you want to go; I guess blood is thicker than water.

Me: I am your blood more than his, Mama, if you don't want to go, we won't.

Mama: No, Megha, I know that I will never be able to get over your father, but it will help me to move on. As he moved on a long time ago, even before the divorce . . . when we were still together.

When I heard Mama's choked voice, I wondered if I was just being too brave for my own good. Keeping to the moral high ground wasn't so easy but I had to begin somewhere and what could be a better place to start than smiling through your own father's second marriage to a woman who broke up your home?

Ooff, the price you pay to be a good person.

Thank God that Papa had not gone over the top – it was a very simple affair. He made me sit by his side all the time, as if to show the small gathering of friends that I approved. Anuradha was sitting coyly like an innocent, young bride – that witch! But when I saw both stealing shy glances at each other, I understood. They both loved each other and to them that was all that mattered. And Mama, she didn't give a second look to her rival. As she had found someone else – to discuss business with, that is. She spent all her time explaining her company's new international marketing strategy to him. And there she'd been, worried about being able to move on or not! I guess she had moved on too, just like Papa, even before their divorce. She was married to her job, only she didn't want to accept it. Rather, she threw a bombshell at me the next morning.

She resigned.

Now this was something I couldn't have imagined even in my wildest dreams – it was even bigger news than Papa's hurried marriage! Did I hear right?

Mama:	Yes, Megha, aren't you happy?
Me:	What do you mean, Mama? When, where, why?
Mama:	Remember the night you got admitted in the ICU? That's when.
Me:	What are you saying, Mama, I don't get it!
Mama:	I quit that night, Megha, but the company wouldn't let go of me. They pleaded for an extended notice period – you know, with my kind of a profile, it's not easy to find the right replacement soon. So it took two months. That's why I was so busy last few days – handing over and all. In fact, today is my last day at my job. I wanted to surprise you. Aren't you super-excited, Megha, we will be together all the time!

Me: Wait, Mama, I need to digest this. But why did you quit? You don't have to feel guilty because of a stupid thing I did! It wasn't your fault!

Mama: Megha, that night when I thought I was losing you – it all made sense. It was I who had led you to the brink of death. Right then I took a sacred oath in my heart that I would make up for it if I got you back. I realised that without you, my life would be so empty, so meaningless . . . I prayed and promised to the God above me that I would be a good mother. And look, you are here – hale and hearty – a champion like before! You should be happy, Megha; we will have so much fun together – mother-daughter time.

Me: Oh Mama, you are a good mother already but are you sure? What will you do? You are not used to sitting idle . . . and I know you don't much like housework either . . .

Mama: I am going to study, Megha . . . Reiki, alternative healing practices, maybe Ayurveda . . . I might be going for some Vipasana courses too . . . but not too soon. First I want to see what it's like – doing nothing at all! You need me, Megha, and I need you. Please be happy for me.

Me: Oh, I am happy, Mama, thank you so much! This is the best surprise I ever got in my life!

So things had started working out for me. I had never even asked for this but boy, it felt good! As it is, coming home to an empty house was a shitty feeling and now I would have Mama waiting for me, to ask about my day at school, dropping me for swimming practice, for tuitions – doing everything for me.

Oh thank you, God, for this wonderful life – for my States win, for letting me show courage and dignity at Papa's wedding, for Tara, for Mama – for everything!

And, of course, for Dolly.

Let's meet up,haven't seen u in a while...
since that night....

U know how it is Dolly, I m not comfortable
coming to your house

U come over na?

Don't worry, Snady Bhaiya is not here

I wanna show u some virus

Oops videos 😃

Damn Typos 😉

Ordered triangle bikini 👙

Smoking hot!!

Ok will come over

Lemme know when

Yes will message u soon

C u 😍 💋

Yes, will wait, I 🖤 u 👍

- *getting reunited with my best friends - done*

And now it was time for me reclaim another lost love – at school

Since the State win, I was reclaiming my 'celebrity-hood', whatever it meant, in school again. The same girls who had been avoiding me before were trying to get into my good books now. Aggarwal Sir, my Maths teacher, was more patient and forgiving than ever, even if I didn't quite 'get' a Trigonometry problem. I got called by Principal Sir again to take charge of the Army Camp coordination. And Mrs Chopra tempted me with the title of Head Girl of the school next year, if I continued with the 'good work'. I was happy with the attention but realised an important lesson that perhaps Nani forgot to teach me and that is:

Everybody salutes the rising sun

And I wasn't going to be one of them. Sorry Mr Kipling, may your soul rest in peace, but I am going to use lines from your famous poem again, hoping that nobody sues me on your behalf:

> *If you can talk with crowds and keep your virtue,*
> *Or walk with Kings – nor lose the common touch,*
> *If neither foes nor loving friends can hurt you,*
> ***If all men count with you, but none too much;***
>
> . . . .
>
> *Yours is the Earth and everything that's in it,*
> *And – which is more – you'll be a Man, my son!*

Before I continue, I wonder if there is a similar poem written for daughters – like, you will be a Woman, my daughter! Or maybe I will get Mama to do it, but poetry is not her forte . . . so I could write and give her the credit. Who cares whose words they are as long as the message gets across?

Please don't read between the lines as there is nothing there, honestly, but take me seriously guys – stay grounded, wherever you are. And be nice to people who don't seem so successful to you – they could be the average kids in class or your poorer relatives or even your domestic help – be a good person. That's what my Nani always says. Even if you become super-successful yourself. And if you read this book, you will one day!! (*Nope – I am kidding, no one can guarantee that, no matter how many self-help books you mug up, and secondly, it depends on* **what you call 'success'**.)

To be honest, a lot of success and adulation is not that easy to handle, either – see what happened to Miley Cyrus? And a whole bunch of others, who have gone into major depression, taken a lethal overdose of drugs, had psychic issues or committed suicide – (and actually died, unlike me ;-)), despite or due to more fame than they could take. So I will make my own quotation and that is:

The setting sun has its own glory of beauty and peace – and that deserves your attention too . . .

So you know what I did? I stuck to my rebellious non-judgmental cool friends in school – Gayatri and Ragini – as for them it didn't matter if I was a setting sun or a rising sun. All that mattered was that **I was and always will be a star.**

Meanwhile — I needed one more tick in my goal list — you know what, right?

Before I delved into it, I needed Mama's permission, who was coping well, too. She joined the neighbourhood yoga classes and finished her level-three Reiki course and an online certification on 'Organic, Healthy Nutrition for the Whole Family'. She was reading a book a day and watched short award-winning documentaries on YouTube. Sometimes, she would bake a cake for me but it wasn't such a great idea as we had a wonderful housekeeper who cooked like those professionals on TV. Mama even let go of poor Goldie Bhaiya, our driver, and chaperoned me to the school, tuitions, swimming, and pretty much everywhere. Yeah, if you are still wondering – she did have the time to read a book a day. An overdriven, overactive, over-the-top, over-over-everything jobless woman – too much time and too little to do! Well, coming back to the Boot Camp – I thought that with her new friendship with an army guy, she wouldn't mind my joining it. Of course.

Mama:	Yes, Megha, go ahead. I like the army and everything associated with it.
Me:	Really, Mama? Think about it. The Foundations course is not a big deal but in October, I might have to join the weekend camp. And then all the way to the demanding Boot Camp during my winter and summer vacations.
Mama	Trust me, Megha, when I say this – go ahead.
Me:	Is that all? What about tuitions? What about swimming?
Mama:	Yes, what about it? Did you not think of it? You should have as you will be the one who has to balance everything. You know you need to work

on your marks. And the National Championships in November. You tell me, can you handle it all?

Me: Well . . . I . . .

Mama: You will have to, Megha. But take it from me – from now on, I will not expect you to be a topper or even win any swimming competition. If you do, I will be the happiest person around. If you don't, it's your battle. From my side, it's all OK.

Me: Oh Mama, why are you angry with me? Why are you saying you will not expect me to win? Have I let you down somewhere?

Mama: Megha, my child, I mean it. I have always been way too ambitious but I don't want to rub it on to my daughter who is . . . well, not me. You are a different person, Megha. Make your own choices. I trust you. And I am with you.

Me: Are you sure, Mama?

Mama: What do you want me to say, my child? You know a lot has changed inside me too over the last few weeks . . . Don't worry about me. Just do what makes you happy. I am happy if you are.

These so-called beautiful words by Mama were actually making me kind of nervous. She sounded too calm and composed compared to her usual self and I wasn't going to believe that it was a good thing. Yes, she was changing. Yes, she was becoming a 'good mother' as she had promised me. Yes, she was giving up control over my life – but a part of me still wanted my old mom back. Now her approval for everything I did was becoming a bit too scary. But I didn't think about it a lot as there's **'a time for everything and everything in its time'**.

And now was the time for some action – the Army Camp!

Maj. Rajput: But before any action, let's just sit and do a **Situation Reaction Test**. In this test some situations will be described to you and you will be asked to respond based on your own reasoning, common sense and presence of mind. Again – no right or wrong answers but don't play around either. Remember – it's not an IQ test.

Me: So how will we know the scores, sir?

Maj. Rajput: As I said, candidates, assessment is our job. Your job is to do the task given honestly. Now get down to work. Sixty situations – thirty minutes. All right, girls – your time starts . . . *now*.

Phew – these army guys: no-nonsense types. And Nani had it in mind to suggest that I could make a good army officer! What a joke. As when I looked at the situations, my mind went blank for a while before I started scribbling. Here is a sample:

```
1.  She went hiking with her little sister and they lost their
    way in the dark.
2.  She was going to the school but saw a dog bleeding on the
    road, of a ghastly accident.
3.  She was studying late at night and around 3 am, she saw a
    shadow entering her neighbours' house.
4.  She wants to go for a party while her parents want her to
    finish homework which will take a very long time.
5.  She went swimming with her friends on the beach but
    suddenly it starts to rain heavily and the tide is rising.
6.  She is travelling abroad alone when she notices that she
    lost her purse that had her passport, tickets and cash.
7.  She comes to know that her best friend is going around
    with her boyfriend.
8.  Her father and mother fight every day and refuse to listen
    to each other.
9.  She has committed a blunder and her mother is now
    confronting her
10. She fails an important exam despite working very hard.
```

As I wrote down the answers, I was tempted to impress Sir with my wisdom and wit but then remembered that I was supposed to apply logic and common sense and not sound hypocritical. Well, it's so difficult if you are an Indian student – a breed that doesn't let go of any opportunity to make it to their teacher's imaginary list of 'good children'. Not just teachers, but about any older person you meet. Remember the countless number of times you recited 'Ba-Ba Black Sheep' to hundreds of visiting aunties and uncles, when you had just started preschool? Exactly. Show 'em how good you are!

Coming back to the story – once we handed over our papers, Maj. Rajput came forward to discuss the next event.

Which was called – can you believe it – the **Snake Race.**

Basically, a group was made to race against other groups while carrying a rolled up tent which (supposedly) looked like a snake! And because in this case, I will have a really hard time explaining what we did, crossing over one obstacle after another, I will have to use these pictures. The bottom line is that this was the most exciting and high-energy task I had ever attempted in my life! The group coordination and bonding, the adrenalin rush, the tempo – it was all enough for me to really give army a serious thought. But of course career planning could come later; for now we had to cross these six obstacles that my school had very generously fixed in the vacant area behind the Kindergarten block, which was now used for the Camp's physical tasks.

- *Joining the Army camp – done!!*

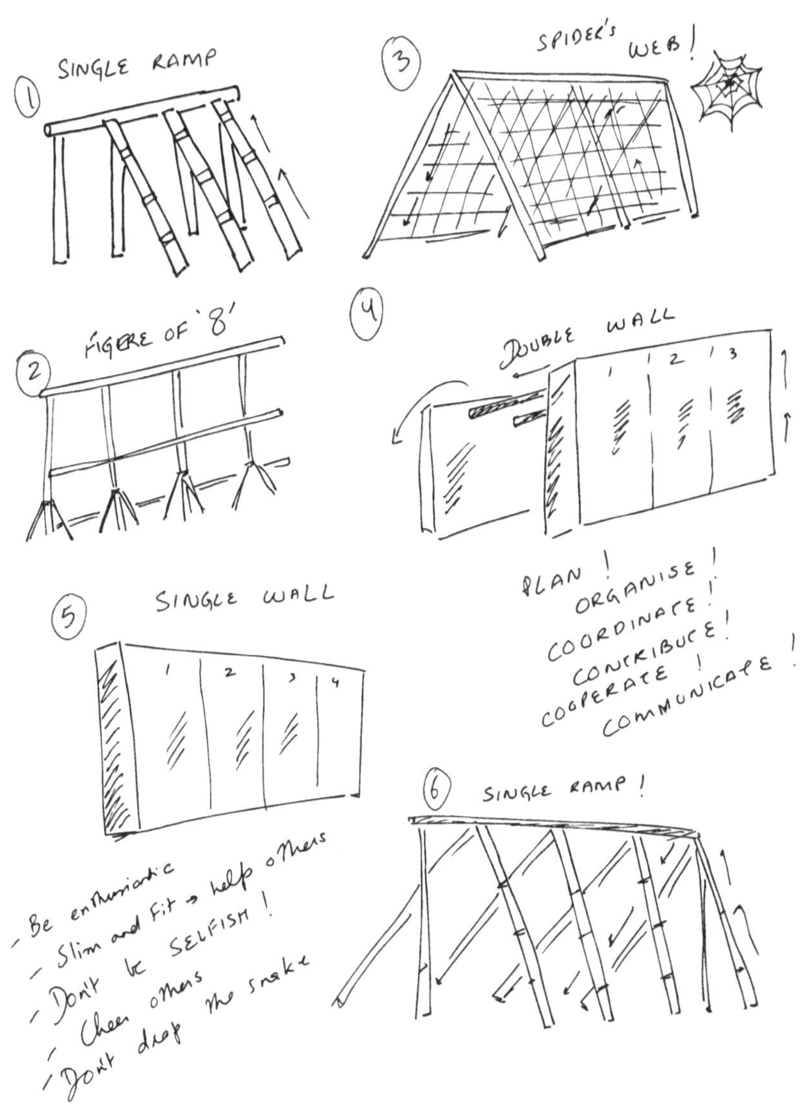

Yes, there was some more 'army' coming and you guessed it:

When Mama came to pick me up from school, there was someone else in the car too. Coach Uncle! He told me that he came over as he was missing us! Yeah, so no I-was-here-for-offical-work-so-thought-of-coming-by-to-say-hello!! Hold on, what did he say, he was missing *us?* What was going on?

Was this my imagination or were they already a couple? Why didn't Mama tell me anything? I had a right to know! So after the usual pizza and pasta, we came home and I waited for them to tell me the truth. And this time the entire truth. Yes, I have a right to be dramatic as well.

Mama: So, Megha, as you know we were together in school. I mean, we weren't going around or anything but have known each other a long time.

Uncle: Actually, you did not have feelings for me, Seema, but I did.

And a pause . . . Imagine what a fifteen-year-old can go through, looking at her so-called uptight mother blushing hotly, while playing nervously with her *dupatta*! And Uncle, his eyes were fixed on Mama . . . *Come on guys, but seriously??!!*

Mama: Yes . . . yes . . . anyway, the point is, Megha, we both like each other. We don't know as yet, but things could develop in the future.

Me: Like what Mama, you too are getting married? Like Papa, couldn't you have waited? What's with you guys?

Mama: Cool down, Megha, we are not getting married. Not as yet. Maybe never, as I have stopped believing in marriage. I cannot commit to anything to either you or Uncle. All I know is that I am in a happy relationship.

Uncle: Yes, Megha, let's see how the future unfolds. If you ask me, I do want to get married, but I don't want to rush your mom. I can wait for her for eternity . . .

Another pause . . . there should be a law against grown-ups discussing their relationships with their children. *Now what, guys? Now what?*

Mama: Basically, it means that your uncle is a part of our lives now; he will be visiting us a lot more . . . You know he loves you a lot.

Uncle: I love you both, actually . . . and I would love to have a champion for a daughter.

Me: Stop it now . . . let me process it all. Rather, come to the point.

Mama: There is no point, Megha, just a request – please accept it and feel happy for us.

At that point, when I couldn't bear those lovebirds any longer I went straight to my room and closed my door behind me. I needed to be alone. And I had to get in touch with my own feelings, as Nani would say, as I was really confused. Mama said that she would do anything to make me happy and now she was forcing me to feel happy about her new romance! I guess it was time for some hard-core meditation.

What I didn't realise then was that soon someone else would be making a re-entry too!

'What are you doing here? Dolly, you said he is in Mumbai!' I shouted at both while getting up to leave.

'Hey, wait, Megha, I need to talk to you. Here me out, girl. Have you forgotten how much we loved each other?' Sandy blocked my way.

Yes, Sandy was back.

'It was a mistake, Sandy. Now let me go, you bastard!' I shouted even louder.

'Calm down, Megha . . . Bhai wants to talk to you. Give him a few minutes, please,' Dolly pleaded.

'OK, go on, but hurry up, I don't have time for your bullshit.' I sat on Dolly's bed, waiting for him to begin.

Sandy: Megha, I don't have any explanations except that I screwed up. You were the best thing that happened to me and I hit you. Please forgive me, Megha . . . and can we ever be friends again?

Was I hearing right?

And how could Dolly be so dumb as to play along with his dirty trick! Didn't she know her own brother? And worse still, she left us alone in the room to continue our talk! If only I could stop staring at those dimples! *Control your emotions, you crazy girl!*

Megha: Perhaps I owe you an explanation, Sandy. It's actually my fault that you still have the balls to stand in front of my face, asking me to forget everything and move on as if nothing happened. The day you hit me the first time, I should have stopped you then. But that time I didn't know why I didn't. Now I do – I wanted to save this damn relationship, just because I thought we had something special going on. I loved you, dammit! But I didn't realise that some things are not worth saving. Especially a relationship with a jerk like you. You have serious issues, Sandy, with your temper and violent streak. And sorry, I am not going to be your punching bag anymore. I am done with the sob stories about your broken affairs, your never-ending struggles and countless failures. And guess what – you deserve the life you have.

Sandy: How can I apologise, to make you believe that I truly am sorry, Megha. Here let me make up for it . . .

As he got up to hug me, the blood in my veins boiled to fill me up with such a rage that I knew it was better I left. But when he actually did hug me and tried kissing me the next moment – **he asked for it**. Like always, he got what he deserved, this time too.

As I stormed out of the room, I looked back to a shaken-up Sandy and said – 'Sorry bhaiya, but we are even now.'

And sorry Nani, but a girl's got to do what a girl's got to do!! So I am not totally following your lessons on forgiveness and don't care if he had his reasons. Some guys shouldn't be forgiven. Specially who hit or hit on girls. Like this @#$%^** ?!! How could he think that there was still a chance with me?!!

Seriously, what's wrong with boys?!!

And Dolly? Yes, she could be forgiven as she was stupid but still wasn't a bad person. But I wasn't sure if we could be friends anymore. With my history with her brother, perhaps it was better that we went our separate ways. But I did not want to make up my mind about her yet and decided to go with the flow.

And concentrate on something more critical – like studies.

The Half-Yearlies were around the corner and I guess it was now time to pay some serious attention to studies. It wasn't just me – all the kids were finding this year really tough. And after my Boards debacle, I had to do something now!

Which was . . . nothing.

Don't get me wrong, it's not that I wasn't interested in doing well anymore. Actually, it was more like I felt I did not have to struggle that much. It wasn't either that I was working extra hard or was stressed out all the time about studies, but somehow, things were getting better on their own. My performance was improving; I was able to focus a lot better in class and wasn't so freaked out about my marks anymore. In my heart, I just knew that I was going to do well.

Do you know why?

Because those **panic attacks**, that anxiety, that extreme nervousness and melancholy **had long gone**.

It wasn't that I stopped caring about my results but I accepted the fact that it was impossible for me to be a swimming champion, do the Boot Camp, fulfil my duties in the school government and still continue being a topper in class. I stopped aiming for a minimum 90 in all subjects, while knowing that I would still not be far behind. It became all about prioritising and finding the balance. Yes, some people can do everything well, kudos to them, but I wasn't going to be one of them – not at the cost of losing myself.

And this chance I took with myself – it paid off

I got an average of 85 per cent

Need I say more?

My marks improve - done!!

Of course, the fact that mama wasn't constantly on my case anymore, brought a lot of relief when it came to my life. However, she herself did not look too charged up about her own life. She became irritable, lazy and slovenly, and stopped going for yoga. The 'always immaculately dressed' woman – I would find her roaming around in her wrinkled floral nighties with unkempt hair and chipped nail polish. She even started snapping for the craziest reasons – like if there was even a speck of dust on the table, if the plates were not squeaky clean, if the tea wasn't strong enough or soup wasn't hot enough or *chapattis* weren't soft enough! Our poor housekeeper – before she quit her job and I had to eat rock-hard cakes for the rest of my life, I had to take some serious steps. But Mama wouldn't listen, she cribbed about the mess in the house, about the clothes I wore, about the traffic, about the late-night news debates on TV – pretty much everything. What was wrong with her? Mid-life crisis? Menopause? I had to bring Nani into the picture right away.

So I called her.

Nani: Oh Megha, I think I know what Seema is going through. It's the same old story.

Me: What is it? She is acting kind of weird these days . . . it's almost scary . . . like it's someone else, you know?

Nani: Yes, darling. It *is* someone else.

Me: Stop it, Nani, you are freaking me out!

Nani: Don't worry. It's not such a big problem. Your mom is dealing with her breakup.

Me: Really? Do you know Nani, Coach Uncle came over and I think Mama is in a committed relationship with him. I doubt she misses Papa.

Nani: It's not your Papa, Megha, it's her job – her career – that she misses.

Me: Oh God, why didn't I see that? You are so right, Nani, it's all making sense to me, why Mama is not motivated enough to look after herself and is always in a bad mood.

Nani: Yes, Megha, she is a workaholic and extremely ambitious. But she left it all as she thought she had failed in her duty as a mother. She thought she could make it up to you by spending all her time, her energy on you. But she should have realised – she would lose her happiness, her drive in the bargain.

Me: She did it for my happiness, Nani . . . She said all she wanted was to make me happy.

Nani: Are you, Megha? You have your mom back.

Me: No, Nani, that's not my mom – that's a sad woman who seems to be giving up on life slowly . . .

Nani: Then bring her back, Megha – talk to her. She needs to get back to her job. I don't think she can take many more weeks of staying at home.

She is not the kind. She had made this mistake once before too, but I guess some people don't learn the first time around. But don't worry. Everything will be all right. I know you will make sure of it.

So was it up to me now, to fix my mama's life? Or should I focus on the Nationals first?

November had started – the festive month, when the weather starts getting cooler and there is an air of excitement around. Time for sweets, lights, crackers and Diwali. Time to celebrate. Especially for me, after my win, for sure.

I was swimming harder than ever before. This time it wasn't for Mama, or to become Head Girl of the school or for a mention in the local newspaper. It wasn't even for Coach Uncle, who believed in me so much, or Papa, who promised that he would come for the finals.

It wasn't for anyone or anything.

The big day arrived (yes, I know – the book has a lot of them, OK let me rephrase.)

The biggest day of my life arrived!! (*better?*)

And this time, the party was in Bangalore! And I would not let it be a repeat of Kolkata. I mean, this time I was going to see the city. With Mama, Nani and that crazy best friend of mine, Tara, around, I had no choice. Coach Uncle had flown in too but he stayed at a different hotel. You know, with his 'could be' mother-in-law and her snooping nature, he decided to keep some distance from us.

Papa too had flown in and for obvious reasons he stayed at a different hotel too. Nani, Tara, Coach Uncle, Mama and I – we were all one big family. Happy but not together.

Now do you want me to get into the details of the Iskcon temple (thanks to my nani), the Lalbagh Botanical Gardens, the Art of Living International Centre (yes, thanks to my nani again) and Cubbon Park, or should I skip it?

I agree with you, let's not lose focus and come to the point. As the race was about to begin:

Commentator 1:	Here we are, super Saturday for the under-17 girls 50-meter freestyle!!
Commentator 2:	Beautiful day and lovely crowd!
Commentator 1:	Yes, it keeps getting better every year. The girls have become stronger and faster over the year. Every one of them seem to be in an incredible form. I heard the defending champion, Sana from UP, has been majorly into Pilates

and lost even more weight. Can she do it this time?

Commentator 2:	Looks like she will. She is pretty competitive and her timing has only improved. But don't forget the others too – Manjeet and Shreelatha are still here. Poor Manjeet is still struggling with a shoulder injury but Sreelatha broke her own record recently… well…how about Megha? What do you think? She had a smooth State win this year
Commentator 1:	Let's hope for the best as she didn't do quite well in the last tournament in Kolkata. In this particular race, she is the underdog but look at the crowd – Megha seems to be everyone's favourite!
Commentator 2:	Here are the girls taking their stance and waiting for the whistle to blow...
Commentator 1:	Yes, all in water, good start for all... halfway through, Sana has taken the lead followed by Shreelatha... both together in sync but look – Megha swims past them and gets ahead!
Commentator 1:	Amazing race...Megha has taken a definite lead though Sana is getting closer...neck to neck – well

	orchestrated...could be anyone's race, Sana goes past, Megha struggling to catch up but one final stroke and she hits the wall. Remarkable story. Over in 50 metres!
Commentator 2:	Megha Deshpande, our girl. Does it in style again — A whopping win. A National record, no less!!

Yes . . . I did it. I did it. I did it. Oh thank you God . . .

Was all I could say before I lost track of what was happening around me. Yes, I have seen the video recording of my race and am embarrassed by my expressionless face when the gold medal got hung on my neck. I also remember how my family got hysterical taking a million pictures of me but I don't really remember how exactly I felt. It wasn't sinking in. Yes, it felt good but I don't have the words to describe what it meant for me that time. I tried feeling excited but somehow it wasn't happening.

And then I thought of the girls who had lost. Perhaps one of them worked even harder than me. Perhaps one of them wanted it even more badly. Perhaps one of them could have won if it wasn't for an injury. Perhaps one of them will take it as a major setback. Perhaps one of them will even give up competitive swimming. And then there would be one. Who will fight against all odds and make a comeback. But that's still not the girl I needed to watch out for next year. Because the girl to watch out for would be me.

Before we go , it's time for another quick recap:

Yes, winning comes with a greater responsibility. A responsibility to be your best version.

So finally, I achieved all my goals:

- *Settling down in school*
- *Getting reunited with my best friends*
- *Joining the Army camp*
- *My marks improving, and most important:*
- *Winning the States and then of course . . . The Nationals*

ALL DONE, DANA-DAN-DONE!!

Something I now wanted Mama to understand and the timing could not have been better. So when we were alone in our room that evening . . .

Mama: Oh God, Megha, I cannot tell you how happy I am for you. You did it, my child!

Me: Yes Mama, it's a big deal – Nationals and all. I wish I could say that I am truly happy.

Mama: What is it, my child, tell me . . . I can do anything for you.

Me: I need you to make three promises to me, Mama.

Mama: Go on, my child, ask me – it's your day!

Me: One, you will go back to work. Two, you will not make my happiness the moral purpose of your life, and three, you will give yourself another chance. With Uncle.

And Mama cried. For a long time. And I got confused. *Did I say something stupid*?

Mama: Oh, sorry, Megha, but I got emotional . . . I can't tell you,beta, how proud I am of you . . . Yes, I am glad you said it, child, as my career is my passion. I feel alive when I am giving presentations, during those so-called boring board meetings – throwing around management jargon, when I am fire-fighting at work, when my team looks up to me for solutions, when the company meets its numbers . . . and I see my own bank balance rising . . . I guess it all sounds too frivolous to most people my age, who are now sick and tired of their jobs and are looking at spirituality and adventure sports for that kick . . . but that's not me. I love working, Megha, I am a typical corporate type. And I wish I wasn't so ashamed of it. But that's who I am . . .

Me: It's OK Mama; it takes guts to accept yourself. And why are you ashamed of being an achiever? Listen to me, Mama, if you really want me to be happy – go back to work. Don't deny yourself. You have worked very hard for your success, your position – don't let go of it so easily.

Mama: I think I will, Megha . . . as soon as we get back . . . maybe I will . . . Or do you want me to hold on for some more time?

Me: You are the adult here, Mama, you know best. And as I said – don't make my happiness the moral purpose of your life. It's not worth it. Go when you are ready and if you ask me – you look so damn ready now.

Mama: But why did you bring Coach Uncle in? We already have something going on . . . you know that, right?

Me: Yes, but I know you are holding back something. If you want to be in a relationship, open yourself to him,Mother, don't be afraid. Even if it doesn't work out in the end. Whatever happens, life goes on, right?

Mama: Oh Megha, you are now talking like Nani, but I am glad. I think I did need someone like my own mother in my life.

Me: Nani is there too, Mama, and it's OK to be vulnerable in front of her. She is your mother. The way you are mine. Talk to her, Mama. She might be a big *pakau* and loves giving advise till your ears bleed but she does it out of love.

Mama:　　　You don't know how happy I am feeling, Megha . . . you really have made a comeback. In a big way.

So that's about it guys. My story.

A story of grit and determination and passion?

Nah – as the cover says, it's a story of a nervous girl with a screwed-up mind who gets her life back. And yes – just like that race – she does it in style.

Yes I am in Class XII now – the year of the Boards. Oh God – not again!!

I passed Class XI with an average score of 82 per cent!! I am no longer the topper of my school and don't want to be either. I have only so much time to study and it's more than enough. And no, it's not a case of sour grapes – if you know me by now.

Since my big win, I realised that swimming meant everything for me. Actually, I have to keep reminding myself that, as now I might be going international. And yes, I get better by the day. Working hard guarantees that. And having Coach Uncle's constant guidance helps too. So now pizzas are completely banned from my life !

I also made it to the Army Boot Camp and will be spending a major part of my summer vacation crossing obstacles. I am still not sure if I am looking at the army as a career but yes, I am not going to spend the rest of my life in meeting rooms like my mama.

Mama got back to her job and the company gave her a big promotion in order to motivate her to keep making more money for them. She is loving every minute of it and doesn't mind the extra headache that comes with a bigger bank balance (sorry, Mom, but I am happy for you, trust me).

Coach Uncle complains that she doesn't spend that much time with him but he asked for it, didn't he? Jokes apart, Mama and he are in love and I am waiting for the day when they will make their relationship official. Nani says it will happen soon.

Taking about Nani, well . . . last month she made her own relationship official. So I have a new grandfather now – a jolly good fellow, as he calls himself!! But he is not interested in following any of Nani's advice – he drinks like a fish, spends his evenings playing bridge at the club, doesn't do yoga and calls meditation 'hogwash'. Basically all he does is have a good time. Despite this he is alive and kicking at eighty!! Perhaps that's why Nani loves him – because he is someone she can't be.

Of course, now the secret about Papa's marriage. You know, he was in a hurry to get married, right? If you have watched enough Bollywood films then I don't have to explain it to you. If you haven't, then read on. Just six months into his marriage – I got a baby brother from another mother!! Now you can do your calculations and arrive at your own conclusion. And no, I am not going to be a 'good girl' by not joining Nani and Mama in the gossip sessions about his second wife. A step-grandfather, a stepmother, a half-brother, a would-be stepfather – the works! Well . . . what to say . . . the family is growing.

And so is my friendship with Tara. We are closer than ever before and have promised to start spending more time together. Some relationships need to be worked on and my friendship with her is so, so worth it.

And Dolly . . . you win some, you lose some. We are not in touch at all but I heard she has moved to Mumbai bag and baggage to try her luck in Bollywood. I don't understand what the urgency was but I guess we are done with each other.

About Sandy . . . well . . . Do you really want to know?

Oh, last year's Ms All Rounder title completely skipped my mind. I won! (*Phew*) But now that I have joined the gang of the Powerpuff girls Ragini and Gayatri, I have started to question the significance of such competitions that create unnecessary complexes in kids. And I totally agree with Mama who says that when you are older and on your own – whether you were a prom queen or a class monitor or the most popular girl in school – it has got nothing to do with how well you will do in life.

And how well you do in life has nothing to do with how successful you are.

Yes, you heard it right. How well you do in life has nothing to do with how successful you are. Being truly successful doesn't mean reaching somewhere. But really being what you are. And staying true to yourself – whether you are a struggling student or a swimming champion or a celebrity in making. You are successful when you are what you are. That's all.

So friends, loosen up. (But if you still find yourself panicking – don't forget to talk to someone you trust.)

Am I missing something . . .? Yes – so did I finally get appointed Head Girl of the school? You decide.

Everything is OK in the end – and since it is OK – It is

THE END

And finally – as promised

A poem by my mother, as I said, *who cares who actually wrote it* ;-) so PTO:

And you my daughter – will be a woman

If you can love a man, completely without any shame

But still not lose yourself in the bargain

If you have gone through heartbreaks, sleepless nights and depression

But still have not lost your passion

If an old romantic song brings tears in your eyes

And still be able to see through his countless lies

If you treat everyone with the same respect

Without giving a damn to how much they get

If you can feel the same confidence in trousers or a mini skirt

And not justify your choices to the world

If you can take a stand for others

Without worrying about their gender

And while standing up for others

Learn to stand up for yourself

If you don't apologise for being an ambitious bitch

And still embrace your duties as a homemaker if choosing to make that switch

While climbing the ladder of success

Help the other girls who need a push

If you stay strong and fight your way through

And don't mind a dash of vulnerability too

If you can live it up, love, laugh, support, hug, and have an opinion

Yours is the earth and everything in it

And you my daughter – will be a woman

ACKNOWLEDGEMENTS

Since I have already covered my wonderful family last time, I don't have to thank them again as honestly I don't think it matters to them a lot ;-) but still – Manish, Siddhi, Anusha, Mummy, Papa, Rashmi and Mona – I love you guys.

My husband is a very private person and hates attention of any kind but I will take a chance by thanking him here as without his love and guidance, I would have been completely lost.

Before I forget, I want to thank Mr V.P. Gumber, my father-in-law too, as he is the only person in this world who is always available and willing to read the unedited versions of my books and keeps me going with his blessings.

Finally: you the reader who has read so far or plan to do it – thank you for your faith in me; I hope I have not let you down. You guys rock and no matter what, you have a special place in my heart. (Of course – **I write for you.**) A BIG BIG THANK YOU to all those who follow my work on Facebook – really, without you, there is no point to it all. And the BIGGEST THANK YOU for those who trusted a relatively unknown author like me and went on the buy my first book – ***Sick of Being Healthy*** – God bless you guys!

But, before ending, I would like to acknowledge some amazing writers and thinkers whose books have greatly influenced me, especially for this particular work. As I mention in the story, the lessons or rules that the central character's grandma teaches her are not a secret revelation and they are certainly not entirely original. I have basically compiled my learning over all these years by reading Ayn Rand, Robin Sharma, Richard Carlson, Richard Templar, Mark Twain and many more. Specially Rudyard Kipling whose poem *If* I have quoted in the book a couple of times and even attempted a feminine version in the end.

But I have to thank my mom who has been forever and still is on my case. Without her wisdom, this book would have been just another philosophical, boring self-help book gathering dust somewhere instead of this rather interesting story that would help the reader too (Yey)!!

So as Bhai says:

Do whatever you want to do but don't trouble your mother!!

PART-3
TEEN
RILOGY
DOLLY

MONISHA K GUMBER

DOLLY
WON'T
A story in free verse...or whatever
PLAY

In the memory of my father

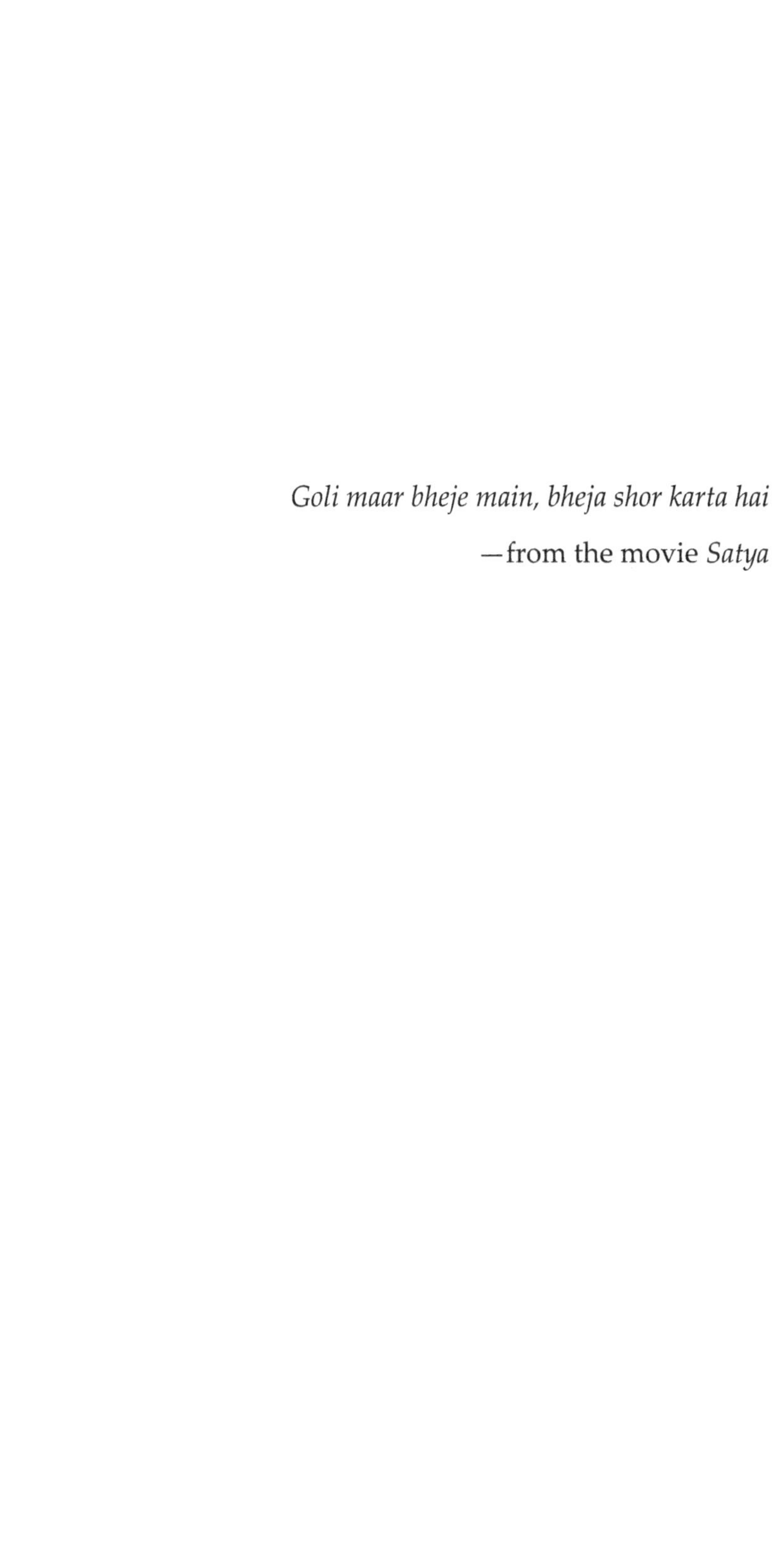

Goli maar bheje main, bheja shor karta hai

—from the movie *Satya*

Part I

Growing-up Pains

How do I start

that it sounds oh-so-smart?

Or should I just concentrate on being me?

—just a pretty face

and a superb figure

Welcome to my world

of make-up, false eyelashes, push-up bras and
report cards

with lots of red lines

Yes. The Dumbo is going to write a book.

Have no expectations

have

nothing to lose

except if you paid to read the book

which I doubt . . .

It's a bright, bright, bright

sunshine day . . .

blue sky above and lush green grass

on which I lay.

Wet kisses on my cheeks

being hugged so tight

somehow it doesn't feel so right.

Uncle is so nice and warm

and frankly,

hasn't done enough to raise an alarm . . .

So my feelings

I learn to fight

even though

it still doesn't feel so right . . .

I see this stunning woman

my mama

walking towards us

Uncle gives her a hug, too

A hug

that should have ended

a minute sooner.

I feel a pang of

jealousy . . .

Towards whom?

They say they are friends,

best friends

But *ladka ladki kabhi dost nahi hote*

Nani and I again watched *Maine Pyar Kiya* on TV
the other day

But they're grown ups

Man and woman

Is Uncle my mother's friend?

Or mine?

Papa and Mama

fight a lot,

all love is lost

You see, Papa, a smart doctor

Mama, an ex-Miss Delhi

Smart and dumb

don't go together

You are the biggest

mistake of my life

Papa lashes out at her

Mama rolls her eyes

because this beauty queen

doesn't have the words

that can hurt

My brother and I

two dumb-bells

taken after our mom

so says Papa

Bhaiya gets beaten up a lot

but not me

I am just a cute little girl

A *kanjak*

Dolly, you are so sweet

like an ice-cream . . .

You know it, don't you?

I could eat you up

He licks his lips

the lift door opens

I run off

but a part
remains

with my
uncle

School starts

Time to get serious

We are big children now

in Class 4, no less!

Come-onnnnnnnn-childrennnnn-dictation-time!

A lullaby

yet my heart beats louder

then fades away . . .

I hear the cruel words

bounce on my empty notebook

Ma'am pulls it away mercilessly

as I try to hold on to it desperately

She looks at me contemptuously

as if I am a criminal

even though she just robbed me

of my self-respect, my notebook

Home wasn't so happy, either

but I loved them all

especially my dad

He was too good

for the rest of us

or that's how

he made us feel.

I ached for his affection

a hug here, a kiss there

None came . . .

Except a shrug of his shoulders

like

Where did I go wrong?

But Uncle filled in for Dad

and gave me

more than I could ever ask for

My handsome Uncle Uday, my hero

Come on, Dolly

let's go high

He pressed

the button of the lift,

we elevated

before he put me down

to play

on the bed

And made me take a God's promise

never to tell a soul

and if I broke it

my mom would die,

the devil would kill her

It was all part of God's mission

A part of me knew

he was making it up,

a part of me believed him

because a part of me wanted

what he wanted

Love

So that Mom could live

forever

That's what I told

myself

Did it hurt?

Or

did it feel nice?

Or both?

After so many years

I still feel ashamed to say

Yes. It did

Sex is not overrated,

it hurts like hell

it feels good

it is supposed to

Both

Can I describe it?

No, I am not good with words

and I don't want to

What Uncle and I had

was too personal

sacred

an act of being loved

finally

But I did it for Mama.

You know that, don't you?

School again.

I jump

from one place to another

One topic to another

School

They called my parents

to say I needed to be

evaluated

professionally

What was that?

They said I was slow. Lost. In zombie land.

It's not just academics

she mutters to herself . . .

she just doesn't respond . . .

and stares away into space

My dad refused

to believe

I was his daughter, after all

Mom did

I was her daughter, after all

Colourful educational toys

jig-saw puzzles, stacking cups, Mr Potato head

some broken crayons

No sweat

Except this doctor

asked me

my favourite colours

my friends

my hobbies and

what did I want to do in life

Yes, grown-ups are crazy

even the well-meaning ones

From the corner of my eye

I see my mom

wiping her tears, her eyes looking elsewhere

I know

she knows

ADHD

Attention Deficit Hyperactivity Disorder

But Dolly is, you know . . . Mama said

kind of lazy

a daydreamer

she isn't hyperactive

Well, the doctor says

there are all kinds

all variations

and depends on the degree of the problem.

But that was me

that was God's way of punishing me

for playing with my uncle

and enjoying it too

instead of praying

for my mother's life

that I

screwed up

Big time

Don't cry, Mama

I will never do it again

Do what, Dolly?

Mom's eyes pierced into mine

I mean, I will learn my spellings

Oh, Dolly!

What will I say

to your father?

That was her biggest worry

I will sue her

she doesn't know a thing

Dolly is my daughter

she can't be

what I can't be

My father

still

hoped

that I could not go wrong

but I did

I had a disability,

a learning disability, as they say

which meant I wasn't normal

I wonder

who is . . .

My friends

Tara and Megha

Tara—funny yet rebellious

Megha—always a winner

read books I dreaded

Bizarre names like *Matilda, Of Mice and Men,
The Wind in the Willows* . . .

What if they found out

that I was different?

So I focus

on a story

Megha is narrating

A movie based on Ruskin Bond's novel

'So, you see, Khatri's life becomes miserable as everyone
boycotts him in the village. Biniya is a kind girl who
sympathises with Khatri and decides that Khatri is the
real owner of umbrella, not her. She gives the umbrella to
Khatri. The village people accept him, then . . . and then . . .
Guys, that's about it . . .'

concludes Megha proudly. As if it was 'her' film.

I can't take it any more

I go home

Dolly, come on in . . .

Uncle holds my hand

gives me a gift

a Barbie doll

My fingers stroke her silky hair

touch her full chest

wrap around her slender waist

feel her long legs

and drop her hard on the floor

who could be envious of a plastic toy?

But what if Uncle notices the stark differences, too,

and stops playing with me?

But Uncle smiles

reassuring me

and I melt

to the taste of refreshing peppermint

So, where have you been?

Wasting time with Megha and Tara?

Papa shouts at me

'So, you see, Khatri's life becomes miserable as everyone boycotts him in the village. Biniya is a kind girl who sympathises with Khatri and decides that Khatri is the real owner of umbrella, not her. She gives the umbrella to Khatri. The village people accept him then . . . and then . . . Guys, that's about it . . .'

I conclude proudly. As if it was 'my' film

Papa's eyes

burning balls of red fire

Phataaaaaaakkkkk!!

I collapse

And this time

I really did zone out

Sorry, it was a blackout

My head still spinning and

an extreme pain

deep inside me

It was the middle of the night and my body seemed
to be on fire.

Mama . . . Mama . . . I called out

Shhhh . . . baby, I am right here

And found my mama next to me

Mama, did you see that? Papa hit me…

I cried while my little body shook

probably to shake off the

betrayal

I remembered those times

when he took me out on drives for ice-cream

when I was still at nursery school

I guess back then it didn't really matter so much if
you couldn't spell 'slide'

as long as you knew how to play on it

'Dolly, I am with you, always . . . no matter
what happens'

We hugged each other to sleep

Thankfully it was a weekend and

despite the filmy slap,

which hurt, by the way,

I was happy

that I didn't have to go to school the next day

School

A place having a loving and supportive atmosphere

where children develop emotionally and academically

where children reach their full potential

a nurturing environment that develops confidence

We all know it's nothing but

propaganda

In reality, for kids like me who felt out of place

who couldn't focus in class,

who were sniggered at,

avoided by most children

it was a nightmare

I was bullied

Everywhere

By the teachers

the nastiest of bullies

at least some of them

Every time I got humiliated by my teachers

I felt tears trickling down my chapped red hot cheeks

More so because I couldn't bear their proud smiles
(my friends')

that they were trying hard to suppress

Children can be cruel

How I wish parents would teach them

the true meaning of kindness right from the beginning,

which is, being nice

to the weak kids in class

and the fat ones, the short ones, the weaklings, the *dheeley*
screws, and all the other kids who don't

fit in

I know you have heard this before

so nothing I will say will do anything more

In other words, school sucked.

I hated every minute of it

sick of those never-ending tests,

the attitude my friends were developing and

that

there was nothing I was good at

Yes, no singing. No dancing. No sports. Nothing at
Annual Day functions.

Not even a hint of extra-curriculars

It was *that* bad

At age nine, I was already destined to be

A F A I L U R E

in life

Meanwhile,

my personal life rocked

more and more

Oh Dolly, it is the best gift you can give to your
Uncle Uday

You are so beautiful, Dolly . . . so soft . . . red cheeks

I can never have enough

of you . . .

My body jerked in response

It felt good

Electrifying

The feeling of letting go and drowning in muck

it liberated me and

I was hooked

I was dirty

Finally

It felt refreshing to admit it in my mind

Uncle knew it, and still accepted me

despite my problems

despite my grades

despite what my teachers thought of me

despite being hated by my dad

He loved me. And that was all I cared for . . .

But remember, never to tell anyone

I promised Uncle

I meant it, you see

For once,

I wanted

to make an elder proud of me

The boat rocked

in the storm

I couldn't

hold on

with a moan . . .

went down

deeper and deeper

in the whirlpool

of my pee

Do you know you could replace the word 'Whirlpool' with 'Suckhole'?

Funny, no?

And so apt for my situation

Oh no, Dolly . . . you did it again.

Mama swallowed a lump in her throat

as she opened the drapes

to let the yellow

light

into the dark room

but the prison

inside me

remained black

You need to get out, Dolly

from your bubble

We have work to do

said my mother

to herself

A dumb beauty

took to Google

and read and read and read

until

she had enough words

to talk about it

Dolly isn't doomed, neither is she mentally retarded

Ok, she can be impulsive, or have problems with communicating and relating to the world around her and has a hard time concentrating

but a lot of kids like her are super intelligent and super talented

If it makes you feel better, then

do you know what little Dolly has in common with these famous people

Justin Timberlake, Michael Phelps, Sir Richard Branson and countless others?

ADHD

said the doctor

No, it doesn't make me feel better

because we don't know even one famous person from our country of a billion-plus people who has this.

But they do, Mrs Nanda

they just don't talk about it.

And that's why

Doctor

I am sad . . . Mama said softly.

So, you see, Mrs Nanda, I knew there was a problem

Aren't you glad you took Dolly to be evaluated
professionally?

said my class teacher, seeming more cheerful than ever

as if she had won a free comb with hair oil.

Kindly look for

a special school

for such children . . .

She can't stay here

Finally. Some sympathy.

All Dolly needs is some support

my mama replied

Like some personal attention in class, some extra time to do her work

some sensitivity

Today it's Dolly

tomorrow it could be your kids

whatever age they may be

Today it's ADHD, tomorrow it could be autism

Times they are a-changin'

adding more and more stress

taking a heavy toll on the kids

Surely as a teacher,

you can see that, can't you?

And have you not seen

Taare Zameen Par?

My mother roared

as if a movie should now

provide credibility

to her claims

of her daughter

wired differently

Oh, I underestimated you

but I see your point

Let's meet in a few days

and discuss

My teacher surrendered.

So Mom had tamed this bully

And that's why they say that

a mother's love

is the most potent force in the world.

I wonder why they consider me dumb

even when

I use such smart phrases

So my mother became

the first therapist

I ever had

Just like your mother

was to you

She asked me to look for

words in a game of

word search,

just five

A daunting task

But she pushed and pushed

and didn't let me give up

I ended up finding more,

even words which

weren't there

in the first place

and even the words I hated.

As I said, mother's love . . .

that starts much before they

push and push

in the maternity room

Girls just have it in them

despite the pain,

too much love to give

sometimes . . .to the wrong people . . . knowingly.

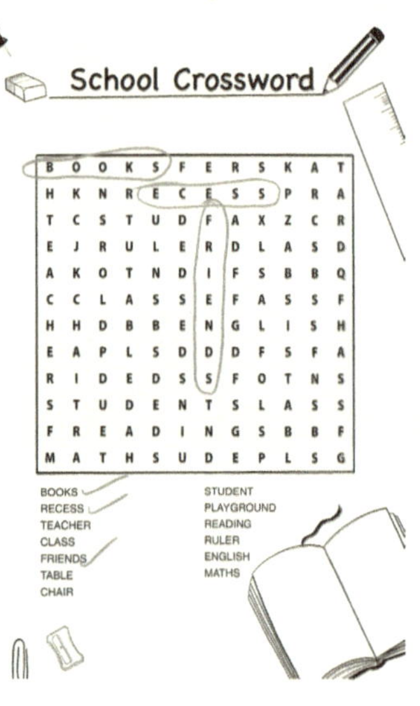

We bonded over

words and words and words

She taught me so many

some of them really impressive

only I don't know

if I always use them correctly

Learning disabilities or not

I could learn now

Ok, at my own pace

in my own way

All children are different

they talk different

play different

look different

learn different

Everyone knows

Then why the labels?

Why brand us for life?

Does it make it any better?

What's the rush to *fix* us?

What's the hidden agenda?

But then . . .

I was too young

and Mama too overstrung

with no respite from the frustration

of having no answers to these unasked questions

Henceforth (wow, I like the ring of this word)

we did

what we had to

and sure enough

I started doing better

and better

I wanted to stand first in class

I studied and studied

But it just didn't happen

I asked my mother

is it impossible

because of the way I am?

Dolly, nothing, nothing can come in your way

just keep trying

Once I knew that

I gave up

trying

Milky white

hair as black as night

big eyes

that, too, light

Already

little girls were mean to me

I didn't want more hate

than my nine years could take

I settled for 'dumb beauty'

even when I had ideas

and theories

and concepts

and what not,

only I could not

express them properly

So I tried to remain deaf

to being called dumb

but couldn't get used to

the shit

especially because the shit was true

Instead of a simple cotton suit

Mama wore

black stilettos

and a skirt

with a red silk top

to a school meeting

and asked them to see

beyond their invisible glasses of racism

that size up, judge and compartmentalise

people

as smart, intelligent, genius, crazy, stupid, slow, gone case,
high class, low class . . .

based on the brands

they wear

on their bodies

or actually

how they speak

words

of the English language

in Hindustan

Mama became a warrior
she fought my case
at school
at home
defended me
believed in me

She didn't care what the doctors said

or what the internet said

Maybe

it would have been easier

if she could admit

that God made me this way

She KNEW I would overcome it

that there was no need for repentance

and it wasn't a life sentence

But my life ended

when Uncle Uday left the city

for greener pastures

or pinker little girls

Armies of hundreds of them

invaded my mind

I surrendered to them as

I couldn't let go of him.

But his body went

without goodbyes

except a call to his best friend

Mama

She felt even more defeated

than I did

What did this man do to his

women?

I just ran away—got on to a rocking horse

in the nearby park

I rocked and rocked

and rocked some more

rubbing myself violently against the saddle

as my poor mama stood watching

with her eyes blinded

drenched in hot tears

It felt good and I continued rocking

to get the same feeling

Uncle gave me

The rocking horse failed me and

I collapsed

on the beast.

Incomplete.

Now her trembling body

drenched in cold sweat

she became super-desperate

despite her belief in me

she started believing

in everything else too

occult-shocult, tantra-mantra,

energy healing, *pir baba* . . .

Maybe something would work?

So that her Dolly could

be like

other girls

Papa stood his ground

wouldn't let her try

anything on me

She promised

And the very next day

took me

to that place

I whimpered

I saw myself descending a black hole slide in the water
park,

a black hole that had no light at the end of it

or maybe no end at all

Look at me! the old woman in a black robe yelled

and shook my shoulders

Let go of me, Aunty . . .

I won't trouble anyone again . . . I howled.

Yes, I knew you were in there

leave her body

out, you witch! and she smacked me with a broom

to chase away the evil spirits

The mother spirit, however,

awakened

in Mama

and she knew

it was a mistake

She rescued me from the dusty dark alley

and promised

to herself

to protect me

from everything evil

A promise made

too late

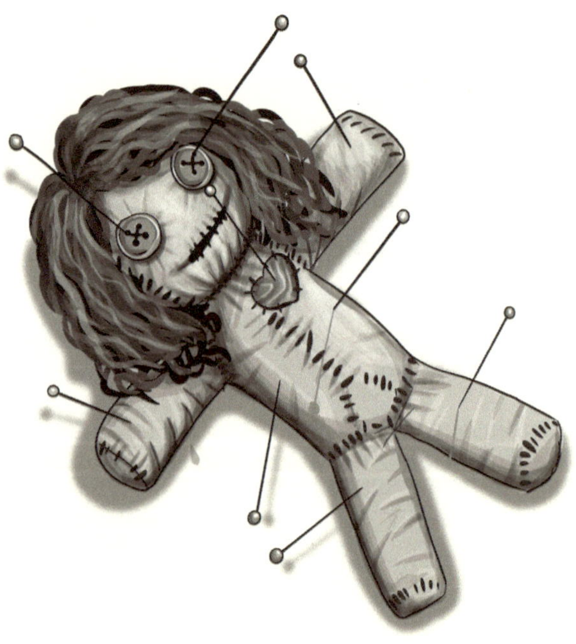

Dejected

heart-broken

confused

Lonely. Very.

Our games in bed had

cast a spell

The intensity of self-contempt combined with

fierce yearning

for the potion of love

rendered me helpless

an addict

on the brink of insanity

But life goes on . . .

We somehow managed

to pass each year

in school

The tag of 'dumb beauty' stayed

even when I could focus

a lot more

on words and numbers

written

on the blackboard,

much like the stories held as hostages

scripted

in my head

struggling to break out

till

I stopped peeing in bed

and

became a teenager

And

Fell in love

with Uncle Uday again

Nearly

Part II

Love is in the Air . . .

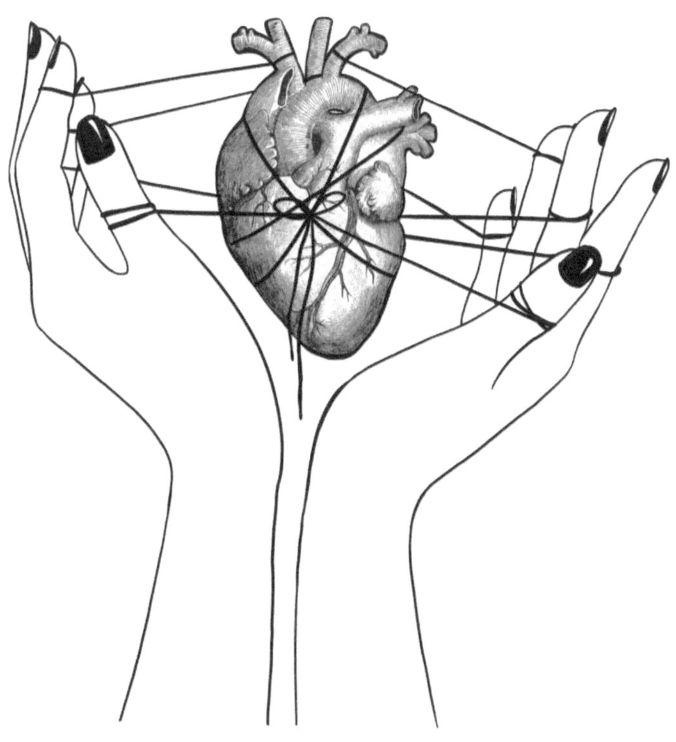

I know it's the wrong time

to introduce the characters

of this story

but I never did

anything right anyway

Tara, Megha, Karan, Mama, Uncle Uday . . .

Sandy, my brother, too

who hardly has a role to play here—

fragments from my twisted mind

from books

written earlier

We all were neighbours

lived too close

for our own good

Is this introduction enough?

Then let's carry on . . .

and take a time leap

just like they do in TV serials

I was now

a really, really pretty teen

like Betty and Veronica from Archie comics.

Somehow

girls wanted to hang out

with me

and show me off to other girls

to evoke jealousies

Why does no one tell them

it's wrong?

Even when I felt vindicated

that now it's my time

as no matter what,

these girls

could never

have half my figure

Even if it was wrong

I didn't want to change it

A recluse like me
welcomed the attention
It was long due
and I deserved it

Tara, my best friend,

was in love

with this guy

I had not paid any attention to

but when I saw him

looking at me

I fluttered my eyelashes

and welcomed him

in my space

even when

I knew

how my best friend felt

even when

she told no one

but all knew

It was Karan

Uday Uncle's son

Until now I did not really notice

but when he looked at me

with the same brown eyes

my body shivered

and reminded me

of his maker

Someone

I didn't even try or want

to forget

and move on from.

The contrition

(you can look it up, just in case)

mixed with recollections

of being in a trance

away from the realities

of the other world

was now my identity

and I craved for it

His voice

a softer version of Uncle's

with the same tone,

his hands

a shade darker,

his hair

thick

unlike Uncle's

But he was the best replica

of my lost love

as his mouth

was exactly his

father's,

brought back the memories

that had never really left me

and it was enough

for the time being

till Uncle came back

and reclaimed me

Well . . . I am in college

Dad lives far-far away

in foreign lands

That's what Karan told me

when I asked him

You go to which school and

what does your father do?

(*besides drive me crazy*)

Little did he know

that his dad has lived in my room

since I was a little girl

What was I to do,

except

settle for his shadow?

At fourteen, the hormones raging in me

were making it impossible

for me

to sleep

without reliving

the moments

from five years back

when I was just a little girl

and now

with my own

chest

rounder than Barbie's

and legs

longer

than hers

Oh that would please Uncle so, so much

I didn't have to do much

just pouted my lips

stroked my hair

acted a bit more

dumb

than I was

to get his attention

I know I hurt my best friend

but

I had to

get him at all costs . . .

but as I said

he came cheap

Young love

so innocent

he sent me

a million messages on Snapchat

cute animal videos

some memes

borrowed from the internet

love poems

that rhymed

funny selfies, too

with a filter that made him look

so much like Uncle

but so unlike him

Uncle had

what his son can never:

the power to possess

Whereas Karan, poor young lad,

even in college

wasn't man enough

to admit

he wanted me

or perhaps he didn't

and he really was innocent—

something that had begun to bore me

as this school girl really wanted to see

who was better

hoping that Uncle was . . .

so I could have no excuse

to get over him

I was desperate,

wasn't used to

this claustrophobia

of public places:

meetings at Comic-Cons,

the society park

or PVRs

If it was love

Karan had to prove it

but I was the girl here

and didn't want to

be too available,

which I was

but exclusive

to his bloodline, though

Yeah,

I am not a bimbo

I said to myself

School

as usual

boring

tiring

irritating

etc., etc.

but I had to still go

since I was just a young teen

and was expected to spend half the day there

even if I spent it daydreaming

in dusty classrooms

reverberating with giggling sounds

stench of half-opened tiffins

passed around during algebra lessons

interrupted by

a loud *Class! Be quiet!*

or in the girl's toilet

spending hours

adjusting my skirt

my hair

my bosom (because it's still school. Ok, boobs.)

applying layers of make-up

to get the

no make-up look

to attract boys

I had

no interest in

And, of course,

you already know

I claim no potential

in Math and Science

or English

though I have come a long way

can focus a lot more

can write a 300-word essay

with commas, apostrophes and capital letters

in the right places

unlike here

where I have the freedom

to write

without any fear of Cs or Ds.

A notebook

confined, limited, chained my thoughts

. . . but this laptop

Where my words are not forbidden

has no judgement from God

or the random Adam or Eve

who would

ultimately read

this shit

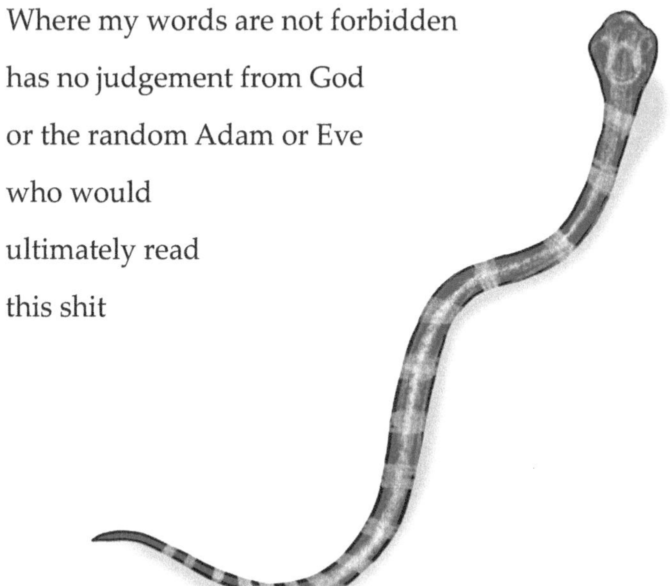

All these philosophies

made me forget

that I have a lover

who just wants to hang out

in groups

What could be more unfortunate

for a cheapo,

a DESPO like me?

Yeah. I know I am called that

sometimes

just for wearing short skirts

that show off my long smooth legs

that other girls don't have

in the peak of winters

Neither do they have

dysfunctional families

friends who have no respect (for me)

a history of sin

for which there is no redemption

committed at an age

reserved for teddy bears when

I played with

a male's private parts

the ugly truth that little girls don't even get to see

leave alone touch and feel.

A past and perhaps

a poignant future of

learning difficulties

that made my mind wander

from a

trigonometric equation

to a word from the thesaurus I can replace 'sad'

with

to my father's stethoscope

to mama's tattoo on her navel

to *bhaiya's* muddy football

to the Barbie Uncle gave me

with her face now

damaged

eyes tired from always staying open

hair in disaster

and shabby old tight-fitting rags

She started looking so much like

I do

from the inside

CURSE

You need to

love yourself Dolly

just look at you

who can match

these features?

this skin?

this figure?

this sense of style?

You are already a knockout

announced my mother

Oh cut the crap, Mama!

I have heard this a hundred times

as if it would

actually

make me

change my mind

Almost forty now

Mama

was holding on

to her youth

by spending all her time

in the gym

or next to the mirror

and she did a

bloody good job of it

We were more like friends

than mother and daughter

A friend . . .who knew nothing

about my dirty dark secrets

chiselled inside me

forever . . .

But my beauty

spread

far and wide

only Karan

still remained untouched

at least physically

But Mama

gave me the confidence

to carve

my own road

a road

that led

to the same lift

the same house

that Uncle brought me to

a hundred years ago

and now

I brought his son to

play

once again

Yes

this was meant to be

As his lips came near mine

I could smell the flavour of the same

refreshing peppermint

As his hands glided down

to my waist

I saw him

Standing at the door

with a wry smile

on his pale face

amused

dejected

in pain

for betraying him

Uncle!! I scream!!

Karan let go of me

What did you just say, Dolly?

Your father . . . I said, hushed . . .

I think he saw us...O shit man !!

My father, Dolly

lives

in Australia

Karan . . . I whispered again . . . he is back

go out and say hello

. . . Look, there is no one

relax, Dolly

maybe you are just nervous

Karan said

all creeped-out as he switched on the lights

of the main entrance

Mama, I swear I saw him

I mean someone

who looks like Uday Uncle

in the building . . .

is he back?

Well, if he is, I am not going to spare him

this time

for leaving just like that

Yeah, Mama, and now

he is back

just like that

You are so beautiful Dolly, so soft . . . red cheeks

I can never have enough

of you . . .

My body jerked in response

I woke up

startled

all wet

only now

it wasn't my pee down there

I need to see him

he is back

but why is he hiding?

Mama, did you find out?

Let's call him over for lunch

your best friend

Dolly, what the hell are you talking?

Uday isn't back

he called me last night

from Australia

said he was thinking about us

Us? You mean me, too? I thought

as a chill ran down my spine

I still need to see him

or

for now

his poor photocopy will do

Karan. The neighbourhood stud

girls swooned over him

guys wanted to be like him

Into music. Sports

And me

A complete package

yet

so incomplete

to me

God, just add those couple of decades

some more suave

and he might come close

to my illicit love

Paint your palette blue and grey . . .

For the first time

I felt a connection

with Karan

as we slow danced

to this tragedy of an artist's life . . .

Now I understand

What you tried to say to me

And how you suffered for your sanity . . .

I almost closed my eyes and felt

Karan's closeness

as if he

would rescue me

from the pain, the longing and the loathing

his father dug deep in my soul

Maybe

I should just give him a chance . . .

and not use him

to fulfil me

I open my eyes

as my body moves to the rhythm

next to his

slowly . . . softly . . .

and I see him . . .

Standing at the door

with the same wry smile

on his same pale face

amused

dejected

in pain

for betraying him

Uncle!! I scream!!

Karan, don't shit me

your dad's there, I saw him

he was looking at us

Dolly, stop playing these games

you don't want to get close

just say so

Karan is now on fire

and I melt

as he reminds me of the same heat

I felt around his dad's body

a long, long time ago

Yes . . . I was just fooling around, I apologise

and feel sorry

for myself

What's happening?

And who is really playing games?

Uncle is back

but no one wants to tell me

Does it mean

they know?

I am like the

pink handkerchief

tied

fluttering in the middle

between the two ends

of a game

of tug of war

pulled viciously

by the son and his father.

Whoever wins

or loses

forgets all about the

dangling piece of cloth

which is now

tossed aside.

With an imagination

as insane as mine

I started fearing

falling asleep

to ward off the random scenes

turning into full-fledged

lucid dreams

of both father and son

together

dissolving in the bed

with me

There came a point

when I wasn't sure

if I was awake

or sleeping

Only the fluorescent numbers

across my bed

confided in me

that there were hours to go

before the morning sun

came in through

to disinfect

my bed

with sweat trickling into

those creases

just like

the creases in my toxic mind

if only I wasn't too lazy

to smoothen them out

My friends

Tara and Megha

said they were worried about me

Tara took me to a workshop

in the society hall

where they teach

girls

how to say no

If only

I'd known

that I had a choice

I listened

and I broke down

I had to tell someone

even if it was nothing but lies

that Karan wanted

to go all the way

(but rather it was me…still we couldn't…because…his
father was always watching)

and it wasn't a lie

as they said I was telling

So he broke up with me

left me completely

on my own

to live out my fantasies

alone

Oh, how much I liked

him

I realised

only after he stopped

taking my calls

and called me

what I was:

M-A-D

Now I didn't know

what was true

and what wasn't

I saw his father

but he did not believe me

and said

I had issues

I had to sort out

and I had to stop flirting

as he was serious

about wanting a real relationship

not just physical intimacy

like me

I guess I was a bimbo

after all

I apologised

I couldn't

let him leave me

just like his father

Maybe if I met him around people

Uncle wouldn't mind

and I was right

Uncle stopped stalking us

so we continued

having our relationship

NOT being taken

to the next level

as I am sure

both my mama

and Uncle

would have disapproved

Here I was falling

in love now

floating in the clouds above

washed by and soaked in raindrops of true love

so clean

no kisses

no fondling

only pure

messages

of I love you baby

on Snapchat

Oh, how it felt

to be that precious girl

the chosen one

that girl who can have anyone

but wants no one except him

that girl who is finally falling in love slowly,
soberly, sweetly

with the handsome stud of the neighbourhood

who had eyes

only for her

Yes. Beautiful people

make love seem

even more pink

than pink teddy bears

We continued

our romance

despite

my record

with his father

I felt

we all could move on

and grow up

A couple of years more

till I was seventeen

and hated school

more and more until it was

just too much

so that

one day

I just quit

Part III

Coming of Age

You can't do that, Dolly!

my mama

laughed at my guts

that reminded her

of her younger self

I am not going there any more, Mama

I have nothing more to learn

than I already know

of which I can't remember

anything at all

What would your dad say?

Dr Aman Nanda's daughter

not even a high-school pass?

And it made her laugh even more

holding back

her tears of sorrow

for a failure of a daughter

of relief

for her daughter didn't have to suffer any more

of revenge

on her husband

whose blood

had let him down

big time

They were separated

but still some more tears remained

in anticipation

of the spiteful sarcasm

she

would be subjected from him

and the whole wide world

that she had failed too

in her most sacred duty

as a mother

But only she knew

she had given me enough courage

to make such a move

which in today's date and time

only the super-crazy or

the super-rich or the super-poor

can.

But here we were

the simpletons

the middle classes

maybe the upper-middle

or whatever

as if it mattered

The fact was

I was free

of the prison they called school

If only I could break free

from the prison of my mind

just like that, too!!

While my classmates slogged

cramming more and more formulas

I stayed at home

and tried to sleep

away the pain

of being called

slow, off, mental case

behind my back

sometimes on my face

while all I could do was

pretend

I did not hear their words

and did not understand

their sneers

that made them feel

good about themselves

simply because

a beautiful girl in their class

was so, so damn stupid

that she didn't stand a chance

of ever, ever

making it in life

and then they could forgive God

for making them ugly

At least they got marks

you know

Whoever invented the idea

that intelligent people

are those who know by heart

the names of

presidents and vice-presidents or
capitals or currencies

of the countries of the world

was the biggest dumb ass to begin with!

That's GK, dude!

So what next, asked Mama

I want to take it easy

Mama shrugged

as in her mind

her lazy spoiled daughter

already had it easy

till she remembered

a difficult childhood

of learning difficulties

and the struggles we had to go through

in order to stay

at a place

that didn't want me

a place

I had just rejected and didn't allow

any more

to squeeze me more and more

into an invisible bubble

a bubble I could not burst

but now could make it bigger so I could breathe

I had to stay inside, I guess

I had secrets to protect

and conspiracies

that made me

But now that I was almost an adult

I knew

or had a divine revelation from the dark skies above

what happened to me

was not fair

Uncle

did not do it so Mama could live

I knew it then

and I laughed

at my sorry state

of pretending to myself

that I believed him

when I did it

because it… kinda felt nice

and now the agony I felt

because I had enough free time

to know

I was so so so so wrong!!

Why did Uncle and I

do this to me??

I was just a baby

how could he, God, how could he??

I screamed and screamed

silently

and my mind split open

created a mayhem of a million pieces

with blood, gore and acid oozing out fiercely

each piece felt a different feeling:

revulsion, hatred, disgust, remorse, paranoia

As I said, I am not so good with words

and anyway, those different feelings

mean the same shame

directed towards

the same thing

a dream

of him, his whole being slaughtered and sliced

into a million pieces too

I will get you one day

Uncle

I promised

to the little girl

There was only one problem

His son

had fallen deeply madly

in love

with a girl

who had snapped herself out of it

just like that

for a greater cause

a higher purpose

When I said I don't love you any more

as I have found someone else

I was almost right

but he didn't believe me

and begged me to stay

I had to break away

as I did not want collateral damage . . .

he

was too precious a boy

too loving and caring

a sweetheart

who had to be protected

from me

But his love for me

was perhaps

greater than my hate

for his father

so I gave up trying

to keep him out of this

Maybe I wasn't strong enough

to stand my ground

or maybe

I did love him

a fact that was coming

in the way

of my fantasises

of tormenting his father

more than he made me suffer now

for the pleasure I experienced then

A pleasure that took my mind off

from the torture of those times

of having a razor-sharp stone

between my legs

its hardness cutting through my insides

for which I made an excuse

bluffed like a pro

every time—

that I had a stomach-ache

that I got hit by a hard ball

that I tumbled down on something hard

in the playground

which weren't lies entirely

Mama believed me

maybe she didn't have the courage to take any more blows

or maybe believing was more convenient

After all everyone knew

I was the clumsy one,

in my own zone,

who hardly paid attention to the outside world

As a little girl

I had to wait

to cry

in my bed at night

with a monster underneath

I couldn't even

make much noise about it

It was as if it was

'a part of life'

like it's no big deal

But now that I was a grown-up—

Ok, you heard it before—

so, like I said, I was older

and wiser

had seen some documentaries

and some primetime news

and even read a book

I realised

I was just used

Abused

And I wondered why

my mama who is as modern, as liberal as it can get

never ever talked about this with me

The more I knew

the more I knew

that it was wrong

Uncle violated my trust

and my mama's

He had to pay for it

and this thought drove me insane

the obsession

to see him suffer

became a trending video

in my imagination

But with Karan

I was back again . . .

this on-off relationship

also became

'a part of life'

like it's no big deal

well…you know

it's complicated

In the life of a teenager

a three-four years relationship

with the same person

is a very serious business

like a lifetime

And even I

had begun to feel

committed

If only . . .

senior wasn't in the scene any more

and I could do something

to wipe off

every trace

of him

from this world

Valentine's day

is a good time

to take your relationship

to the next level,

something I used to insist

even when I was younger

But today

Karan did

and as usual

I did not

want to have a choice

It was dead quiet

except

our murmurs, our giggles

in his empty house

the same house

that brought back memories

Thank god

they had got a new floral sofa

and had painted the walls light yellow

So his lips

came close to mine

I closed my eyes

tight

to stop me from seeing

images from the past

and as his shivering hands

explored those angles and curves

I could feel

his presence again

Standing at the door

with the same wry smile

on his same pale face

amused

dejected

in pain

for betraying him

Uncle!! I scream

again

Karan, you dog!!

You are fucking with me again!

Don't tell me

he isn't back

Look, he is watching us!

I pointed towards Uncle

who stood

watching,

his eyes

piercing into mine

Karan! Look at him, your father! I shouted

Dolly! Stop it, you bitch . . .

no one's here

except you and me

Oh yes . . . oh yes . . . he is not there

so I am blind or a psycho?

Is that what you are saying?

You father and son!! In the whole goddamn world

was it only me

you both could find to mess around with??

As we turned back

Uncle

escaped

I fled too

to my mama

I cried

and cried

and cried

Sorry, Mama

I was making out with Karan

and Uncle saw us

My mama

who is as modern, as liberal as it can get

oh, I am repeating myself again

sorry

my mama

couldn't understand

why I was crying

and saying sorry

for being with my boyfriend

She knew about it and did not

really mind

so, what was the ruckus about?

Oh yes . . . Uncle saw us

Dolly, my baby

Uday isn't here

he hasn't visited India

since years

trust me *beta*

he called me from Australia just this morning

How about trusting me, Mama?

I blasted her

For once

when I am saying

he is here

he is here

He is just hiding

and why does he keep calling you?

Mama then realised

there was more to it

She begged me

to tell the truth

and when I refused stubbornly

despite hoping

that she would keep begging

she begged me again

to come with her

to see someone

she trusted

. . . I saw him three times

in Karan's house

I mean

it's his house . . . too

And what were you doing then? I mean anything in
particular or

common

to all these three times?

Yes . . . me and Karan . . . we were

sort of . . . close . . .

kissing and all . . . you know

The first two times . . . it was a couple of years back

and last time . . .

just last week . . .

Uncle is back . . .

I saw him . . . in flesh and bone

but they say I am lying

The doctor didn't want to talk any more she knew

there was so much more

and I wasn't ready

to let the monster out

My mother didn't ask me

any more questions

She just became sweeter

just like she was

when the first doctor revealed the naked truth

of my learning disabilities

ages ago

She was worried

there was something even murkier and savage

waiting to be exposed

though

she sort of had a very good idea by now

evidenced by the dark circles around her eyes

that she lay awake every night

praying

hoping

against hope

that her worst fears wouldn't come true

about her best friend

and her daughter

At my next appointment

we were ready

as it had weighed me down so much

and I was so injured

and so, so tired

that either I could fall flat on my face

with a thud

just like they show in movies

or

be my own hero

decide to stand up

with my fists closed

my teeth clenched

and blood finding its way out through

my combat uniform

a cross between Manikarnika and Bahubali

and to make it even more intense

say out aloud a motivational quote

a Sanskrit *shloka* would be perfect

Obviously, I didn't know any

so I made up my own:

'There is nothing that can get me'

But instead

I was cool

I let out

the steam

revealed those scars

and opened up

about how stupid I was

to allow this person

to control my very being

by playing a game

that shows no sign of ending

And that was quick!

Surprisingly

what I had lived and thought of

for thousands of hours

I summed up in just a few minutes.

as you know

I don't know

how to bullshit

and go on and on

to describe

my fucked-up stories

of pain and anguish and lust and deceit

It could have been so tragic, so shocking,

so sensational

if it had happened to a drama queen

who could throw tantrums

break some glasses

or play with complex words

unlike a Dumbo like

yours truly

Well . . . Mrs Nanda, said the doctor

I am afraid

she has got something.

It looks like . . .

well . . .

schizophrenia

combined with the usual anxiety issues . . .

She sees people

who are not there

she's delusional

or it's a hyperactive imagination . . .

to put it mildly

but it's a mental illness

we could try counselling

or medication . . . if needed

I am so sorry . . .

I need to run some more tests

to confirm

I am so sorry . . .

Here, have some water

Her treacherous past

her learning difficulties . . .

do you know

if this ADHD was acquired or was she born with it?

Maybe it's because of the abuse

we can't say for sure

it remains a grey area

but her current psychological issues

have manifested from

her episodes

with that predator . . .

a trusted one of the family, yes?

as usual

hmm . . .

I am so sorry, dear . . .

The doctor seemed heartbroken

What a nice lady, was all I thought

What a nice lady

said Mama too

on our way back

home

What were we supposed to do?

Mama did not

have a plan

She was tired

of Google already

and said she had done with reading for life . . .

so we decided

to give us some time

and let the grief

of the diagnosis

of the abuse

of the betrayal

sink in . . .

After all, what was the fuss?

Unlike then, which seemed like yesterday,

when I had to still get passing marks

to stay in school—

it was not like

Mama would throw me

out of the house, was it?

Would she?

I locked myself

in my room,

let the monster from

underneath the bed

come out

and laughed:

Hey, you don't have to hide any more

you can live with me

forever

Uncle Uday

on the other hand

disappeared

Karan broke up with me

one more time

maybe couldn't handle the situation

but this time

I needed him

more than ever

as Uncle came only

when Karan touched me

I had to see Uncle

one more time

Mama, look . . .

I have gone through shit

I am still not dead

Why are you behaving

as if

it's the end of the world?

It never is, my dear girl, it is never

the end of the world

Karan, please

I beg of you

will you make out with me

just this last time?

We can break up after that.

I need my answers

otherwise

I can

never move on

I did that

against

my doctor's advice

because

even my mama thought

that's the only way

we could move on

Yeah, my mama

was either very stupid herself

or believed in me just too much

for her own good

But still, my baby . . .

if you have to confront him

let's go and see him

in Australia . . . in person

or if you want to kill him

then let me do the honours

Mama fidgeted helplessly

with raging rivers of black molten lava

erupting from her furious eyes endlessly

Mama, I just need answers

from the man who stands watching

when I get touched by

another man

Karan, my precious one

gave in

when

he heard the whole damn saga

and why I wanted to be kissed by him

He has a good heart

unlike where he came from

a miserable place

You see, Dolly

my father, your Uncle Uday

left us, his family

one fine day and never came back

You don't know

how much I hate him

I have questions too

but I will let you

tackle him first

Karan, my precious one,

was sounding

crazier than even I was . . .

You see,

people

with troubled childhoods

never really grow up

and keep doing stupid things

With my mother's permission

I went again

to the same house

where his son was waiting for me

a boy, nervous

and yet

with a kindness

a strength of character, as the cliché goes,

that made me melt into his arms

despite my selfish intentions

to resolve my own issues

through this shadow

we both waited for

With streams of tears

running down to our mouths

we kissed and kissed

and tasted the salt

in each other

We knew

we were both in fact

applying balm

to each other's wounds

And sure enough

Standing at the door

with the same wry smile

on his same pale face

amused

dejected

in pain

for betraying him

Uncle!! I scream!!

yet again

Uncle . . . I turned towards him

and moved Karan's hands

from behind

over myself

guiding him

to places

Uncle had touched

my manic body now blazing

Don't stop, Karan . . . I ordered

I had to make sure

the father stayed

long enough

Me: Why are you back, Uncle?

Uncle: I cannot believe you would become a bad girl, Dolly

Me: Uncle, was I a bad girl when you had me?

Uncle: No, you were good

I loved you

and you loved me

and I thought

you will always love me

even if I left

I had given you

enough memories

to last a lifetime

Me: Uncle, do you know what you did was wrong?

Uncle: You were a part of it, Dolly

You wanted me, as I wanted you

Me: I was a little girl, Uday, you bastard

I was a little girl

You vomited your vulgarity all over me

made me impure for life

you robbed me

even when I had

nothing to give

your claws dug into my chest

that shuddered with pain

and took away my soul

burnt it mercilessly

then put the ashes back in . . .

And now, why are you back? Tell me what brings you
back?

Uncle: I came back

to say sorry

will you forgive me?

for a sin committed for which no punishment is brutal
enough

I was a demon with blood in my hands

I was a murderer of the spirit of an innocent child

but Dolly, never ever think it's your fault

forget what I said before

never think you are impure

because of what I did

you are pure . . . as pure as your mother's love

but will you forgive me, my dear little girl, my *kanjak*?

Me: Even if it's too much to ask for

I forgive you, Uncle

for I need to save myself

from my wrath

for I need my sanity

back, too

if I ever was sane

and when I know

I was never 'normal'

to begin with . . .

Uncle: So long, Dolly . . .

Uncle vanished

for good

It was all over

Or so I thought

Just then Mama walked in

her face

evaporated of all colour

What happened, Mama?

I asked

even though I had something

more important, more exciting to share

Karan, my child . . .

cried Mama

I just got a call from

Australia

Your dad's colleague . . .

he said your dad . . . met with an accident

. . . passed away last night . . .Uday, that son of a bitch!

Oh he will burn in hell!

 am so sorry

We all hugged and cried over our loss

Part IV

Closure

I regretted the impossibility

of seeing him suffer

and crying out in pain

and pleading at my feet

to forgive him

but I already did

I just needed to remind myself

again and again . . .

They say

- Stop telling yourself these negative stories about yourself

- You are God's creation, a miracle

- Be your best version

- Unburden yourself from your past

and blah blah blah.

But then, what's the rush again?

Why is a long long long

grieving,

a very very very

sad

period full of guilt and filth

not allowed?

Why couldn't I be left alone

to figure it out

myself?

I had started feeling secure in this place . . .

indulging myself in the soothing

comfort food

of self-pity

I also understood very well, I needed to get out

and waited for that time to come . . .

delaying it as much as I could . . .

I knew I couldn't jump-start the healing

but I had to start somewhere

It was now a year

that

he had left

And Karan, my precious one

the original hero

he had to leave too

for higher studies

promising

that he would come back for me

soon

I believed him

as I had started to believe in everything, too

He had his own demons to fight

and needed that space

While

I continued having trouble sleeping

and bouts of panic attacks here and there

But slowly . . .

from black

the sky started looking blue again

from yellow

the French fries golden

the Snapchat filters made me laugh again

I started missing my friends too

and it was time

to go back

to school

Knowledge is a powerful tool

let us not take it away

from kids

who have to acquire it

with difficulty

what you call learning difficulties

or disabilities

if at all it matters

The fact of the matter is that

kids like me

and all other kids too

just need respect

It was the last year in school

though when I left before

I had told everyone

I did it to become a model

As I was just confirming a stereotype

that beautiful girls = dumb = models

and of course

it validated them

and the gossip mongers created even more hype

But this time

even if it was kind of awkward to come back

I had to be honest

I needed to prove

that I wasn't finished

I was an interesting work-in-progress

And it did not mean

better percentages

it meant

more confidence

more positivity

more style than I already had, why not?

And

a resounding belief that no matter what

There is nothing that can get me

I know it's all *gyan*

but there has to be something good

that you can take away from

a sickening, wretched life like mine

so read more books

watch more movies

Bollywood best

play more sports

make your bed

talk to your mom

motivate that friend

mend some fences

don't judge

see a therapist if you have to

work through your problems

face your fears

dare

Be good.

Even if it's a paradox

And so, so unfair at times

this is the only shitty world we've got

so, if we can't fight it

we join in

Joining in can be fun sometimes

And who says we can't still change the world?

Of course we can

That's why we are here

People close to you can be weirdos

but they are your own people, your own friends, your own
family

even when rebelling is a young person's second nature

sometimes

you sit back

and believe

and sure enough

everything will be alright

Maybe I haven't been able to give you your

Happy Ending

but I continue breathing . . .

and just as the proof of the pudding is in the eating

the purpose of life is in the living

Mere jaisa koi hard'ich nahi hai

—from the movie *Gully Boy*

ABOUT THE AUTHOR

Monisha K Gumber is an Indian author of immensely popular Teen Novels called SICK OF BEING HEALTHY, DYING TO LIVE(a part of 'Memorable Books of 2017' on Amazon India) and finally the third in the teen book series DOLLY WON'T PLAY. She also ahs another novel called BAHIR to her credit meant for older readers and is about a Pakistani woman's survival in the Middle East. All her books have been in the bestselling list of their categories. Monisha is an Army brat and has moved around all over the country and says that her background has made her more accepting and humble. Like most people from her generation she has the usual MBA and many years of corporate experience till she decided to move into the arena of writing. She hopes to write entertaining, simple yet inspirational stories that make a difference. Through her work, she raises serious issues like low self-esteem, negative body image, academic pressures, child abuse, Immigrant lives in her signature lightweight style. She is also passionate about alternative healing and wishes true health and happiness for all. Currently she lives in Abu Dhabi with her family including two dogs and two cats. She is also pursuing a Doctorate in Business Administration.

ABOUT THE ILLUSTRATOR

Pankaj Singh Rathour is a multidisciplinary artist who has worked with Monisha K Gumber to create illustrations for her Teen Novels. Pankaj has no formal education in Arts but his sheer passion for arts has made him a popular artist in India. He is a self taught artist and a B.com (hons) graduate.

After completing his college in 2017 he started working in a construction company. To his amusement, he found his passion and inspiration for Art while working with numbers in his office. He works as an accountant in the day and as an artist at night. He has a growing online community of thousands of ardent followers. According to him art is what makes him a better person and gives his life a purpose